The Jedburgh Branch

by
Roger Jermy

© Oakwood Press & Roger Jermy 2021

Published by Oakwood Press, an imprint of Stenlake Publishing Ltd, 2021

British Library Cataloguing in Publication Data
A Record for this book is available from the British Library
ISBN 978 0 85361 754 9

Printed by Claro Print, Office 26, 27, 1 Spiersbridge Way, Thornliebank, Glasgow G46 8NG

From the same author:
The Eyemouth Branch (ISBN 978 0 85361 364 0)

Northern Northumberland's Minor Railways:
Volume One: Brickworks, Forestry, Contractors, Military Target railways
and various other lines (ISBN 978 0 85361 703 7)

Northern Northumberland's Minor Railways:
Volume Two: Colliery & Associated Lines
(ISBN 978 0 85361 704 4)

Northern Northumberland's Minor Railways:
Volume Three: Sandstone, Whinstone & Gravel Lines
(ISBN 978 0 85361 705 1)

Northern Northumberland's Minor Railways:
Volume Four: Limestone Industry Lines
(ISBN 978 0 85361 706 8)

Title page: A '4MT' 2-6-0 has finished its shunting at Jedburgh and heads vigorously out of the station platform with the goods train. On this occasion it consists of four standard mineral wagons, a wooden-sided open wagon, a box van plus the guard's van at the rear.
Bruce McCartney Collection

Front cover: 'J37' class 0-6-0 No. 64608 of St Margaret's shed in Edinburgh waits to restart the Jedburgh pick-up goods train from Ormiston crossing on 1st April, 1961. It is awaiting the guard climbing back into his van having delivered a can of water to the crossing keeper's cottage which had no piped water. Having dropped off a green BR(SR) van at Jedburgh the return goods consists of one loaded 'Vanfit', one loaded 'Shocvan', the parcels van and the brake van. The photographer, a railway employee, travelled back to Galashiels on the footplate.
Rae Montgomery

Rear cover, top: In June 1963 a group of schoolboys watch Ivatt '4MT' class 2-6-0 No. 43138 prepare to leave Jedburgh with the goods: one open wagon, one closed van and the brake van.
Bruce McCartney Collection

Rear cover, lower: Railway Clearing House map of the Scottish Borders, 1907.

Oakwood Press, 54-58 Mill Square, Catrine, KA5 6RD.
Tel: 01290 551122 *Website*: www.stenlake.co.uk

Contents

'J35' class 0-6-0 No. 64463, this locomotive was allocated to Hawick, but probably based at its sub-shed St Boswells. It awaits departure from the passenger platform at Jedburgh. Its train consists of the six-wheeled van which sufficed for much of the road van traffic in the 1960s. The locomotive looks grimy and work-stained, typical of many goods engines at this time. *Hugh Davies/Photos of the 50s*

A commercial postcard of Jedburgh Abbey.   *Author's Collection*

A commercial postcard of Auld Bridge, Jedburgh.   *Author's Collection*

Chapter One

Introduction and background

O, grey old town of Jethart, The magic of thy name!
Thy wand'ring children love it, It speaks to them of 'hame'.

Jedburgh (or *Jethart* in old Scots) was formerly the county town of Roxburghshire in the Scottish borderland. Today the old county names have largely disappeared and Jedburgh is now located in the administrative district entitled the 'Borders District' whose headquarters and administrative centre is at Newtown St Boswells, near to Melrose. The main transport artery is the A68 trunk road which passes through the town.

For over 100 years Jedburgh was connected to the British railway network. A seven-mile-long branch, with three intermediate stations, ran northwards to a junction at Roxburgh. This linked with the line which ran approximately east-west, linking Newtown St Boswells (on the Edinburgh-Hawick-Carlisle so-called 'Waverley Route') with Tweedmouth on the East Coast main line (linking Newcastle with Edinburgh).

Jedburgh

'Thou raise the slogan with ane shout
Fy Tinedaill to it! Jethart's here'.

The town of Jedburgh sits astride the Jedwater, a small river whose tributary burns flow down from the Wauchope Forest and Carter Fell located to the south of the town. Carter Fell forms part of the Cheviot Hills separating old Roxburghshire from Redesdale in Northumberland, England's most northerly county. A mid-1850s description of the town, appearing in the local newspaper, the *Teviotdale Record*, referred to the surrounding scenery as appearing uninteresting but that 'if visitors had inhaled the miasmata [*sic*] in some of the swamps in England and inter-tropical regions, they would fully appreciate the pure atmosphere and variegated scenes around.'

To the north of Jedburgh the Jed flows into the River Teviot, a major tributary of the Tweed, whose broad valleys run in an approximately south-west to north-easterly direction. Along this valley was constructed the highway, now the A698, which links Coldstream and Kelso towards the east, with Hawick to the west. This road intersects, at Bonjedward, a couple of miles to the north of Jedburgh, with the generally north-south route of the highway, now the A68(T), linking Newcastle-upon-Tyne (58 miles to the south), Jedburgh and Lauder with Edinburgh (48 miles to the north). In the 1930s this road was described as passing 'through varied, romantic scenery' in the Jed Valley.

Jedburgh possesses the ruins of an abbey, founded in 1147, and records show the existence of an earlier priory and a church dating back to the 9th century. Through history the town has been the site of markets for horses, cattle and corn as well as for meat. Local hiring fairs for farm workers and servants were traditionally held at Jedburgh. At the time of the coming of the railway to Jedburgh *Chambers Gazetteer of Scotland* referred to the chief trade of the town as being the manufacture and sale of flannels, tartans, carpets and stockings and the spinning of woollen yarn. Since then its industries over the years have been based on local agriculture with textiles, principally woollen goods, tanning, grain mills and glove-making being prominent. The woollen industry was reputedly started in about 1728 according to A.E. Wallace, a railway parcel clerk at Jedburgh station, writing in the magazine of the London & North Eastern Railway (LNER) in the 1930s. More recent industrial activity has included electrical engineering products and the manufacture of artificial silk (rayon).

Today tourism is the principal industry with visitors to the ruined Jedburgh Abbey, to the Castle Jail and museum, also to Queen Mary's House which contains the museum of Mary, Queen of Scots. Roadside retail outlets sell woollen and other products though most items are not made locally!

Roxburgh

The present-day small village of Roxburgh, close to the site of the former Roxburgh Junction railway station, lies some two miles to the south-west of the site of the ancient and historic Roxburgh. The original trading burgh was, in the Middle Ages, as important as Edinburgh, Perth, Stirling and Berwick-upon-Tweed, being Scotland's capital for a short time when the king, David 1st of Scotland, resided there. Its trade was related to its position in the middle of the Tweed Valley, a richly fertile agricultural area. Its position on the River Tweed allowed shipment of agricultural goods and products downstream to the seaport of Berwick.

An engraving of Roxburgh castle.   *Author's Collection*

The town was subject to repeated battles during the Scottish Wars of Independence but its final capture in 1460 saw the town and its castle destroyed. Lacking a route to the sea after the English captured Berwick in 1482 it had little reason to rebuild or even exist! Today the village is a quiet rural backwater approached via unclassified roads. Its most prominent edifice is the magnificent viaduct formerly leading the railway to Kelso over the River Teviot.

Kelso

Though Kelso was not located on the Jedburgh branch all of its earliest trains also served Jedburgh on their way to and from St Boswells. Later the Kelso and Jedburgh services remained inter-linked and it is appropriate to mention briefly details of the importance of the town of Kelso in local railway history.

Like Jedburgh, Kelso is a small market town. It dates from the formation of its abbey in 1128. Much of the wealth of the town is derived from the monk-craftsmen who lived there. Its first bridge was an important river crossing which was washed away in the 1797 floods. Access to the town from the south bank of the Tweed was resumed when John Rennie's bridge was completed in 1803. This bridge is reputedly a smaller version of the Waterloo bridge over the Thames, also designed by Rennie. Kelso has never been a town associated with large industries.

Its principal present-day tourist attractions are Floors Castle and its ruined abbey. Like Jedburgh, Kelso is a 'rugby town' and was formerly the destination of special trains bringing or taking away supporters.

A commercial postcard of Kelso bridge and abbey.   *Author's Collection*

St Boswells

Like Kelso, St Boswells features strongly in the story of the Jedburgh branch although it is important to recognise that there is a distinction between the two villages: Newtown St Boswells and St Boswells itself. The first local station at this location on the Edinburgh to Hawick line was opened as 'Newtown Junction' in 1849. Later, when the branches to Reston and Kelso were operational its nameboards read 'St Boswells – Change for Kelso, Jedburgh, Earlston, Duns and Berwick'. In 1853 its name was amended to 'New Town St Boswells' but in 1865 it became simply 'St Boswells'. The station was located in what is known today as Newtown St Boswells, the village simply named St Boswells being some two miles to the south-east. Historically Newtown St Boswells was a regional communication centre with various road links to Selkirk, Jedburgh, Melrose and Galashiels, also Duns, Kelso and Berwick. It had several watermills and was a centre of grain milling. Much cattle was moved through the station, though its importance declined after the local rail lines closed in the 1960s. There is some commuting to Edinburgh especially since the restoration of the rail link between Tweedbank and Edinburgh.

St Boswells village was, for many years, an agricultural centre for cereal crops, peas and root crops. The rest of the local community were connected with the demands of the residents: for example bakers, butchers, publicans and bankers. The hunting season brought many visitors to the village at which the kennels of the Duke of Buccleugh were located. The Buccleuch Arms hotel was constructed as a result. A horse-drawn taxi service linked the village to the station at Newtown. Other visitors, as at Kelso, arrived for the high quality salmon fishing on the Tweed, and for the annual gypsy fair, which evolved from a sheep fair and wool market into a selling point for horses and cattle. A munitions factory at nearby Charlesfield brought troops and civilian work to the area in World War II.

A commercial postcard of the Buccleuch Arms. *Author's Collection*

Chapter Two

Early railways in Roxburghshire and the Borders

This chapter describes some of the railways that were planned for Jedburgh and Roxburghshire in the first half of the 19th century. Some did not progress much beyond the planning stage; others came to fruition. Their details are included to provide background to the Jedburgh line, and, hopefully, will help to explain how, and possibly why, Jedburgh station came to be at the end of a single-line branch rather than on a more major trunk railway line.

The earliest discovered references to the planning of railways close to the Border in Roxburghshire appeared in the *Scots Magazine* in the year 1810. Two linked articles featured in the editions published on 1st May and 1st June. The authors, for the article is written in the plural using 'we', performed some serious research, quoting Merton Dalrymple and Thomas Telford to support their suggestions. Referring to the already successful railway lines linking Kilmarnock and Troon and Lord Elgin's line at Dunfermline, these proposals involved a line, with the use of some inclined planes, from Glasgow to Berwick, which is carefully detailed in the magazine. Leaving Glasgow the line would follow a route taking it close to various industries and canals, then passing by way of Peebles, the north bank of the Tweed, the south side of Melrose, then avoiding Paxton House but heading on 'the most direct route to Berwick'. Both horse power and machinery were to be used to move the goods on the line. Its purpose would be to move goods from where they were produced in abundance to where they were much needed. For example grain from the fertile area around the Tweed could supply the demands in Lanarkshire. Imported goods into Berwick's port could be supplied to the Tweedside districts and cotton could be sent down from the Lanark Mills to Glasgow. Other materials to be transported on the line would include coals, lime, iron, timber and manufactured goods. There was to be no provision for the transport of passengers. The expected revenues from the different traffics were detailed and, in conclusion, the authors considered that, after deductions of £10,000 per year for the expenses of 'repairs, collecting tolls, inspection and management' a return of 12 per cent would remain for the proprietors. The line appeared on the second edition of Kirkwood's *Map of Scotland* which was published in 1812. An advertisement for this map appeared in the *Caledonian Mercury* of Saturday 6th June, 1812.

Kirkwood's map also included the proposed railway from Berwick to Kelso. This railway was sanctioned by an Act of Parliament dated 31st May, 1811. The *Caledonian Mercury* newspaper had reported on 14th March, 1811 as follows: 'We are happy to learn, that the bill for making the railway between Berwick and Kelso, is now before parliament, and that there is little doubt of that measure being carried into effect, so as to meet the general approbation of the country.'

The line, first projected in 1809, was to run from Spittal, on the opposite side of the River Tweed to Berwick, via Coldstream (where the Tweed would be crossed by means of a bridge) to Kelso. At that time Spittal was a part of a detached portion of County Durham, rather than Northumberland. The bridge at Coldstream would convey vehicles and pedestrians in addition to the railway traffic.

The Act of Parliament was noteworthy in that, for the first time, the carriage of passengers was authorized. The company could make charges for the conveyance of light goods or parcels not exceeding 5 cwt in weight but these charges were not to exceed 2*d*. per mile.

In 1814 a surveyor by the name of Alex Kinghome produced a report entitled *Practicality of uniting Glasgow with the Kelso and Berwick Railway and of extending a Branch upwards to near Ancrum Bridge*. Two possible routes were selected from Old Melrose (next to the Tweed) though in the absence of an accompanying plan it has been very difficult to ascertain the precise routes. The first route would have included a section which arrived at Kelso having passed Nether Nisbet and crossed the road from Nisbet to Kelso. Then it would have traversed the Ormiston Lands passing to the south of the village of Roxburgh. The second surveyed route would have produced a line passing Newtown, Maxton and Riddlestone (likely the present day Riddleton), turning southwards to pass a location referred to as 'Trows' before terminating near Ancrum Bridge. At Melrose these proposed lines would have linked up with the Glasgow line and at Kelso with the first alternative linking with the Berwick line at Kelso.

The papers of the 2nd Viscount Melville, now deposited in the National Library of Scotland, identify plans for another railway, this time from Dalkeith, via Stow and Galashiels, to St Boswells Green and Hassenden [*sic*] on the Teviot to provide transport to an area of country 'hitherto deprived of coal and lime'. One of the signatories to the scheme was a certain Walter Scott, of Abbotsford. This line was surveyed by the Scottish surveyor, Robert Stevenson. Stevenson's survey and report, dated 22nd May, 1821, included a possible extension via

Abbotsford from the River, Tweed.

A postcard of Abbotsford, home of Sir Walter Scott, from the Tweed. *Author's Collection*

Maxton to Kelso, though not to Hawick. The line would have involved gradients as steep as 1 in 42. It would be laid with 70 lb. per yard rails and have a single line with four passing points per mile. However, the engineering of the alignment would allow for doubling of the track if needs became pressing.

This scheme was revived in 1825 when a letter from Walter Scott contained the following: 'I am the sharer to the extent of £1,500 in a railroad, which will bring coals and lime here at half price, and double the rent of the arable part of my property, but is dead outlay in the meantime'.

As with the early Glasgow & Berwick Railway none of these proposed lines were constructed. Disagreements amongst the Directors regarding such matters as the cost of the bridge over the Tweed and the purchase of land, caused the Berwick & Kelso scheme to be placed in abeyance. However the idea of constructing the line did not fade completely as *The Scotsman* newspaper of 11th December, 1824 contained a notice that a quorum of the proprietors of the Berwick & Kelso Railway Co. requested that a special general meeting of the company be held on the 17th January, 1825. The meeting was planned to be held in the Royal Exchange Coffeehouse in Edinburgh for the purpose of appointing a treasurer and clerk, also an Engineer and any other such officers, in regards to subscriptions and in regards of surveys which may be necessary previous to the beginning of works. A committee was also to be elected to manage the affairs of the company. The leading promoters included Hugh Scott, John Spottiswoode and Andrew Bonar. Once again there was no start of the line's construction. At this time £22,500 was subscribed to add to £32,000 already subscribed towards the building of the line.

The Berwick & Kelso Railway's name appeared in the press once again in 1836. On this occasion it was the *Durham County Advertiser* that contained a notice of a special general meeting of the company's proprietors to be held at Mrs Margaret Sang's Inn in Coldstream on Wednesday 5th October. The meeting was called, on this occasion, by a more distinguished group of individuals including the Earl of Buccleugh, Lord Polwarth, David Milne (later David Milne-Hume of Paxton House) and George Baillie of Mellerstain House in the Borders. The meeting was to ascertain the present state of the company, also to discuss a report, made by the sub-committee of the Border Association for the Encouragement of Agriculture which recommended the immediate commencement and execution of the railway. Once again there were no immediate consequences relating to the building of the line and it would be a further 15 years before the line would be built from Tweedmouth towards Sprouston, near Kelso. In fact the Berwick & Kelso Railway was dissolved in February 1838.

In passing it is worth mentioning that road communications over the border from Jedburgh and Roxburghshire were also being discussed in the 1820s and 1830s, with alternative routes for improved communications between Edinburgh and Newcastle being considered. A report was printed at the direction of a general meeting of the heritors and turnpike trusts after a meeting held at Jedburgh on 25th November, 1829. It was entitled *Report of the Roxburghshire Committee upon the Road from Edinburgh to London via Jedburgh*. Two 'inland' routes across the border were apparently under consideration, the first being via Wooler, the second via Jedburgh. The report concluded that the route via Jedburgh was the more direct of the two. It involved passing through Dalkeith, Soutra, Lauder, and St Boswells Green before crossing the Teviot at Ancrum Bridge. Thence it would proceed to Jedburgh and follow the River Jed to Carter Fell. This section would have been in the area of the Roxburghshire Turnpike Trust. Beyond the Carter summit it would descend through Otterburn in the Elsdon Trust area reaching Newcastle via Ponteland (in the Ponteland Turnpike Trust area). The road length, after the straightening and 'every possible improvement' suggested by surveyors Telford and McAdam, was measured as being 96 miles in length. The maximum gradient (with the exception of one or two short lengths) would be 1 in 25. It would, it was suggested, result in greatly improved through communication between Edinburgh and London and an acceleration of the mails, not to mention the benefits to the inhabitants and road users of the intermediate towns, including Jedburgh. The building of this toll road made the Percy Arms at Otterburn, south of Carter Bar, an intermediate stop for the *Chevy Chase* coach running between Edinburgh and Newcastle and for the *Blucher* coach which linked Jedburgh with Newcastle. This road over Carter Bar eventually became the A68 trunk road though, as we shall see, there was the possibility of a railway line over the same route.

In the 1830s there were already a few railways in operation both north and south of the line of the border. South of the border a provisional committee of the Newcastle & Carlisle Railway met in 1825 publishing a route for a railway between Carlisle and Newcastle quay. A Parliamentary Bill was submitted in 1826 and despite some difficulties the Newcastle & Carlisle Railway Act was finally passed in May 1829. Work on the line started in 1830 and the line was

Carter Bar in the 1950s.   *Author's Collection*

built to the standard gauge. Several more Acts were required before its completion. The initial part of the line was opened between Hexham and Blaydon for goods traffic and shortly afterwards for passengers on 9th March, 1835. Steam locomotives hauled the trains. The western section between Greenhead and Carlisle opened on 19th July, 1836 and the line was extended eastwards from Derwenthaugh to the Redheugh terminus at Gateshead on 1st March, 1837. The remaining gap between Greenhead and Haydon Bridge, near Hexham, was finally opened in June 1838, the 18th of that month being chosen for the opening as it was the anniversary of the battle of Waterloo.

North of the border existed the Edinburgh & Dalkeith Railway (E&DR) which was opened in stages from 1831 to convey coal from the various coal pits near to Dalkeith to a depot at St Leonards, to the south side of Arthur's Seat, the rocky summit which dominates part of the Edinburgh skyline. It had branches to Leith and a small harbour near Musselburgh. This line used horse-drawn wagons and was built to a gauge of 4 ft 6 in. using cast-iron fish-bellied rails. The line involved a steeply-graded tunnel (1 in 30) through which wagons were drawn by cables powered by a stationary steam engine. A private businessman, Michael Fox, operated horse-drawn passenger carriages over the line from 1832.

In 1839 the E&DR made a most unusual, and perhaps unlikely proposal, namely for an extension from Dalkeith towards Coldstream, then across the border to Wooler, Whittingham and Longhorsley to Newcastle. The route was surveyed by George Rennie in 1838. Not surprisingly the proposal was considered impracticable, by Morpeth and Newcastle surveyor and engineer E. Bowman, on the grounds that the route was 'too hilly', though the gradients would have been compatible with the nature of the Edinburgh & Dalkeith's existing lines which used stationary engines and horses. Furthermore the E&DR was constructed to the 'wrong' gauge, being incompatible with the lines being planned and constructed northwards from York to Newcastle and Newcastle to Edinburgh. It was hardly a candidate for an important cross-border route. An Act of 1845 allowed the purchase of the E&DR by the North British Railway (NBR) in 1845 and much was converted to the standard gauge.

The Edinburgh & Glasgow Railway was authorized by an Act of Parliament dated 4th July, 1838, though thoughts of linking the two cities by rail dated back to 1824. The contract to build the line was let at the end of 1838 and its construction involved some complex engineering: cuttings, embankments, tunnels and viaducts. The line opened for passenger traffic on 21st February, 1842.

By the end of the 1830s decade four rail routes across the border were under serious consideration. The first of these was an East Coast route from Newcastle via Berwick and Dunbar to Edinburgh. The second possibility was a more 'central' route from Newcastle to Edinburgh via Hexham, Jedburgh and Galashiels. The third and fourth were 'West Coast' routes heading north from Carlisle either via Dumfries, Kilmarnock and Paisley, or via Annandale and Carstairs which would link up with the Lancaster & Carlisle route to the south. The third route was longer and provided inferior connections to Edinburgh whereas the fourth would need to pass through the Southern Uplands with steep gradients but would provide a route to Edinburgh from Carstairs.

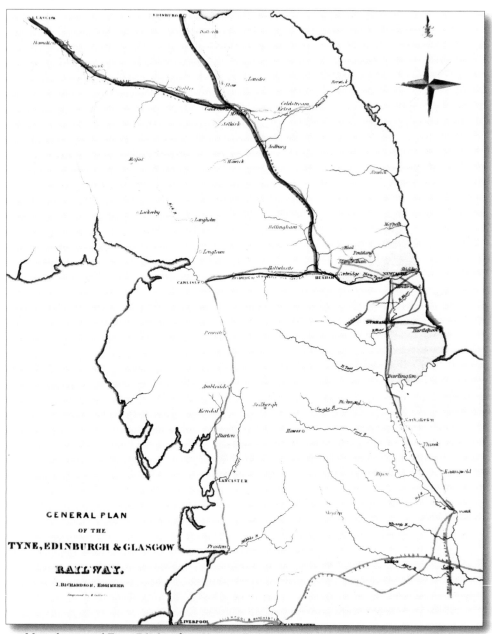

Map of proposed Tyne, Edinburgh & Glasgow Railway, 1836.

Jedburgh Historical Society Collection

It was in *The Scotsman* of 13th August, 1836 that a report appeared of a public meeting which had been held in Jedburgh to consider the expediency of constructing,

... a MIDLAND LINE of RAILWAY up the NORTH TYNE and REED WATER, by CARTER into SCOTLAND, with branches to Edinburgh and Glasgow [*sic*].

The meeting was well attended by local businessmen and dignitaries and chaired by William Oliver Rutherford, the Sheriff of Roxburghshire. A first resolution was passed which stated that the construction of such a line was desirable as a means of connecting the cities of Edinburgh & Glasgow with the English cities of York and London. Such a railway would lead to an extension of commerce, create a demand for coal, lime and ironstone, afford increased employment and (presumably referring to passenger traffic) facilitate intercourse with remote parts of the kingdom.

The second resolution referred to the advantages of the line passing through the 'centre' of the country rather than a coastal line to the east or west. A committee of management was established to liaise with other local committees and a law agent was appointed to work with the secretary for the committee for Northumberland, based in Newcastle. A bank account was established for the paying in of subscriptions or other monies.

A second public meeting was held at the Royal Exchange Coffee House in Edinburgh on 16th August. This was chaired by Peter Lamond, the Lord Dean of Guild, and attended by dignitaries, advocates, bankers and merchants. Several resolutions were passed. The first welcomed the construction of a railway route between Newcastle and Edinburgh 'by the nearest and most practicable line'. Secondly they recommended that the route, recommended by Stephen Reed, a Newcastle solicitor, and approved by Joshua Richardson, civil engineer of Newcastle, be approved, namely from Newcastle via Carter Fell into Scotland, thence via Jedburgh, Melrose, Galashiels, Peebles and Penicuik into Edinburgh. Such a railway could have a branch into Glasgow from Peebles both of benefit to that city and the project as a whole. Another resolution called for Richardson to study the countryside through which the railway would pass and work out a comparison between the costs of construction and the probable revenue once completed.

An article in the *Newcastle Journal*, dated 2nd July, 1837, mentioned that Richardson had been busily engaged for nearly 12 months in acquainting himself with the 'stratification and districts' through which this line would pass. The article went into great detail of the route that Richardson proposed including his estimate of the length of the tunnel required under Carter Fell, the gradients of the line and other constructional difficulties. Richardson considered the cost of construction to be nearly £1½ million with the expected revenue being just over £300,000 per annum with a net profit of over £200,000 after expenses. A comment was made that the promoters of the alternative route, the line from Berwick to Edinburgh passing near Haddington, had long been 'entirely inactive'.

It was at the end of August 1838 that the promoters of the coastal route from Newcastle to Edinburgh met 'to employ a professional gentleman of such acknowledged eminence and talent, to make surveys and fix upon the line as would be calculated to put an end to the controversy that has so long existed as to the east, or coast line, and the middle line'. Who was appointed? None other than George Stephenson who was present at the meeting and expressed his readiness to start work without delay. Stephenson's report was dated 12th September, 1838. It detailed the route which he proposed for the railway from Newcastle via Berwick, Grantshouse and Dunbar. He commented on the level nature of the low ground over which much of the line would be built and the facility of extending branches to the nearby towns and villages via the river valleys. He contrasted this with the problems of Richardson's 'middle route'. He concluded that this 'is the only feasible and desirable line of railway with levels to which locomotive steam power can be advantageously applied between the town of Newcastle and the cities of Edinburgh and Glasgow'.

A letter from 'a friend' to *The Berwick Advertiser*, dated August 1838, but appearing in the 8th September edition, provided supportive evidence to Stephenson's conclusions on the proposed Newcastle-Edinburgh link. The author went into great detail regarding the lengths of the line, the need for an expensive tunnel on the middle route, the need for an expensive viaduct to cross the Teviot, extensive embankments and cuttings, not to mention the steep gradients. Not surprisingly he came to the conclusion that 'It may be safely assumed that the East Coast route would be the most productive one'.

There was some continuing support, however, for the inland, or middle, route which would have put Jedburgh on the main line to Edinburgh, particularly from the prominent persons inhabiting the county of Roxburghshire. The Commissioners of Supply and Heritors met at Jedburgh in June 1839 to reiterate their support for a line through the county. In the event, despite this support, the 'middle' line was not built. The Royal Commission looking into the possible rail routes between England and Scotland decided in favour of the 'West Coast' route through Carlisle.

The North British Railway, formed in Edinburgh in 1842, was supported by the Edinburgh & Glasgow Railway. It realized that as an 'internal Scottish railway' a line southwards from Edinburgh towards Dunbar would fail to attract backers compared with a line linking Edinburgh and Berwick with a view to linking up with the English lines already approaching Berwick from the south. Accordingly the NBR applied for, and obtained, an Act of Parliament (in 1844) to build a line from Edinburgh to Berwick-upon-Tweed. Construction proceeded quickly and the line was opened to traffic on 22nd June, 1846. Bridges across the Tyne at Newcastle and across the Tweed at Berwick were necessary before the NBR line could become a part of the through route between the English and Scottish capitals. The York & Newcastle Railway and the Newcastle & Berwick Railway amalgamated to form the York, Newcastle & Berwick Railway in 1847 and later, with further amalgamations in 1854, it became the North Eastern Railway (NER).

Meanwhile the North British Railway had acquired the Edinburgh & Dalkeith line in 1845. This was considered as a 'jump-off' point for a railway from Edinburgh to Hawick. Starting off as the nominally independent Edinburgh & Hawick Railway it became part of the NBR in 1845. The line, involving costly gradients and a winding route, climbed from the South Esk Valley to a summit at Falahill before dropping down to the Gala Water reaching Galashiels. From here it passed into the Tweed Valley and on to Melrose, St Boswells and finally to Hawick. The line opened in November 1849. Much later, in April 1864, this line which became known as the 'Waverley Route', was extended to Carlisle, with the Border Counties line from Hexham joining it at the remote Riccarton Junction.

The *Kelso Chronicle* reported on 30th May, 1845 that a meeting of the Jedburgh Farmers' Club had taken place on 1st April. It reported that the club was of the opinion that it would be of the greatest importance to Jedburgh, Kelso and the intermediate district if a line of railway were to be constructed from the Edinburgh & Hawick Railway near St Boswells to communicate with these towns. Their views were transmitted to the Directors of the NBR. A few days later representatives of the local farmers were allowed to address the railway committee at the House of Commons, as reported in the same newspaper of 10th April, 1846.

In 1846 the NBR, as reported in several newspapers including *The Scotsman*, obtained an Act to build three lines emanating from the Waverley Route, namely from Galashiels to Selkirk, St Boswells to Kelso and Roxburgh to Jedburgh. In May 1847 it was reported that plans had been drawn up for the Selkirk and Jedburgh branches and that plans, sections, specifications and contract drafts would be available for inspection by potential contractors at the NBR offices at St Andrews Square in Edinburgh. In addition the company's assistant engineer would be available at the Bridge Inn, Galashiels on 8th April and at the Spread Eagle Inn, Jedburgh on 9th April to point out the routes of the proposed branches. Tenders were invited. However, neither the Selkirk line nor the line to Jedburgh was built at this time.

The Spread Eagle Inn on the High Street in Jedburgh.   *Author*

The Kelso branch was, however, constructed from St Boswells towards Kelso. Initially it gained a temporary terminus at Wallace Nick in 1850 as the line did not have the full support of the Duke of Roxburghe for entering Kelso. The following year a station was constructed at Kelso. This was, however, inconveniently sited for the town, being on the south side of the river.

The Newcastle & Berwick Railway was authorized to build a branch from Tweedmouth on the south side of the Tweed, near Berwick, by an Act of 1845. It initially terminated at the village of Sprouston and was opened for passenger trains on 27th July, 1849 by which time it was under the auspices of the newly-formed York, Newcastle & Berwick Railway (later NER). It is recorded that some goods services operated prior to this date. Sprouston was about two miles from the site of the future Kelso station. The line was extended to Kelso to make an end-on junction with the NBR line from St Boswells at a location known as Sprouston Junction. The *Kelso Chronicle* reported on 23rd November that work had recommenced on the extremity of the embankment below Mellendean farmhouse. The newspaper understood that the only remaining obstacle to the joining of the NER and NBR lines was the want of an arrangement with a certain Captain Scott of Wooden relating to the value of the land to be occupied by the line. The *Chronicle* also stated that the railways would have to look at their freight charges carefully as it was cheaper to buy coal at Nisbet (brought by carters from the Northumberland collieries) than it was to buy direct from the railway stations near Kelso.

It might be assumed that once the lines were joined, on 1st June, 1851, that they would provide a through route for trains between the Waverley Route and the East Coast main line; however both the NBR and the NER operated their lines to Kelso as separate branches, often with very poor connections for any through passengers. Kelso thus got its railway station and train services operated both to Tweedmouth and Berwick to the east, and St Boswells to the west. However, the powers granted to the NBR for the construction of the Jedburgh branch were allowed to lapse and travellers to and from the town were required to take one of the carriages which made (often unsatisfactory) connections with the trains at St Boswells, Hawick or Kelso.

Kelso viewed from the south side of the River Tweed.   *Author's Collection*

Chapter Three

The Jedburgh Railway:
Proposals, postponements, plans and permissions

For five years after the initial granting of permission to the North British Railway to build the branch line to Jedburgh no construction work took place. Eventually permission to build the line was in danger of lapsing.

The *Kelso Chronicle* of 23rd January, 1852 published an editorial article entitled 'Our Branch Railway'. The first part of the text read as follows:

> We hear of projected railway branches in various directions, but never a syllable on our defunct Jedburgh branch. Can anybody tell what has become of it, or what the Directors of the North British Company think on the subject? They have certainly broken faith with the inhabitants of this locality - the requisite Parliamentary powers having all been obtained, and a prospect held out of no time being lost in commencing with the scheme.

The article went on to accept that 'bad times' had depressed railway progress in the late 1840s but it expressed the view that the recent increase in trade should have provided encouragement to go on with the scheme. The author of the article considered that a single line from Jedburgh to Roxburgh or 'Stockster' would be cheap to construct and that the necessary land could be acquired economically as the landowners would see the benefits. The article ended with a plea for the inhabitants to call on the NBR to 'implement their engagements', and the 'landed gentlemen of influence' to stir themselves towards giving the locality the benefit of a railway, before it is too late. The last point bears reference to the fact that Jedburgh was one of the last of the border towns not to have a railway.

The same newspaper, at the end of April 1852, reiterated the necessity for efforts on the part of the council, magistrates and inhabitants to bring a railway to Jedburgh. It commented that even the very small town of Lauder was in the process of submitting a Bill for a railway. Traffic to Jedburgh was considered to be six times that coming into Lauder! Jedburgh was the site of the circuit courts, the sheriff courts, fairs, cattle markets and various other sources of passenger traffic apart from the traffic in 'materials'. It emphasized that, with changing conditions, the cost of constructing the line would be about half that when the application was made for the Parliamentary Bill by the NBR.

The readers of the newspaper did not have long to wait. The *Kelso Chronicle* contained a notice in its advertisements column of 12th November, 1852 headed:

JEDBURGH RAILWAY
FROM
JEDBURGH
TO THE
ROXBURGH STATION OF THE KELSO BRANCH
OF THE NORTH BRITISH RAILWAY

Clearly research must have been undertaken and meetings held before this notice could be published as it was a detailed document.

First of all it announced that the capital for the line would be £40,000 in the form of 4,000 shares of £10 each. An initial deposit of £1 per share would be required.

A provisional committee had been established, numbering some 14 gentlemen, mainly from Jedburgh, but also from Oxnam, Lanton, Langlee and Hunthill nearby, with Henry James Thomson, the Provost of Jedburgh, being the first named. The Engineer was named as Henry Johnston Wylie and the solicitors were Richardson, Loch & MacLaurin, of London, and James F. Wilkie of Edinburgh. The appointed bankers were the British Linen Co. and the Western Bank of Scotland and the interim secretaries were listed as Messrs Laing & Stedman, Writers, of Edinburgh.

The Engineer, Henry Johnstone Wylie, was a young man at the time, being just 30 years of age. According to the Institute of Civil Engineers, of which he was a member, he had a knack of managing contractors and workpeople with a 'far-seeing eye for economy in construction'. He was associated with the Selkirk & Galashiels Railway, the Bridport Railway (in Dorset), the Kirkcudbright Railway, the Galashiels & Peebles, and the Berwickshire Railway.

The notice in the *Chronicle* referred to the fact that the state of the money market had prevented the Directors of the NBR from making the double-track Jedburgh branch in 1846. It was now considered that a single line of track, such as laid on the St Andrews branch would suffice. The notice went on to describe Jedburgh as being situated in one of the best-peopled, agricultural and manufacturing districts in the south of Scotland. It referred to the existing use of carriages for passenger traffic to Hawick, Kelso and Belses stations and the use of horse-drawn carts for the goods and mineral traffic. It stated that the demand for raw materials and the need to transport manufactured goods was great. There was a constant demand for drain tiles, lime, manure and coal. Also there was a need to transport fat cattle, sheep and corn to markets to the north and south. The view was expressed that this inconvenience could be overcome by building the railway. The estimate of £40,000 for the purchase of land, the building of stations and the line's construction had been arrived at and there were contractors who would do the work for this price. An invitation was extended for subscribers to purchase shares in the railway.

Even in those days news travelled quickly and the *London Daily News* of 15th November referred to the Jedburgh Railway as being one of the 'new British railways projected'.

On 25th November the *Edinburgh Evening Courant* repeated a notice which had first appeared in its 10th and 18th November editions regarding the incorporation of the company and its intention to construct a railway from Jedburgh to the Kelso branch of the NBR. It stated the intention of the Jedburgh Railway to submit a Bill to Parliament for the building of a line from Bongate, in Jedburgh's Royal Burgh, to a point on the North British line close to Roxburgh station and the village of Roxburgh. It would pass through several parishes: Jedburgh, Crailing, Eckford and Roxburgh. The usual clauses were included referring to compulsory purchase of lands, deviation and closure of roads and watercourses, the levying of tolls for the use of the railway and the entering into of agreements with other companies for the making, maintaining and working of the line. In particular, sections of the notice referred to the future relationship with the NBR as regards the working of the line. A map of the line, also plans, levels and sections of the line, would be deposited with the Sheriff-Clerk of the County of Roxburgh and in each relevant parish and burgh. A copy of the notice was to be placed in the *Edinburgh Gazette* to appear before the 30th November. Finally it was the intention to deposit copies of the Bill with the House of Commons on or before the 31st December, 1852. The notice was issued by the Edinburgh and London solicitors to the railway, dated 2nd November, 1852. A copy of the notice duly appeared in the *Edinburgh Gazette* of 26th November, 1852.

The *Kelso Chronicle*, for long a proponent of the building of the line, could not conceal (in its 26th November edition) its pleasure at the announcement. The newspaper rejoiced at the common sense of the proposals. It,

> ...will confer upon the district a boon of no inconsiderable magnitude ... The forecast for the transport of coals, lime, farm produce and manures has been ascertained from correct data and the passenger traffic by coaches from Jedburgh to the existing railway considerably exceeds that from Hawick, the terminus of the line.

The newspaper considered that the 7 to 10 per cent dividends forecast by the promoters should be confidently expected.

The *Edinburgh Evening Courant* of the 4th December and the *Brechin Advertiser* of 14th December contained a statement of the 'Projected Scottish Railways' which were lodged in the railway department of the Board of Trade on 29th and 30th November of that year. The list included the Jedburgh Railway as well as other 'local' lines such as the Peebles Railway and the Hawick & Carlisle Railway.

All would have seemed to be progressing smoothly. However, this was not the case. The *Dundee Courier* of 12th January, 1853 contained a short article entitled 'Abortive Railway Companies'. It read: 'Of the 157 railway companies that lodged plans and sections in November, 30 are not able to proceed this session, in consequence of not having lodged the necessary deposits with the Accountant-General and other causes'. A partial list followed but the names of both the Hawick & Carlisle and the Jedburgh Railway were included. Back, almost, to square one. The inhabitants of Jedburgh would have to rely on carts and carriages for some time yet!

The system of conveyance by carriages was not working in a satisfactory way. The *Chronicle*, on 23rd September, 1853, described some situations which were cited as being commonplace. Passengers on arriving at Belses station on the last train from Edinburgh, expecting to continue onwards to Jedburgh by carriage, would arrive at this station to discover no coaches present. The eight mile journey on foot was a long and dreary one when faced by ladies. An invalid applying for a ticket at Edinburgh could not be provided with details about completing the journey from Belses to Jedburgh by carriage. On assuming, again, that a carriage would be available he arrived to find none thus having to complete his journey by hobbling along the road quoted as being 'the bleakest corner in the county of Roxburgh after dark'. Blame was apportioned to the carriage providers, and, most of all, to the NBR. However the article ended by hoping that these grievances would be of short continuance and that a strong movement would be made for the construction of a branch railway so that the local inhabitants 'will be pushed along to and from our doors like every body else [sic]'. However it would be over 12 months before further plans were published. In the meantime travellers had to rely on the various coaches to link them to the railway system: the Chevy Chase to Newcastle and Belses, the Highflyer to Kelso and the (apparently unnamed) coach to Melrose.

On the 3rd November the Kelso Chronicle contained an editorial item which referred to a notice in the advertisement column of the same edition. The notice was the Prospectus for the next attempt to create the Jedburgh Railway. As usual the newspaper was unequivocal about its support for the efforts to achieve this. 'The advantages to our county town and the adjacent districts will be great'. The paper was pleased that the landed proprietors, through whose properties the intended railway would pass, had awarded their aid to the scheme. 'We cannot but conceive that the shareholders will find it a paying line, and that many agricultural and commercial advantages will be secured in this district of the county'.

Returning to the notice in the advertisement column it was headed: 'Prosepectus of the Jedburgh Railway'. It is immediately obvious that the numbers and composition of the acting provisional committee had changed considerably since the previous notice some two years earlier. The number of members had been increased to 18 with 13 of these being new compared with the November 1852 list. The names added included William Oliver Rutherford, the Sheriff of Roxburghshire, Sir William Scott of Ancrum, Baronet, Henry James Thomson, Provost of Jedburgh, J. Moreton Craigie, Sheriff-Substitute of Roxburghshire, various landowners, a medical doctor and several local merchants. The capital was amended from £40,000 to £35,000 to be derived from 3,500 shares of £10 each. The deposit was raised to £1 5s. per share.

Henry Johnstone Wylie was replaced by Charles Jopp, civil engineer, of Edinburgh. This may have been because Wylie was involved on the Selkirk & Galashiels line at this time. Messrs Dalmahoy & Wood of Edinburgh were appointed as the new solicitors and Richardson, McLaurin & Loch, of Westminster were appointed as the Parliamentary agents. The bankers became the British Linen Co. and the National Bank of Scotland.

Jopp was born in about 1821 in Old Machar, Aberdeen. He was educated at Edinburgh Academy and Edinburgh University. He became articled to railway engineer John Miller of Leithen for six years, becoming his principal assistant. He was in charge of much of the construction of the NBR network, including the Stirling & Dunfermline, the Devon Valley and the Forth & Clyde Junction railways. On Miller's retirement in 1850 Jopp became Chief Engineer to the NBR at the young age of about 29. In the 1851 census he was described as a Civil Engineer of the company Miller Jopp Mash in Edinburgh. Later he became involved, amongst other schemes, with Shankend railway viaduct (1862), Leaderfoot viaduct (1865) and the Waverley station hotel and market scheme (1866). He became a Member of the Institution of Civil Engineers on 4th December, 1855.

As a young man Jopp had been a keen field sportsman, enjoying hunting with hounds. He was a philanthropist and a member of the episcopal church, serving as a vestryman at St Paul's, Edinburgh, and St Baldred's at North Berwick.

Jopp made a fresh survey of the line and his estimate of expense for the Jedburgh Railway's construction survives in the Parliamentary records. It reads:

Jedburgh Railway
(Incorporation of company and construction of railway from Jedburgh to the Roxburgh station on the Kelso branch of the North British Railway; Arrangements with North British Railway Company.)

I, Charles Jopp of Edinburgh, Civil Engineer, do hereby estimate the expense of making and constructing a railway commencing at or near the Four Mile Bridge at Jedburgh and terminating by a junction with the Kelso branch of the North British Railway at the Roxburgh Station, to be called the 'Jedburgh Railway', with all proper works and conveniences under the authority of the Bill under the above written title herewith deposited and according to the plans and sections of the said railway and works deposited in the Private Bill Office of the House of Commons, at the sum of Thirty five thousand pounds sterling.
Dated at Edinburgh the twenty sixth day of December, Eighteen hundred and fifty four years.

(Signed) Charles Jopp

The text of the Prospectus referred to the line serving 45,000 acres of the best agricultural land in the south of Scotland and the large area of pastoral land to the north of the Cheviot range with its superior breed of sheep. It referred to the 1846 Parliamentary approval for the line granted to the NBR which had by this time expired. The Prospectus doubted that the original scheme, with its double line of rails and expensive construction (£90,000) would have been productive but stated that the new proposals for a more-cheaply built line would be successful. It quoted the support from the Marquis of Lothian and the Earl of Minto through whose estates some six miles of the line would run. The Proprietors had been in touch with contractors who were confident that the line could be completed within the amount of capital to be raised. Arrangements with the NBR to work the line had almost been concluded for 50 per cent of the net traffic receipts. The support already received suggested that Parliament could be approached in the ensuring session. An application form was attached below the notice.

A week later, on the 10th November, the *Kelso Chronicle* contained a brief article under the heading 'Jedburgh line of railway'. It commented on the launching of the scheme and the unanimous support expressed for the project at the recently held public meeting in Jedburgh. 'We would earnestly call upon the landed proprietors and the community in general to come forward and give their hearty support to a scheme which is intimately bound up with the welfare of the district, and which, from the explanations laid before the meeting, must prove lucrative and remunerative.'

The *Morning Chronicle* of the following day contained a report of the meeting referred to in the *Kelso Chronicle* article. The meeting was chaired by the Sheriff of the county, William Rutherford. Present were a considerable number of tradesmen of the town, farmers and representatives of landowners. Rutherford introduced Charles Jopp, the Engineer, who detailed the course of the proposed line to the meeting. He said that it was a line that was easily determined as there were no obstacles which could swallow up money. As others had done previously Jopp compared the proposed Jedburgh line with the St Andrews branch in Fife.

The next speaker was James Stevenson, the Procurator Fiscal, who reported the data on which the cost of the project had been calculated. He said that the estimated cost would be £35,000 and that with the forecast traffic a profit for the shareholders was easily within reach. He referred to the two principal landowners on the route who had expressed a willingness to ask only for a fair valuation for the required land for the work. He ended by saying that a very considerable number of shares had already been taken by inhabitants of the Burgh. John Ord moved the adoption of Stevenson's report. Finally the Chairman pointed out the benefits that would accrue to the town, whose air was 'more salubrious and dry ... than in either Melrose or Kelso'! Before the meeting finally broke up considerable additions were made to the list of shares that had been taken up.

The meeting was reported in other Scottish newspapers, though the *John o'Groat Journal* of Friday 24th November appeared to make an error with its date, stating that the meeting had taken place on the previous Tuesday (i.e. 21st November).

The *Kelso Chronicle* (17th November) contained the notice relating to the submission to Parliament for leave to bring in a Bill for the 'making and maintaining a railway, with all proper works and conveniences'. It was stated that the line would commence at a point near Flour Mill bridge over the River Jed in the parish of Jedburgh and terminate at or near Roxburgh station in the parish of Roxburgh, both ends of the line being in the county of Roxburghshire. As usual with such notices it went on to describe activities which would be associated with the building of the line: diversion of roads, streams and rivers, possible deviations and matters concerning the transfer of lands to the railway. It described the

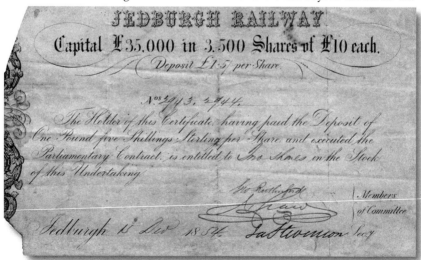

A Jedburgh Railway share certificate for two shares, dated 18th February, 1854, and signed by two committee members and the Secretary Mr Stevenson.

Jedburgh Historical Society Collection

arrangements for the working of the line by the NBR. It ended with the usual references to depositions of plans, sections and books of reference in the House of Commons and in access points in the local towns and parishes. The *Edinburgh Gazette* of the same date duly published a copy of the notice.

The *Caledonian Mercury* of 4th December published a 'Board of Trade List of New Railway Bills' and the Jedburgh line followed other applications made by the Great North of Scotland Railway (Huntley to Nairn), the Glasgow & South Western Railway (various branches) and others such as the Aberdeen to Peterhead and the East of Fife line.

The *Kelso Chronicle*, for long a keen proponent and supporter of the Jedburgh line, reported on 23rd February, 1855 that the Bill had been introduced in the House of Commons on Friday 16th February by Hon. J.E. Elliot and Sir H.F. Davie. Sir John Elliott was the Liberal MP for the county of Roxburghshire whilst H.F. Davie (his full name and title being Sir Henry Ferguson-Davie, Bart.), was the member for nearby Haddington in Lothian. (Elliot was later to gain some notoriety for introducing a Bill to Parliament for legalising marriage with a deceased wife's sister!) The *Chronicle* reiterated that it looked forward to the satisfactory completion of the line of railway.

The Act of Parliament giving the go-ahead for the line was dated 25th May, 1855 and on 29th June the *Kelso Chronicle* gave notice of the first ordinary meeting of the Jedburgh Railway Company to be held in the Spread Eagle Inn, Jedburgh on Saturday 14th July at noon for the dispatch of ordinary statutory business. It was signed by 'Will. Oliver Rutherford, Chairman, and J.A. Stevenson, Secretary to the Company'.

All of the deposited plans associated with the 1852-3 and 1855 Bill applications, together with the Bills themselves and House of Lords and House of Commons committee reports, are held safely in the Parliamentary archives which is available via www.portcullis.parliament.uk.

Plaque on the wall of the Spread Eagle Hotel: 'the oldest licensed premises in Scotland'.
Author

Monteviot House Nr. Jedburgh.

Monteviot House, the seat of the Marquis of Lothian.   *Author's Collection*

Minto House, the seat of the Earl of Minto.   *Author's Collection*

Chapter Four

The construction of the line

The construction of the line was authorized by the first ordinary meeting of the Jedburgh Railway Company which was held at the Spread Eagle Inn in Jedburgh on Saturday 14th July, 1855. A report was submitted to this meeting by the Directors and a copy appeared in the *Kelso Chronicle* on Friday 13th July.

The report informed the shareholders in the company that the Act of Parliament incorporating the Jedburgh Railway Company had received the Royal Assent on the 25th May without opposition. The Directors, on receiving notice of this resolved to proceed with the construction of the railway immediately. In their Prospectus they stated that the railway had the support of two important local landowners over whose land the Railway would pass. These gentlemen were named as the Marquis of Lothian and the Earl of Minto. The Marquis' seat was at Monteviot House, near Jedburgh, whilst the Earl's main residence was at Minto House, near Hawick. Both of these gentlemen had agreed to sell portions of their land to the railway at a reasonable price. The Earl of Minto had taken shares in the company rather than being paid for the land, whilst the Marquis had agreed for part of his payment to be received in shares.

The report, according to *The Scotsman* and the *Kelso Chronicle*, said that the NBR had agreed to work and maintain the line for 50 per cent of the gross revenue until it reaches the sum of £3,500, and if the revenue exceeded that figure the percentage payable to them should reduce on a fixed scale. The agreement by the Act of Parliament was limited to 10 years. The Directors calculated that the return to shareholders would be 4 per cent per annum.

In practice there were three principal landowners who owned the land which the railway required. At the start of the line in Roxburgh parish, of the 29 areas of land required, all bar four belonged to the Duke of Roxburghe, two of the remainder belonging to the NBR. There were several lessees or 'occupiers' of the land. In Eckford parish all of the 24 areas of land required were in the ownership of the Marquis of Lothian with just two major tenants. Similarly in Crailing parish the Marquis was the principal landowner, with just one pasture not belonging to him. In Jedburgh parish about two-thirds of the land required to be crossed was part of the Marquis of Lothian's Estate with the remainder owned by the Earl of Minto. Again there were several tenant farmers of the land.

One vexed question was the site for the construction of Jedburgh station. A meeting between the railway company and the town council in 1855 resulted in animosity with the railway opting to build their station on the 'cheap side' of the town boundary. The rates were cheaper on the north side in the county area compared with the Jedburgh Burgh area. The alternative sites favoured by the council were, firstly, at Hartrigge Park, closer to the town centre (today the site of Stratheden Gardens). This would have required a costly bridge over the Jed and would have required payment of higher rates. Secondly a station could have been constructed at Queen Mary's, even closer to the centre and located

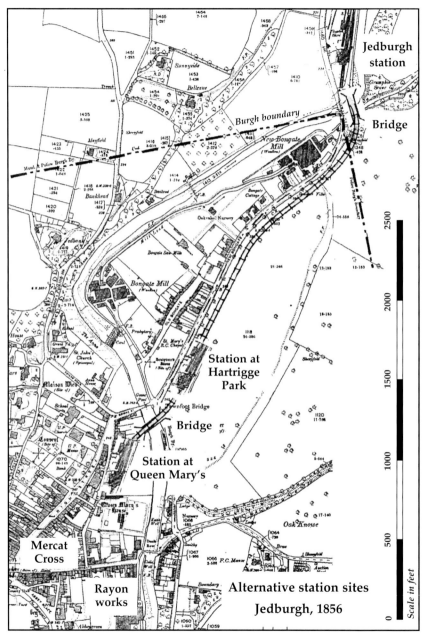

Based on an Ordnance Survey Map.   *Crown Copyright*

just to the north of Queen Mary's House. This was the council's second choice. It would have required the construction of two new bridges over the river, including one just to the south of the Toonfoot (Toonfit) road bridge, also requiring payment of higher rates! The chosen station site, almost a mile from the centre, was to be the subject of much discussion over the ensuing years.

The contractor appointed by the Jedburgh Railway was David Gillespie of Causewayhead near Stirling. He was born in about 1809. He was the son of a cotton weaver. In the 1861 census he describes himself as a contractor employing 66 persons and in 1871 simply as a contractor, in both years living at 2 Crag View, Causewayhead in Stirling. A local trade directory described him as a 'railway-contractor'. He is believed to have been associated with the building of the Stirling & Dunfermline Railway and some others in Scotland. By 1858 he was also the proprietor of the Clackmannan Brick, Tile & Fire Clay Works. He was a benefactor of Dollar Academy at Stirling though there is no evidence that he studied there. He was a member of the Stirling & Bannockburn Caledonian Society. He was also keen on field sports and took part in angling competitions, gaining, for example, the first prize in a competition held by the Alloa Angling Club. He landed 18 lb. of fish; the second prizewinner landed just over 6 lb. Gillespie also bred draught horses, which, no doubt, were used on his contracts. After completing the Jedburgh contract he assumed responsibility, according to the *Stirling Observer*, for maintenance of the line and stations for the Forth & Clyde Junction Railway.

The Jedburgh line was staked out and the contractor was ready to proceed with some of the heavier aspects of the work as soon as possession of the land was obtained. The contract with Gillespie required the work to be completed by 1st October, 1856. However, the Directors expressed an opinion that if more funds became available then the railway could be finished and opened for traffic in advance of that date.

Gillespie's contract required him to construct the railway and associated works, plus stations, with the sum to be paid to him (quoted variously in the press and at meetings as £28,000, £28,500 or £29,000) being well within the capital sum authorized by the Act of Parliament. The Directors' view was that, after the costs of construction were paid, and with the level of traffic that they anticipated, an annual dividend of 4 per cent would be paid to shareholders, though at that time only £26,000 of the authorized capital of £35,000 had been subscribed. Gillespie was to be remunerated partly in paid-up shares as the work progressed.

A report, signed by the Chairman, William Oliver Rutherford, included the names of the Directors named in the Act: Oliver Rutherford, Andrew Whitelock Mein, William Dodd, John Ord, J.S.E. Fair and Charles Kerr. The report stated that the Directors recommended that Thomas Riddell replace Oliver Rutherford who wished to stand down.

Charles Jopp's map, *Plan and Section of the Jedburgh Railway* is dated 1854 and, like his estimate of expense, is part of the Parliamentary archive at Westminster. The map shows the proposed extent of the line, enlargements of areas where full detail could not be shown on the main plan, plus sections across the line at important road crossings. The limits of deviation, permitted during construction, appear also. Linear distances on the map are measured from the junction with the Kelso branch at Roxburgh and are in the imperial units used at the time: miles, furlongs and chains (one furlong is 220 yards, that is, just over 201 metres whilst one chain is 22 yards i.e. just over 20 metres).

On the map the proposed line leaves the junction on a gentle curve of four furlongs radius and descends on a downward gradient of 1 in 106 for just over three furlongs. Just beyond the station limit is shown the 25 ft high road overbridge with a 16 ft arched span. The gradient changes to a short upward section of 1 in 105 to a point opposite the house 'Redstead' where the line is on a curve of six furlongs radius. The line levels out for just over three furlongs almost as far as a small bridge over a burn where the left-hand curve is of three furlongs. At a point 1 mile 2½ furlongs from the junction the line leaves Roxburgh parish and enters Eckford parish on a downwards gradient of 1 in 420. The gradient changes to 1 in 110 down and is shown crossing the road at Ormiston on the level, necessitating the road being raised by 5 ft with the road approaches to the crossing on gradients of 1 in 20. (In actuality a bridge was constructed to take the railway over the road. Ormiston station was constructed immediately after this bridge though stations are not shown on the map.) A succession of small cuttings and embankments characterize this first section of the line.

After the road crossing the line is shown as quite straight and level for about two miles. Then the line changes to a very gentle downward gradient of 1 in 500. A level crossing is shown across a very minor road. Curves of five and then four furlongs radius follow over a section of about a mile. The line then traverses part of Crailing parish from approximately the 2 mile 5½ furlong to a point 4 mile 5½ furlongs from the junction at Roxburgh. In this section the gradients change from 1 in 600 up, to 1 in 115 down. A burn in a culvert is crossed at 4 miles 1 furlong. Shortly after this is the Nisbet road crossing immediately after which Nisbet station was built. The crossing is shown as exactly level.

From Nisbet the line is shown as level for 1½ furlongs, crossing a footpath close to Nisbet Boat House on the level. The gradient changes to 1 in 150 down with a small bridge taking the line over the leat (shown as 'The Lead' on the map) from Nisbet Mill. The track becomes quite straight on an upward gradient of 1 in 180 before making another road crossing, in this case the road needing to be raised by some 3 ft to make the crossing level. The track then continues level for the crossing of the line over the River Teviot. (This is normally referred to as the 'Teviot Bridge' but sometimes as 'Nisbet Bridge'.) No indication is shown on this map of the nature of the bridge, though it was originally wooden, being replaced later by a metal girder bridge which was painted black. Local ganger Jim Hay's recording for the Scottish Borders Memory Bank refers to this as 'The Black Brig crossing the Teviot' though the term 'Black Brig' has also been applied to the bridge crossing the Jed.

After the Teviot Bridge Jopp's map shows the rail track, carried on a shallow embankment, descending on a gradient of 1 in 180 towards a point five miles from Roxburgh. The embankment at this point was pierced by a small bridge, really a viaduct, supported on wooden, later concrete, piles, usually referred to as the 'Boss Brig.' This was located on the opposite side of the Teviot from the Nisbet Mill farm. It was a wooden structure on piles which allowed flood water to drain away from the nearby Haughs with the aim of prevention of undermining or damage to the railway's foundations. (The term 'Boss' is an old Scots word meaning 'hollow'. 'Boss Brig' is thus the 'bridge over the hollow'.)

The line is then shown as entering into the Jedburgh parish. For the next four furlongs the line rises at 1 in 193 with a succession of curves, left, right then left, of two to three furlongs radius. Mount Hooly House is on the east of the line. The curves take the line from the valley of the Teviot into the valley of the River Jed (or Jedwater). The line follows the Jed for the rest of its distance to the planned station at Jedburgh. At the 5 miles 4 furlongs point (just after the unmarked site of Jedfoot station) the line crosses the main Kelso and Crailing to Jedburgh road on the level. No works were necessary to adjust the level of the road for the crossing. The line is then level for 2½ furlongs with a bridge to take the line over the Jed in the middle of this section. (This metal bridge, identified as a 'viaduct' on some Ordnance Survey maps, replaced the original wooden one later in the century. It was, like the Teviot bridge, painted black and, as mentioned earlier, was also referred to as 'The Black Bridge or 'Black Brig'.) The line then becomes curved, firstly to the left, then to the right, both with radii of two furlongs. The gradient changes to an upwards one of 1 in 174. The line was designed to pass Bonjedward mill with the sharpest curve on the line, about 1 furlong 2 chains radius, nearby. From a point about 6 miles 6½ furlongs the gradient switches to 1 in 1066 upwards as far as the terminus. Jopp's map indicates the need for the diversion of the original public road, and the creation of a new level crossing, before the terminus is reached at just over seven miles from Roxburgh. There was a difference of just one foot between the height of the start of the line at Roxburgh Junction and the station site at Jedburgh!

The local Teviotdale newspaper, the *Teviotdale Record*, informed the public in mid-August 1855 that the formation of the railway had already commenced at a location near to Ormiston on the north bank of the Tweed. The newspaper lamented the fact that the Directors had not seen fit to hold a ceremony for the turning of the first sod, though it was admitted that this would have served no useful purpose other than publicity. However, it was felt that a ceremony, involving the people of the district, would have been a good idea. The paper also lamented that no-one from the shareholders or Directors had seen fit to keep them informed of such matters as the commencement of works (actually on 6th August, St James' Fair Day), the terms of the contract and the arrangements with the North British Railway for working the line. They had been totally unaware that the works were in such a forward state! 'The railway was commenced at Ormiston, without any ceremony, not even in the presence of the chairman, the secretary, or the auditors of the company.'

By early December it was reported (in the *Kelso Chronicle*) that works upon the line were progressing with considerable rapidity. Near to Nisbet, where the railway had to cross the River Teviot, a large number of piles had been sunk. The bridge, to be constructed in wood was said to be of such solid construction that it would resist the Teviot even its wildest moods. Over 200 navvies were already at work between Nisbet and Ormiston. The reporter expressed the opinion that, assuming that the weather continued to be favourable in the winter months, such substantial progress would be made ensuring that the work would be completed by the date of 1st August, 1856. This would afford local residents the opportunity to attend St James Fair at Kelso with less cost and fatigue than hitherto. It predicted that the opening of the railway would bring 'a good time coming' to the whole of the district. The *Illustrated Berwick Journal* used the same article, in its entirety, in its edition of 15th December.

However, the weather during the next fortnight was not as kind as had been hoped. The *Westmorland Gazette*, published 'over the Border', reported that the River Tweed had completely frozen up for a week and the severe freezing conditions had caused the surface of the Teviot to become coated with a thick layer of ice. A rise in temperature and heavy rain caused a very rapid thaw to set in and the river, swollen with extra water to a higher level since the great flood of February 1831, carried down huge icebergs! These carried away a quantity of loose timber from next to the Teviot bridge. Some scaffolding on which a group of men were working was washed away by the force of the water and they barely had time to escape before the entire structure was borne away by the current. Sections of the embankment near to Nisbet were completely washed away. However, conditions rapidly improved, repairs were effected, and progress on the works returned to normal.

As happened all too frequently during railway construction at this time, the navvies engaged in the work let themselves down. The Teviotdale newspaper reported that in mid-February 1856 there had been a 'disgraceful breach of the peace' at Crailing Tofts, not far from the line, on a Sabbath evening. A band of drunken navvies had engaged in a fight amongst themselves and a number became seriously injured. The police were sent for but by the time that they had arrived the ringleaders had fled. However, their identities were well-known and it was anticipated that they would soon be apprehended and taken into custody. It was suspected that the source of spirits which had caused the drunkenness had been obtained from an illegal source in the village of Crailing. The local inhabitants were said to be petitioning that a police force be stationed at Crailing on each Sabbath day to prevent a recurrence.

Despite these setbacks the unusually fine weather of early 1856 allowed the work to make very satisfactory progress especially on the section of line between Nisbet and Roxburgh. The bridge over the Teviot was also reported (by the *Illustrated Berwick Journal* towards the end of March) as being in a very advanced state. Likewise the bridge over the Jed, in the neighbourhood of what was formerly called Waulk Mill, had also been started. Some of the piles had already been driven into the ground. The article, and a similar one in the Teviotdale newspaper, predicted that there was every probability of the works being completed, and the railway opened for traffic, by the month of August allowing the 'Jethart Folk' to get a trip to the St James Fair on 5th August.

The local *Teviotdale Record* newspaper contained further details. The 'spiles' for the Teviot bridge were nearly all anchored into the ground creating a formidable array of wood and iron. On 2nd January, which rather than New Year's Day, was a local holiday both young and old were seen wending their way towards the Teviot in order to get a view of the bridge under construction.

The actions of the 'Monkey' (pile driver) in driving the ponderous blocks of wood into the river bed was a source of astonishment.

The *Illustrated Berwick Journal* report coincided with the advance notice of the second ordinary meeting of the shareholders, which, once again, was to be held at the Spread Eagle Hotel. The date of the meeting was 25th March, 1856, the notice being published on 1st March. The report placed before the meeting stated that the works on the line had made steady progress and that the Directors had made inspections from time to time. They were able to corroborate the report which the Resident Engineer had made of the work being in a 'forward and satisfactory state'. This engineer was, of course, Charles Jopp. In his report to the Directors he mentioned that despite the inclement weather, which had been experienced for part of the construction time, the work was half-completed.

He reported that the heaviest cuttings on the line, between Old Ormiston and the Junction with the Kelso line at Roxburgh, were very nearly finished. The bridges over the rivers were also well advanced. The Teviot bridge was to be completed within a month, whilst the one over the Jed, recently commenced, would be completed in the course of about six weeks. The masonry of the only two public road bridges on the line would be completed within about a fortnight. A considerable portion of the fencing had been erected and upwards of 560 tons of permanent rails, 140 tons of chairs and upwards of 9,000 sleepers had been delivered. The permanent way had been laid for a length of about three miles and the contractor was continuing to lay down the 'forming' (foundations) and was complete for another one mile. The plans for the various stations and gate keeper's lodges were finished and nearly all were in the hands of the contractor, the execution of these works being proceeded with immediately.

The Engineer concluded his report by stating that he had no doubt that the works for the line would be completed, and that it would be opened for traffic, by 1st August. To achieve this, the contractor would only have to continue at the same rate in the favourable summer months as he had in the winter. No doubt it was this report which provided details for the brief article in *The Scotsman* referring to the satisfactory progress on various parts of the line and the probability of it being opened by the month of August.

By the 22nd April newspapers were reporting that on the north side of the Teviot towards Roxburgh Junction the line was almost complete. The bridges over the Teviot and the Jed were almost ready for their rails, whilst from the Teviot towards Jedfoot Bridge the line was rapidly assuming shape and form. As the land here was below the level required for the railway it was necessary for an 'island' to be created on which the rails could be laid. Temporary rails had been laid to bring in construction materials to a field on the adjacent farm of Mounthooly. From the new rail bridge over the Jed (a short distance above the old stone road bridge) as far as 'Mr Stenhouse's mill' the work was very advanced. Picks, spades and wheelbarrows were involved in some heavy cutting work beyond this point at a location referred to as 'the foot of Harden'. Nearby the course of the Jed had been successfully diverted a little from its former course 'to give place for the career of the "warm water hero".' To what this refers is not known! Towards Jedburgh the trackbed skirted the side of the road until the end of the tree plantation where a further small deviation of the Jed had been made. Work was proceeding to divert the route of the turnpike road. Instead of its existing alignment it was to be diverted to the right (i.e. towards the west) in order to make room for the station near to the road bridge over the Jed. The newspaper reported that the constructions of the stations were now 'let' though it believed that they were three in number: Jedburgh, Jedfoot and Nisbet. The station at Old Ormiston (later Kirkbank) was not mentioned. In the same article the newspaper reporter deplored the apathy and indifference of some of the local landowners, who, it was felt, should have been investing a quota in the line rather than turning their backs upon it. As a result there was still some unappropriated share capital, which state of affairs was shortly to be discussed with the NBR who would be operating the line when it opened.

There were two further setbacks before the work was completed. In mid-May whilst several navvies were engaged in the 'Cut' on the line nearly opposite the new mill, a heavy portion of the bank collapsed engulfing two of the workmen. After considerable efforts on the part of their colleagues they were extricated. One of the men suffered a shoulder dislocation and both of them received bruising. A week after the accident they were reported as recovering well.

On the 17th June the *Teviotdale Record* reported that the works in connection with the line were approaching completion. The cut opposite Mr Hope's Mill, which had proved to be a serious obstacle, was all but finished and the short space between this point and the Jedburgh station site would soon be completed with the efforts of many men being concentrated there. A further source of delay had been overcome by the proposed erection of a screen as the rails had come very close to the road at Bonjedward. This would cost a sum of about £200. Some considered this to be a waste of money as it was considered that the noise of passing trains would be the same with or without the screen. Horses were more likely to be frightened by this if they could not see the train rather than having it in view. If this screen were considered important then there were other places equally deserving of a screen. A letter to the newspaper, signed by 'Tiviotdale' [sic] described such an incident at a neighbouring station where a horse, unable to see the source of sound from a locomotive, had become almost unmanageable, but, on its coming into sight, had become submissive and quiet. The letter's author urged the trustees not to urge the erection of the screen. The local turnpike trustees held a meeting to discuss the erection of this screen. The prevailing view was that the screen would be 'productive of evil'. It was also stated at the meeting that the majority of the public, and those conversant with the matter, were not in favour of the screen's erection.

At the same meeting the trustees received a petition from Mr Scott of the Spread Eagle Inn and Mr Govenlock of the Harrow Inn, asking for a reduction in tolls due to the event of their running omnibuses between the station and their respective hotels. Their request was granted and it would be necessary for them to pay just one half of the normal dues for such traffic.

The newspaper report of the 17th June said that the stations were assuming shape and form but would not be fully ready for use at the time of the line's opening which was expected at the end of July or the beginning of August. The newspaper welcomed the appointment of William Hartley as the new station master for Jedburgh: 'a better and more deserving person could not have been appointed'.

A newspaper published and printed many miles away from Jedburgh, the *Dumfries and Galloway Standard*, predicted on 18th June that the Jedburgh Railway would be opened on 18th July. The significance of this date was that this was the occasion of the St Boswell's fair-day [*sic*], the greatest market for rural produce in the south of Scotland!

On the 1st July the Teviotdale newspaper (and the *Border Advertiser*) reported that the work on 'Our Branch' was being prosecuted with great vigour with men working day and night on mounding and rail-laying. The rails between Roxburgh and Jedburgh were now almost complete. Trucks laden with material were being drawn over the length of the line by horses but it was expected that the 'iron horse' would, very shortly, take their place. The first locomotive was expected to arrive on about the 9th July and the line be opened for traffic on either 16th or 18th. However, a good deal of work remained to be done in adjusting the rails into position and sloping and dressing the sides of the ballast. The rapidly rising stations were creating an air of anticipation of cheap trips in the inhabitants of the town of Jedburgh!

The *Border Advertiser* in its 11th July edition said that the government inspector was expected daily to arrive to make his survey of the line. They were inadvertently in error in publishing this as the day before, the 10th July, the line was inspected by Lt-Colonel Yolland with Captain Gratton of the Royal Engineers. His subsequent report to the Board of Trade was dated 19th July. This detailed document provides much insight into the construction materials and methods used. He referred to the line as starting 'at a siding' at the Roxburgh station of the NBR and terminating 7 miles and 13 chains away near to Jedburgh bridge. He said that land had been taken for a single line only, with the various bridges being constructed accordingly. The width of the line at foundation level was just 15 ft. The rails were 'double-headed' and laid in lengths of just 20 and 16 ft. The rails, weighing 65 lb. per yard, were laid in cast-iron chairs (of Ransome & Mays patent) weighing 20 lb. The rails were held in the chairs by oak 'keys' with the chairs being fixed to the sleepers by means of 'oak tie-nails'. The sleepers were made of larch whose average size was 8 ft 9 in. x 9 in. x 4½ in. with the smallest measuring 8 ft 0 in. x 6 in.. The sleepers were spaced 2 ft 9 in., 3 ft 3 in. or 4 ft 0 in. apart and were laid on ballast consisting of gravel and sand not less than 1 ft 9 in. in depth. Yolland described the line as being in good order. He referred to the line having some considerable embankments and cuttings but required that the line be regularly subject to careful inspection because of the likelihood of flooding in some areas.

Colonel Yolland described the three underbridges on the line. One was of stone and brick with a segmented arch of 26 ft 6 in. on a skew. The second consisted of stone with cast-iron girders of 25 ft 6 in., also on a skew. The third was built with stone abutments and timber beams. He also detailed four wooden viaducts, the largest being the 144 ft one crossing the River Teviot. This he described as being amply strong and well-constructed on piles.

Five level crossings had been sanctioned by the Companies Act. He remarked that several of these had very little road traffic passing over them. The gates at the crossings closed both the railway and the roads when necessary. He noted that the lodges (crossing keepers' buildings) were still in the process of construction. He remarked on the sidings at Ormiston, Nesbit [sic] and Jedfoot and the stations at these points but noted that the fencing of the railway was incomplete and that the turntable at Jedburgh station had not yet been erected.

In mid-July newspapers reported what was described as the second serious accident since the construction of the railway had commenced. A young boy, playing with friends had been pushing wagons to and fro. Unfortunately he was crushed between the buffers and was killed. This incident is described more fully in a later chapter on accidents and incidents.

Returning to Colonel Yolland's report he noted a number of requirements that were required if he was to sanction the opening of the line. Firstly, a pair of points at Roxburgh needed attention. They were weighted to stand open for the main down line of the Kelso branch instead of for the sidings. He required that the 'handles' (presumably the operating levers) for the branch distant signals should be closer to the stations at Roxburgh, Nesbit [sic] and Jedfoot stations. In addition a distant signal was required to be erected to the south of Jedward mill. He required the lodges to be completed at Jedward mill and Ormiston level crossings and, finally, that the turntable be erected at Jedburgh station.

Towards the end of his report he referred to the fact that he had had a telegraphic dispatch on the 18th July from the line's Engineer stating that the requirements about the signals had been attended to. He had also had a letter from the Chairman and Secretary of the Jedburgh Railway Co. requesting permission for the line to be opened at once if they undertook to erect the turntable within three months of their letter. This 'telegram' explained why the Directors were so keen to have the line opened as soon as possible. Firstly they stated that there was a number of fairs and markets held in the district in July and August, and secondly, that they were making exertions to encourage summer passengers.

The Directors had corresponded with Jopp, the Engineer, and he referred to the fact that the NBR, contracted to work the line, had undertaken to provide a tank engine to work the line, making the immediate need for a turntable unnecessary.

Bearing all of this in mind, Colonel Yolland recommended to the Board of Trade that sanction be given for the opening of the line subject to the following four conditions:

That only one engine in steam be permitted on the line at one and the same time
That the engine be a tank engine
That the company undertake to erect the turntable within the period of three months, and
That the speed on the line be limited to 20 miles per hour.

The *Teviotdale Record* celebrated its first year of existence on 15th July, 1856 and contained a very extensive editorial essay relating to the opening of the Jedburgh line and to railways generally. It started with reference to the celebratory trip which the shareholders were to make along the line and to the dinner, to be held in the Spread Eagle Hotel. It referred to the fact that the undertaking of the Jedburgh line, first proposed some years previously, had been deferred on account of the reckless speculation that had reached its climax under the reign of George Hudson. However, wiser commercial principles had now been applied. The editorial described the Jedburgh line as being 7¼ miles in length with a subscribed capital of £35,000. The contractor's estimate for the building of the line was £28,500 and he had completed the work within the specified time. The line had been made with praiseworthy economy. The editorial expressed the hope that the Directors would exercise a wise discretion in determining to carry both passengers and goods upon moderate terms. It noted that they had resolved to run no trains on the Sabbath.

The auctioneer James Fairbairn placed an advertisement in the *Kelso Chronicle* for the sale of some of the plant used in the line's construction. The newspaper's date was 30th September, 1859. To be sold were some 80 waggons [*sic*], 22 tons of service rails, a piling machine with a crab winch and some 'dobbing carts'. No advertisement has been found for the sale, after October 1859, of the remaining plant; perhaps it was already sold privately or had been moved for use at the site of another of Gillespie's contracts.

The reference to 'praiseworthy economy' was to rebound on the railway in future years. On many occasions the use of cheap gravel and sand ballast, rather than more substantial stone ballast, was to facilitate wash-outs of parts of the trackbed following flooding, as hinted at by Yolland in his report. It was also necessary later in the century to replace the original timber bridges with more substantial stone and metal constructions and finally the relative lack of facilities at Jedburgh station (inadequate lighting and sheltered waiting areas) were to become a regular source of complaint from travellers.

However, the *Record* reminded readers that at the end of the previous century the coach known as the *Jedburgh Fly* took two days to travel the 50 miles to Edinburgh over roads with an execrable road surface, and that at that time the saddle and the packhorse were the established methods of conveyance. Even in more recent times, with an improved road surface, the journey to Edinburgh had taken at least 4½ hours. But now 'the Royal burgh of Jedburgh has sworn allegiance to the railway. The road has yielded to the rail.'

Indeed, the *Border Advertiser* reported on 4th July, 1856 that the 'old fashioned stage coach' would no longer run between Kelso and Jedburgh; the one remaining coach continued to ply between Jedburgh and Belses.

TO RAILWAY CONTRACTORS AND OTHERS·

SALE OF RAILWAY PLANT, &c.

To be Sold, by Auction, at Roxburgh Station, on the Line of the Edinburgh and Kelso Railway, on Thursday the 13th of October next,
A PORTION of the PLANT used in the Construction of the Jedburgh Railway, consisting of
80 WAGGONS, 22 TONS SERVICE RAILS, a PILING MACHINE with CRAB WINCH, a Number of DOBBING CARTS, and a good many other articles, suitable for Railway Contractors.
Terms, Cash.
The Sale will commence at 11 o'Clock A.M.
JAMES FAIRBAIRN, Auctioneer.
Kelso, Sept. 22, 1859.

Advertisement from the *Kelso Chronicle* of 30th September, 1859.

Chapter Five

The opening of the line

The inaugural train

The *Teviotdale Record* of the 29th July, 1856 reported in detail on the opening of the line which had taken place on Friday 18th July. It referred to the energy of the contractor, Mr Gillespie and the zeal of the Board of Directors, coupled with the able services of J. Stevenson, the Procurator Fiscal as Secretary in giving the shareholders and public a line some two months before the specified opening time. This was a feat not often accomplished at that time. The government inspector was well satisfied with the stability and the construction of the railway, paying compliments to Mr Gillespie for the manner in which the contract had been fulfilled. It reported that the inspector was rather displeased that there was no turntable at the Jedburgh terminus but understood that this would shortly be remedied. He had made no comment about the lack of gas lighting at the station and between the station and the Bongate bridge or the lack of telegraphic communication to Jedburgh. Unfortunately the Jedburgh band could not play at the opening as it had a prior commitment. However, the Lauder band substituted!

After the inspector had expressed his general satisfaction, the Directors and others made a visit to the town, presumably to partake of some refreshment. They were accompanied by the band playing music. They then returned to Jedburgh station for the inaugural train to Roxburgh and back. Apparently there was some slight misunderstanding as to the qualifications for being on this first trip. However, when the train pulled out of the station there was a goodly number of members of the fair sex and some non-shareholders on board. The train consisted of 16 first class carriages and a splendid saloon which had kindly been provided by the North British Railway. A considerable crowd had gathered to witness the train's departure and their enthusiasm was not diminished by a short rain shower which fell at about 1 o'clock. The newspaper referred to all social classes being present, rich and poor, grave and gay, old and young, all wishing to witness the departure of the 'iron monarch'! Once all was ready the train started its journey, leaving the station amidst the applause of the assembled multitude, the sound of cannon reports and the tunes from the band who occupied an open carriage at the front of the train! At the start of the journey the 'screen question' was tested by the numerous horses and vehicles stationed along the road. The lack of distress on the part of the horses provided a strong argument for its non-erection!

On arrival at Jedfoot the train stopped for the band to play a tune for the assembled small crowd. The train resumed its journey passing cows in an adjacent field capering and jumping with their tails on end. Having crossed the Teviot by the new and massive wooden bridge, the train arrived at Nisbet station. Here there was another hearty greeting from the assembled crowd. Once again the band played a tune. A few minutes after departure from Nisbet the train arrived at Ormiston station for a brief stop where some additional passengers joined the train. After a few more minutes the train arrived at Roxburgh having taken about 25 minutes for its journey from Jedburgh.

At Roxburgh station abundant refreshments of wine and cake awaited the excursionists. After partaking of these there was time for a stroll around the village of Roxburgh, a visit to the church and churchyard or a short walk to peep at the 'stupendous bridge' over the Teviot on the railway line to Kelso. After a short time it was necessary for the participants to rejoin the train, which, after a brief stop at Ormiston, rattled along the valleys of the Teviot and Jed entering Jedburgh station to the enthusiastic applause of the large crowd which had remained to see the returning train. Participants were well-satisfied with their first trip on the line. Immediately on arrival the gentlemen from the train formed into procession order and proceeded over the bridge towards the town with banners flying and headed by the band. The ladies presumably returned to the town in carriages, though they were not to take part in the continuation of the celebrations, the dinner at the Spread Eagle Hotel.

The day had been declared a public holiday and so some 300 other members of the local population were able to be carried to Roxburgh Junction in an excursion train (according to a 1952 report appearing in the *Jedburgh Gazette*) and it was reported that, according to the diary of a Mr Thomson of Roxburgh, 'much whisky was drunk'.

The celebratory dinner

At 4 o'clock in the afternoon about 100 gentlemen sat down to an excellent dinner at the Spread Eagle Hotel on the High Street in Jedburgh. Unfortunately details of the menu appear not to have survived!

John Ord, the Chairman of the Board of Directors of the Jedburgh Railway Company, presided over the occasion. He was accompanied, on his right and left, by Messrs Jouat and Cheyne, two of the Directors of the NBR. Also seated at the cross table were local dignitaries Thomas Riddell, J.M. Craigie (Sheriff Substitute), J.S. Darling (Kelso's senior magistrate), Revd Messrs Purves and Barr, J.S.E Fair, J.M. Grainger (Provost of Jedburgh), George Roberts (Provost of Selkirk), Thomas Ord and George Wilson. Charles Kerr was the vice-chairman for the occasion supported on his right by A.W. Nein, William Dodd and James Stevenson. The body of the hall was filled with other tables at which were seated shareholders, officials and invited local dignitaries.

After the meal there was a request for Divine Blessing from Revd Purves. There followed a long succession of toasts: to Her Majesty the Queen, Prince Albert and other members of the Royal Family, to the success of the Jedburgh Railway, to the health of the landed proprietors (including the Duke of Roxburghe, the Earl of Minto and the Marquis of Lothian), the Duke of Buccleuch, the local clergy, the Chairman and Directors of the Jedburgh Railway, Messrs Cheyne and Jouat of the NBR, the Secretary of the Board, Mr Kerr (Vice-Chairman of the Board but referred to as the Croupier), Mr Jopp (the Engineer), 'Prosperity to Agriculture, Manufacturers and Commerce', the army and the navy, Mr Rowbotham and other officials of the NBR, the Provost and magistrates of Jedburgh, prosperity to the Selkirk Railway company, prosperity to Kelso, and so on. There was much mutual congratulation!

The speeches touched upon a variety of subjects, such as the railway stimulating the development of local roads to promote the prosperity and advancement of the community, and to infuse the life and commerce of the town. The facilities of railway transit and traffic would be brought to the doors of Jedburgh's inhabitants. Its tradesmen and manufacturers would be able to carry on their business to advantage and even the humblest of persons would feel the benefit of being supplied with coal and other things more regularly and with cheaper prices.

Speeches of reply were, of course, made to all of the toasts proposed. As if that were not enough, music and songs enlivened the proceedings between the speeches and the company did not break up until about 9 o'clock in the evening.

The start of the passenger train services

The *Kelso Chronicle* displayed, on 25th July, 1856, an advertisement from the Jedburgh Railway which was dated 17th July. This advertised that the passenger train service on the branch had commenced running and that the service would consist of four trains in each direction. The first, with accommodation for first, second and third class passengers, would leave Jedburgh at 6.40 am and arrive at Roxburgh at 7.07 am (Edinburgh arrival, by connecting train at 9.33 am). Subsequent trains would leave at 9.10 am for Roxburgh (arrive 9.37) and Kelso (arrive 9.58), 10.40 am (arrival at Roxburgh at 11.07, Kelso at 11.17 am and Edinburgh 1.36 pm) and finally at 5.10 pm (arrival at Roxburgh 5.37 pm, Kelso at 5.47 pm and Edinburgh 8.05 pm). The 10.40 am train would not carry third class passengers.

In the reverse direction a train would leave Kelso at 7.00 am and Roxburgh at 7.15 arriving at Jedburgh at 7.42. A departure from Edinburgh at 7.25 am allowed passengers to leave Roxburgh at 9.46 and to arrive at Jedburgh at 10.11. The next train to Jedburgh arrived at Jedburgh at 2.19 pm having left Roxburgh some 27 minutes earlier (with a connection from Edinburgh departing at 11.20 am). This train also did not carry third class passengers. The last train of the day into Jedburgh was scheduled to arrive at 7.25 pm with departures from Edinburgh advertised for 4.30 pm and from Roxburgh at 7.00 pm. On Fridays the train scheduled to arrive at Jedburgh at 2.19 pm (the 1.41 pm departure from Kelso) would run 29 minutes later throughout on its journey to Jedburgh.

Each passenger train was to serve all of the stations on the Jedburgh branch, namely Jedfoot Bridge, Nisbet and Old Ormiston. There was no mention in the advertisement of any through carriages, in either direction, between Jedburgh and Edinburgh.

A few days before the line opened the *Kelso Chronicle* announced that the *Chevy Chase* coach had ceased running between Jedburgh and Belses (on the so-called Waverley Route) with effect from 16th July.

The *Teviotdale Record* in its edition of 17th January, 1857 remarked that since the opening of the railway, about six months previously, no fewer than 7,574 passengers had travelled on the line. It commented that this was nearly double the entire population of Jedburgh!

Fortunately the book of the Returns to the Board of Trade for the year ending 31st December, 1858 provides further indication of the passenger traffic on the new rail line. After this date the details of the Jedburgh branch traffic were subsumed into the NBR's returns.

In 1858 there were 3,325 persons purchasing first class tickets on the line whilst 7,983 travelled with second class tickets. The number travelling third class was just 4,609 but the largest total of all was that of the fourth, or Parliamentary, class passengers which totalled 8,164. The grand total was thus just over 20,000 passengers. The total would not have included through tickets to the line's stations from other companies on the railway network. The fare's charged per mile by the Jedburgh company were 2.23*d*. in first class, 1.75*d*. in second, 1.26*d*. in third class and 0.99*d*. per mile in the Parliamentary class. The last figure was fixed at 'no more than 1*d*. per mile' by law. In addition 56 dog tickets were issued.

The Jedburgh Railway and the NBR agreed from the start that through tickets be made available to Edinburgh, Portobello, Niddrie, Eskbank, Stow, Galashiels, Melrose, Newtown (St Boswells), Belses, Hassendean, Hawick, Kelso and Selkirk. The through fares were calculated by adding the Jedburgh line fares to the North British fares from Roxburgh. An example was a Jedburgh to Hawick first class ticket priced at 2*s*. 6*d*. with second class tickets priced at 2*s*. and third class at 1*s*. 9*d*. Some reduced fare tickets were available on Saturdays.

In August 1861 the Post Office announced that henceforth all mail would travel to and from Jedburgh by passenger train. It was considered that this arrangement would speed up the delivery of the mail compared with hitherto, when the horse-drawn 'Jedburgh Mail Gig' had been used. As a result the mail gig was withdrawn from service.

By 1863 there were six advertised passenger trains from Roxburgh to Jedburgh and seven in the reverse direction, an indication either of optimism or of the success of the passenger traffic on the line.

The start of the goods train services

The line opened for goods traffic on the same day as the public passenger service. The timetables, appearing in the local press, referred only to the passenger trains and there was no indication of exactly when the first goods trains would run.

However, it is possible to collate information from several sources to give a picture of the early goods traffic on the branch. These sources include the contemporary advertisements made by various concerns in the local newspapers, the Board of Trade returns for the line and the information provided in the first working timetables which included the goods workings.

Both before, and around the time of the opening, both the Jedburgh Railway and local business concerns were advertising the facilities they would be able to offer, and items that they would be able to supply, as a result of the opening of the line. For example the NBR announced that they had made arrangements for Jedburgh to be placed on the same footing as other local towns as regards the transmission of small parcels. Copies of the regulations relating to this were to be available from Mr Hartley at Jedburgh station.

Before the arrival of the local branch railways, coal for the Kelso and Jedburgh areas had largely arrived by horse-drawn carts from the Shoreswood Colliery over the border in the north of Northumberland. References can be found to up to 40 carts waiting at this colliery each morning for this traffic. However, the Shoreswood and Scremerston Coal & Lime Co. was one of the first to install an agent, Andrew Dunn, at Jedburgh and to advertise in the Borders' newspapers the facility for the delivery of coal, lime, bricks and pipes by rail. In 1856 coal was offered at Jedburgh for 14s. 10d. per ton and lime for 13s. 11d. per ton, with slightly cheaper rates for the other branch stations, though only full truckloads could be supplied to Old Ormiston, Nisbet and Jedfoot.

Also in 1856, William Hartley, who was, of course both station master and agent at Jedburgh, was offering, soon after the branch opened, both English coal (from, for example, Killingworth and Backworth) and Scottish coal (from collieries such as Pencaitland and Prestongrange) in various qualities: 'best', 'smithy', 'splint' and 'dross', at prices to match.

By July 1856 the Shidlaw Brick & Tile Works, located near Carham between Berwick and Kelso, was advertising free delivery of drainpipes, tiles and bricks to all stations on the Jedburgh branch, with prices available on application to their Clerk of Works, George Barnes.

Then in May 1857 advertisements began to appear for the possible delivery of 'superior quality' imported guano and dissolved bones from the port of Leith, for use as manure on the fields. Samples of these products were able to be inspected at W. Brown's on Castle Street in Jedburgh. Wagonloads could be delivered to Jedburgh station.

It is perhaps appropriate at this point to mention that soon after the start of traffic the NBR approached the Directors of the Jedburgh Railway Co. with a view to the latter extending the goods facilities at each station. They requested additional sidings for the traffic, the erection of weighing machines, improved loading banks and other works which would improve the efficiency in working the line. The *Kelso Chronicle* stated that the Directors agreed, at a half-yearly meeting, to comply with several of these demands and the works were carried out immediately. The Directors felt that no additional accommodation or works would be needed unless a considerable increase in traffic should render them necessary. (Works completed at the same time included the finishing of the painting of all of the station and gatekeepers' houses, plus the construction of an embankment on the north side of the Teviot for the protection of the line against erosion from the river waters.)

The Board of Trade returns for the year 1858, soon after the line opened, showed that some 2,552 tons of coal were carried on the branch together with 3,444 tons of 'other minerals'. Into this category would have been entered the lime, fertilizer and other materials referred to above. The grand total was thus 5,996 tons. To this were added 3,634 tons of 'general merchandise' plus items of livestock. For example 165 cattle, 1,340 sheep and 152 pigs were moved along the line, a total of 1,657 animals. Some 41 horses and five carriages were also transported by rail. Jedburgh station could load or unload both carriages and horses, though the other branch stations could only handle horses. Horses were transported for any distance for 2s. 6d., ponies for 1s. 9d. whilst carriages and carts were charged at 3s. 6d. The price of a dog ticket was set at just 3d.

There was thus plenty of variety in the goods traffic on the branch. The revenues from the passenger, parcels and goods traffic allowed the Jedburgh Railway Co. to pay a dividend to shareholders of 3 per cent in 1857 and 2¾ per cent in 1859, for example.

As the first surviving working timetable, including details of goods workings, for the NBR dates from 1863, some seven years after the opening to Jedburgh, it is not possible to be precise about the timings of the first goods trains on the line in the 1850s. The 1863 timetable indicated that a trip working leaving Kelso at 8.50 pm would forward the goods traffic for the stations on the branch. Similarly the working at 7.10 pm from Jedburgh would take direct to Kelso all goods and 'foreign empty wagons' which it may not have been able to remove to Roxburgh in the day's earlier trips. There was a reference to the branch engine working all of the goods traffic between station and station and also between the branch stations and Roxburgh. The same timetable indicated that the 8.41 am, the 2.05 and the 8.33 pm passenger trains from Newtown (St Boswells) should, if necessary, run as mixed trains carrying goods and livestock traffic in the Roxburgh and Kelso direction. The 6.30 am, 1.15 and 7.30 pm passenger trains from Kelso were to run as mixed trains as required carrying livestock from Kelso and Roxburgh towards Newtown. All of these trains made connections with Jedburgh branch trains at Roxburgh. There was also a through goods from Edinburgh to Kelso at 7.15 am arriving at Roxburgh at 12.35 pm and Kelso at 1.00 pm, whilst in the reverse direction a goods left Kelso at 2.15 pm (Roxburgh 2.35 pm) arriving back in Edinburgh at 8.30 pm.

Other matters

Not everyone was happy with the facilities provided at the station at Jedburgh on its opening! The *Teviotdale Record* first raised the question of the lighting at the station very soon after the line was opened. Almost 12 months later it was still a matter for disquiet. Part of an article in the *Teviotdale Record* of 1st August, 1857 is reproduced here:

Tis nearly a year since we first referred to the disgraceful state of matters then existing at the railway station and road leading thereto. In the intervening space of time we did certainly expect to see some steps taken in regard to the laying down of pipes and fitting up of lamps on this our principal thoroughfare, and we are sorry to report that notwithstanding all the meetings and talkings about the matter, we are about to enter another winter's campaign on the same dismal footing.

The dark nights being now setting fast in, a solitary lamp enlivens the arrival of our last train, which is considerably augmented by the red glare of the engine's fire, but combined, the light is barely sufficient to enable a recognition of an arriving friend.

On the 29th of the same month the same newspaper reported that there was shortly to be an agreement between the interested parties whereby the residents of Bongate, and the passengers using the railway, would be 'cheered and enlightened by their way on the introduction of gas lamps from the railway station to the bridge at Townfoot': 'Better late than never'.

> To a stranger utterly unacquainted with the locality the dreariness of arriving at a railway station in a pitch dark night with the walk of upwards of half a mile to the town in utter darkness is no joke indeed. The other night a passenger by a late train lost his way and had to apply to the station master to set him on his road.

The cost of carrying the gas to Jedburgh station was stated by the *Kelso Chronicle* to be about £65 with £22 10s. being paid by the gas company, £22 10s. by the Jedburgh Railway with the road trustees contributing £10. The resulting deficiency of £10 was paid by the treasurer of the town council.

On 20th November, 1857 the *Kelso Chronicle* noted that it was two months since the gas company had decided to extend the gas supply to Jedburgh station. They were pleased to announce that the work was complete and the new light eliminated the former dismal melancholy that reigned at the station. Five public lamps were shortly to be erected between Old Bongate and the bridge thus making the principal thoroughfare into the town what it ought to be. In a note of humour it said that the only people 'kicking against' this liberality are the lads and lasses, who will be compelled to extend their walks beyond the boundary of the lighting improvements so as to pop the question in the dark.

In the event it was not until January 1858 that the *Teviotdale Record* was able to report that the last of the four lamps between the railway and the foot of the town had been erected and though they were set up at wide intervals would prove to be of consequence to the comfort of passengers of night trains. (A simple calculation shows that the gas lamps would have been erected at least 200 yards apart.) The article referred to another recent incident, before the turning on of the lights, in which a gentleman had missed his way at Bongate bridge and instead of going across it, found himself suddenly immersed in the River Jed below!

The Jedburgh turntable was duly installed and it appears on the first Ordnance Survey map of Jedburgh dating from the early 1860s. No doubt hand-held oil lamps had to be used in the gloom at the station when the locomotive was placed into the shed at the end of the day. The nature of the coaling facilities available at Jedburgh shed at this time has not been discovered.

It was not until the Jedburgh branch had been open for two months that the Directors of the NBR proposed that the electric telegraph, which was already in use on the lines to Hawick and Kelso, be extended, with the agreement of the respective line companies, to Peebles, Selkirk, Jedburgh and Berwick. Even when it was introduced, for both railway business and passenger purposes, there was some dissatisfaction. It was not possible, for example, to send messages from Jedburgh after 8.00 pm. In the event of a physician needing to be called from Edinburgh it would be necessary to get to Roxburgh to use the apparatus there to make the call. There were other instances of telegraph messages from Edinburgh to Jedburgh taking four hours to arrive rather than the 10 minutes that was normally promised. This could easily result in passengers from Edinburgh arriving at Jedburgh in advance of the telegraphic message they had sent before their departure from the capital!

When the Jedburgh line opened, smoking on its premises and in trains was not permitted. However the *Teviotdale Record and Jedburgh Advertiser* contained a statement, in its 24th December, 1859 edition, that first and second class smoking carriages were to be attached to all trains worked by the NBR, presumably including the Jedburgh branch that was worked by this company. However third class smoking carriages were not included in these arrangements. Presumably there were third class passengers who ignored the regulations and smoked out of the view of railway officials!

Until its formal absorption into the NBR the Jedburgh Railway duly held its half-yearly ordinary meetings. After due notice of one month being provided these took place at the Spread Eagle Hotel on the High Street in Jedburgh, the meetings starting at 1.00 pm. The meetings received a report from the Directors, including a financial statement, and conducted any other business connected with the company.

Occasionally it was necessary for extraordinary meetings to be called. One such took place, also at the Spread Eagle Hotel (but at 11.00 am), 'for the purpose of determining whether or not a train or trains, for the conveyance of the mails and passengers, should run on Sundays to and from the Roxburgh station'. This meeting took place on 5th November, 1856. Such Sunday trains did not appear for a few years. Presumably the Directors felt that the meeting would not be sufficiently long to interfere with their lunch arrangements. However, the question of trains running on the Sabbath was a vexed one and the discussions were protracted. These meetings are dealt with more fully in a later chapter.

The staff of Jedburgh railway station at its opening

The first census after the opening of the Jedburgh Railway, made in 1861, can provide an indication of the railway staff who worked at the station soon after its opening.

The gentleman appointed as the first station master and agent was William Hartley who would occupy this position for a further 40 years! He lived at the station house close to his place of work with his wife and large family of six children. Three more children would be added before 1871.

After holding the post at Jedburgh for a few years he was promoted to the position of station master at Galashiels but after a few weeks he decided that he preferred working at Jedburgh and returned, working there until his death in 1896.

Hartley's clerk at the station was a 16 year old, James Brown, who lived with his sister and brother-in-law close to the station at 21 Bongate. He appears not to have made a career with the railway as 10 years later, and having moved next door to No. 22, he had become a commercial traveller.

The station had three porters. William Young lived with his family at 5 Bongate and had two lodgers, both working at the railway. One was John Wright who was a locomotive fireman and the other was Frederick Wright, a railway engine cleaner. Young was still living at the same address but working as a porter 10 years later. Just along the road, at No. 9 Bongate lived Thomas Bryden with his wife and family. He also took in a lodger to supplement his railway income, whilst at 28 Bongate lived the youngest of the trio of porters, Robert Purves.

Apart from John and Frederick Wright already mentioned, there were two other men associated with the trains who were resident at Jedburgh. William Moffat was an engine driver resident with his family at 4 Boontrees, and James Taylor, a guard, living at 21 Bongate. James had a lodger, James Brown, the young clerk mentioned above.

There were several railway surfacemen and labourers living in or near Jedburgh. George Lamond a surfacemen lived with his family at Monklaw Cottages near Jedburgh. Lamond's stepson, Thomas Redpath, also a railway surfaceman, lived with him at Monklaw. William McLauchlan was another railway labourer who resided in Jedburgh. He lodged with a police constable, Archibold Hoggarth, and his family in what the census records as 'Cartle

Street', perhaps meant to be 'Castle Street' for the police station is on the road leading from the town to the castle and jail. Andrew Hope, a railway labourer, lived at Bonjedward railway crossing and may also have been responsible for the crossing gates there, whilst John Fiddes, also resident at Bonjedward, was another railway labourer.

At Jedfoot railway station just outside Jedburgh lived the newly-married George Borthwick, the first station master here, along with his young wife, Mary. George would later leave the Jedburgh area becoming a railway porter and later a brakesman. Fortunately a photograph of George Borthwick survives (*left*), albeit much later in his railway career.

A link to the Jedburgh Railway?

The Jedburgh Railway had only been operating for barely four months when plans were deposited for another railway which would include a branch to the Jedburgh line near to Jedfoot station in the Teviot Valley.

Let us outline the context of this line. The Newcastle to Carlisle Railway had opened up the main part of its route, via Hexham, in 1836. In 1853 a line north, from a junction near to Hexham, was proposed to open collieries which were believed to exist near Plashetts. The Act for what was known as the Border Counties Railway (North Tyne Section) was given the Royal Assent on 31st July,

1854. Construction of the line commenced on 11th December, 1855 with the cutting of the first sod. By 1858 the first length was opened and passenger trains were running as far as Chollerford (this station was later known as Humshaugh).

Far to the north was the Hawick branch of the NBR. Conceived as the Edinburgh & Hawick Railway it had obtained the Royal Assent for its Act in 1845. Construction proceeded from Portobello East Junction, Edinburgh, via Gorebridge and the first, terminus, station was opened in Hawick on 1st November, 1849.

On 29th November, 1856 plans were deposited with the Clerk of the Peace for Northumberland and his counterpart in Roxburghshire. They were entitled: 'Plans and Sections of the Border Counties Railway Teviotdale Section – Extension to Belses with a Branch Therefrom.' This railway was planned to link the Border Counties Railway from the Parish of Falstone, in particular The Belling, near Plashetts, northwards to the Hawick branch near Belses, the junction being 44½ miles from Edinburgh. There were no places of real significance on the proposed route, much of the line being planned through areas with very low population. A branch was planned to leave the Belling-Belses line near the River Teviot, running eastwards to join with the Roxburgh Junction to Jedburgh line near Jedfoot. The 'main' line was to be 32½ miles long with the planned branch being 2½ miles in length. The engineers for the line were John F. Tone, already the Engineer on the line north from Hexham, and Francis Charlton.

The line would start in the upper reaches of the North Tyne Valley and pass Deadwater, crossing Liddel Water and reaching a summit at Note-of-the-Gate (printed as 'Note O'th Gate' on the plans) where there would be a short 362-yard tunnel under the watershed. The line would then follow the hillside above the Wanchope Burn continuing to descend into the valley of the Rule Water before its confluence with the Teviot. The line would cross the Teviot on a viaduct and then use the Ale Water valley to head towards Belses. The ruling gradient would be 1 in 100 and the line would be sharply curved in places to allow this to be achieved. On the English side the line would require purchase of land from several landowners including the Duke of Northumberland, Sir John Swinburne, Lord Douglas and the Hon. Walter Elliot. In Scotland the land would need to be obtained from Sir William Francis Eliott [sic], the Duke of Buccleugh, the Earl of Minto, the Marquis of Lothian and the Duke of Roxburghe.

The branch to near Jedfoot was to start in a field called Weaseldean on a farm by the name of Timpendean (owned by the Marquis of Lothian), and terminate at a junction with the Jedburgh line adjacent to the milepost indicating the distance of 54 miles from Edinburgh, 'in the parish of Jedburgh in the county of Roxburghshire'. This branch was to be level for its first few yards, then descend on a gradient of 1 in 289 to the 4½ furlong point. It was then to rise on a gradient of 1 in 495 for a further three furlongs. A slight rise at 1 in 1375 would follow for 2½ furlongs before a downward slope at 1 in 70 for 1 mile and 2 furlongs would bring it to the junction. 'Arching' would be required, approximately 35 ft in height and 50 yards in length, for the crossing of the Jed about two miles from the start of the branch. Gentle curves of between three and 4½ chains radius would be required. The final patch of land was described as being 'Railway station house, booking offices, platform, siding, railway, works and appurtenances', this being the existing facilities of the Jedburgh Railway. The owners of this land were described as the 'Jedburgh Railway Company' and the lessees as the North British Railway.

The *Caledonian Mercury* newspaper (1st December, 1856) reported on a meeting held at Jedburgh to discuss this railway. Several local dignitaries were present. It referred to the junction for Jedburgh as being located at 'Wester Fodderlee', a name not used in the deposited plans. The report also mentioned a spur to the Hawick line at Hassendean, south of Belses, again not mentioned in the plans. The proposed line was described as involving 'easy construction' and with 'curves of a favourable character'!

It is not surprising that this ambitious plan came to naught. Trains for the two principal towns to be served by the route, Hawick and Jedburgh, could only have been reached via reversals at the junctions at Belses and Jedfoot respectively. Local traffic would undoubtedly have been sparse. The Border Counties line did, however, open to Falstone on 2nd September, 1861. It was extended northwards to Riccarton and completed in mid-April 1862. Because the connecting Border Union Railway was unfinished, the goods service did not start until 24th June, 1862, followed by the passenger service on 1st July, just a week later.

In consequence the Jedburgh branch remained as a stand-alone branch rather than becoming part of a through railway.

Railway Clearing House map of 1907 showing the Jedburgh branch and environs.

Chapter Six

The line described

To describe a train journey along the line let us view it through the eyes of a mother and her young, but lively and enthusiastic son, making a journey from Kelso station to the end of the branch at Jedburgh in the first few years of the 20th century. We imagine their start as Kelso station because that was where the Jedburgh train started, even though the branch-proper was not gained until the junction at Roxburgh.

The couple were a little early for their train and so had a minute or two to absorb some of the railway scene. From the ticket office and waiting room they emerged onto the platform and climbed over the footbridge. This provided a vantage point to look over towards the goods sidings, the sheds and the more distant locomotive shed outside which a rather dirty engine was standing. The sidings held a variety of different wagons, some of which were being unloaded by men, some of whom were railway staff in their uniforms whilst others were presumably carters linked with the carts or others associated with local industrial or commercial premises. Noises mingled: the sounds of the locomotive, the cattle being loaded and the calls of the workmen. The young boy was fascinated by all that was happening.

After looking at the tall signal box and huge water tank on the platform they were shown their way, by the kindly station porter, to their first class compartment in the short passenger train already waiting in the loop platform and they made themselves comfortable. It was no time at all before a shrill whistle sounded. There was an answering 'toot' from the locomotive and the train was off. The young boy had insisted that the windows be left ajar so he could hear the sounds of the engine and smell its smoke and steam. Immediately the train passed under the Yetholm road bridge and clanked over the crossover as it struggled to accelerate up the steepish 1 in 71 gradient. A minute or so later the engine noise diminished as the train passed over the minor summit. From here it was all downhill to Roxburgh Junction on the 1 in 150 slope. Our youngster's nose was pressed up against the left-hand window, only moving away briefly when a burst of smoke rebounded from the walls of the Jedburgh road overbridge. Heiton sidings came into view with several wagons and vans standing or being unloaded.

'What does NB stand for, Mummy? That's what is painted on the trucks.'

'That stands for the North British Railway, dearest. We're travelling on a North British Railway train.'

Heiton sidings disappeared from view and the train whistled and slowed slightly as it approached the viaduct, crossing over the steep-sided Teviot Valley with the river at its centre. The train pulled into at Roxburgh Junction, its first stop. The small boy was puzzled as the engine, from his window viewpoint, appeared to go forward on its own leaving the carriages behind. Shortly afterwards the boy rushed to the other side of the compartment as the engine appeared going in the opposite direction on the adjacent line. A slight

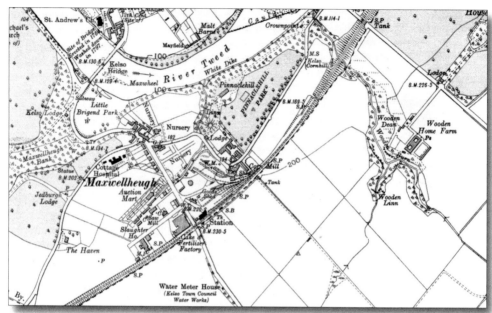

Kelso station, reproduced from the 6 inch Ordnance Survey map of 1923.   *Crown Copyright*

This early 1960s view shows the road approach to Kelso station with the extension to the ticket office underneath the awning. The Scammell three-wheel tractor has either dropped off some traffic for the railway or is awaiting the delivery of some goods by the next train.   *ARPT/J.M. Boyes*

The nearer bridge and embankment carry the start of the Jedburgh branch over the road from Roxburgh village to Nisbet, whilst the bridge further away carries the double track of the Roxburgh to Kelso section. This view can be contrasted with the 2019 photograph on page 221.
ARPT/J.M. Boyes

Roxburgh station building viewed from the direction of the Jedburgh branch platform. Note the 'new' enamelled sign replacing the former wooden NBR version, the advertising posters, the neatly painted platform edges and the well-tended flower border in the foreground. *ARPT/J.M. Boyes*

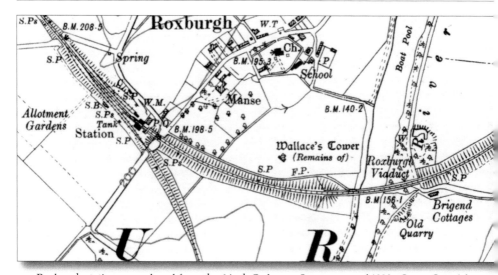

Roxburgh station, reproduced from the 6 inch Ordnance Survey map of 1923. *Crown Copyright*

Kirkbank station, reproduced from the 6 inch Ordnance Survey map of 1923. *Crown Copyright*

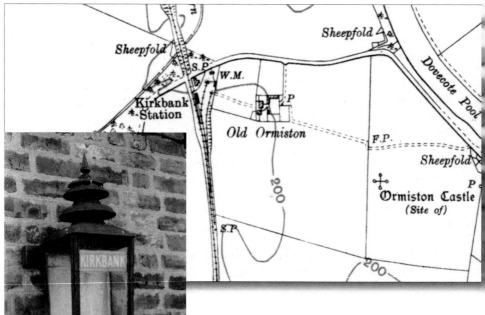

The North British Railway station lamp housing facing the platform at Kirkbank survived right up to the closure of the line. The paraffin lamp which it would have contained had been removed by the time that this late-1950s photograph was taken.   *Photos from the 50s*

jolt soon announced its arrival on what had been the rear end of the train. More whistles and the train was propelled forwards, clanking across some crossovers. Mother and son were still puzzled as the whole train then changed direction and pulled into a curved platform which they had seen on the left whilst coming to a stand in the station. 'I think we must now be on the branch line', said mother.

More whistles and then a porter could be heard calling across to the guard as their train started to accelerate once more. The boy's attention was still on the left-hand side as he watched the cattle in the fields. A line of trees hid the course of the Teviot. After a minute or two the train started to slow again. The boy spied a cart on the road running under the railway, and station buildings appeared on his side of the train. Kirkbank was the first stop, though no passengers were waiting on the station. A slamming door indicated that some travellers had found their destination, handing their tickets to the uniformed gentleman on the platform, who then exchanged a few words with the guard. He then waved his flag and caused the train to start to move off again. The boy's attention was held by some bustle in Kirkbank sidings where some sacks of something very dusty were being unloaded onto a cart from another wagon with 'NB' on the side. Sounds of the bleating of some sheep emanated from a loaded van awaiting collection. All too soon all of this disappeared from view as the train rumbled over a crossover and accelerated. The boy noticed a large house from the window and the river became easier to see. The sounds from the engine appeared to be coming from the right-hand side so he crossed over to the right and saw that the line was curving towards that side. 'Be careful and don't play with the door handle or window, dearest.'

A plantation of trees caught the boy's eye on the other side of the train as he turned around. Then the train whistled and started to slow markedly. There was another sharp 'toot' and the train passed over a road crossing, entering another station. The boy was intrigued by the gates across the road. He read the word 'Nisbet' on the station sign. Here a couple of ladies with baskets were waiting and an equal number dismounted from the train. A door slammed and moments later, with a further 'toot' the train moved out of the platform and passed the station sidings where the boy noticed a couple of laden coal wagons awaiting unloading next to a long platform. A fine view of the river then appeared on the left with the green meadows, on this occasion showing no sign of the previous winter's flooding, stretching towards the horizon.

'Mummy, we're going over a long bridge!'

'That's right dear. We will be crossing over a big river called the Teviot.'

He raced to the other side of the compartment.

'Be careful, dear!'

The river gradually disappeared from his view and cows in the meadow on the haugh on the opposite side attracted his attention and caused him to return to the left-hand window. Absorbed in his view of the cows, the rumbling sound, made as the carriages passed over the Boss Brig, passed unnoticed by the boy.

Once again the train started to slow. Another station came into view, first of all the two sidings housing several wagons and then the platform itself with its station buildings. Mother saw the station sign. 'This is Jedfoot station, the last

This 1950s view of Kirkbank station shows the new platform edging and it appears that the building and fencing has received a 'lick of paint'. The point rodding by the track emanates from the ground frame which is under the sloping roof of the shed near the platform end. The twin sidings appear to have no railway business at this time.   *Armstrong Railway Photographic Trust*

Nisbet station in the 1960s looking towards the level crossing. Note the ground frame in the hut on the platform, the slightly down-at-heel station buildings and the signal post bearing the home signal protecting the crossing plus a fixed distant for the crossing near to the River Teviot.
Armstrong Railway Photographic Trust

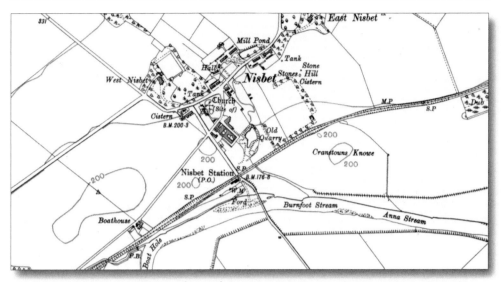

Nisbet station, reproduced from the 6 inch Ordnance Survey map of 1923.   *Crown Copyright*

Nisbet station looking south-west over the level crossing gates in July 1952, four years after its closure to timetabled passenger trains. Note the station building with the entrance to the village Post Office located in the middle of the picture. In the distance is the home signal by the yard entrance.   *Armstrong Railway Photographic Trust/C.J.B. Sanderson*

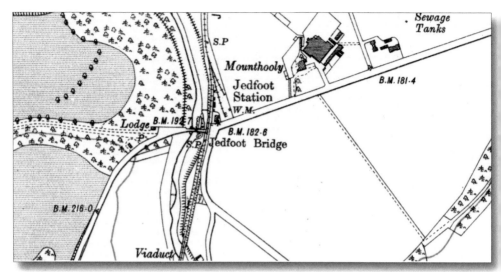

Jedfoot station, reproduced from the 6 inch Ordnance Survey map of 1923.   *Crown Copyright*

This 1963 view shows the Jedfoot level crossing over the Kelso to Jedburgh and Hawick road, the site of a road traffic accident in 1938 which caused the demolition of the gates. Beyond is Jedfoot's station platform and to the right, beyond the station master's house and fuel tank lies the station yard.   *David Stirling*

Jedfoot station on 26th July, 1951, still looking in near-pristine condition despite the passenger train service having finished some three years previously. Note the loading gauge over the siding in the goods yard. *Armstrong Railway Photographic Trust/C.J.B. Sanderson*

This trackside view of Jedfoot station shows the sidings in Jedfoot yard with a solitary mineral wagon, perhaps having brought a load of coal. The loading gauge spans the nearest siding. The sidings could only be shunted by trains heading away from Jedburgh. There was no headshunt or loop. *Bruce McCartney*

This is the view to the north at the point where the exit from Jedburgh goods yard joins with the road from the platform, run round loop and shed. Note the point protecting the running line and the two signals: the starting signal for trains leaving the yard and the home signal for approaching trains. The slaughter house site and oil depot were located to the east of the line here.

David Stirling

Jedburgh station, reproduced from the 25 inch Ordnance Survey map of 1918.

Crown Copyright

one before Jedburgh.' The boy noticed yet another gated road crossing as the train left the station. His mother, looking out of the opposite window, noticed the road bridge over the Jed with a couple of carts and a carriage from the Bonjedward direction awaiting the opening of the crossing gates so that they could proceed towards Crailing village or perhaps Kelso.

'Mummy, here's another bridge!'

'Yes, that will be the bridge over the Jedwater.'

The train accelerated alongside the Jed, and the boy noticed, on the left, the buildings of Bonjedward Mill and the New Mill without comment. A sports ground came into view as the train whistled and started to slow down. A 'toot', perhaps indicating the clearing of the signal, allowed the train to pick up speed slightly before the boy, whose attention was attracted by some men shouting, crossed over to the right where he saw an old grounded carriage body, then a plethora of wagons, not all with 'NB' on the side, standing in the sidings. This was Jedburgh. The men, whose calls had attracted his attention, were unloading the wagons, some with open doors revealing their contents, others with their doors closed. Mother, looking out of the opposite window, had spied the slaughterhouse on the left but decided to keep quiet about this.

'I wonder if Grandpa is here to collect us' said mother.

'There he is!' exclaimed her son as a portly gentleman standing on the platform smiled and waved his hand towards his grandson who was peering out of the window.

Jedburgh station before the overall roof was removed. Note the locomotive shed on the left-hand side and the piles of locomotive ash. The station platform has wooden edging to the otherwise ash and gravel surface. Regularly-spaced gas lamps are located against the platform fencing with the station running-in board on the right-hand side.

Bill Lynn Collection

The door was opened and mother and son climbed down.

'Hello m'dears! Had a good ride?'

Neither of our travellers were frequent railway travellers on the line and they would not have been aware of the need, at Roxburgh, for the locomotive to run-round the train prior to accessing the Jedburgh line. At Kirkbank they would not have noticed the details of the small signal cabin, the station buildings or the gentlemen's cast-iron building with its urinals.

At Nisbet, the importance of the station for both the railway and the inhabitants of the nearby Nisbet and Crailing villages would not have been realized. In fact the station building there housed not only the station staff but also the village post office and store in a room fronting onto the platform!

The crossing keepers' cottages at both Ford, between Nisbet and Jedfoot, and Bonjedward had also been passed without comment. Finally at Jedburgh the carriages of their train in the single platform had hidden the locomotive shed from the family's view as the boy became preoccupied with telling Grandpa about their journey! However, he would not, in any case, have spied the goods engine as it had already left Jedburgh some hours previously.

Jedburgh station, after the cessation of passenger trains, shows some changes compared with the previous picture! The platform has been refaced and shortened, in addition the overall roof and the tracks to the shed have been removed. Despite these changes the station retains a neat appearance.   *Bruce McCartney Collection*

Chapter Seven

Signalling and the permanent way

Signalling

At each end of the single line, at Roxburgh Junction and at Jedburgh (opened in 1894), there were signal boxes, manned by a signalman. At the intermediate stations the levers were located by the station buildings for operating the appropriate points, also the signals which ensured safety at the entrance to the sidings, and at the level crossings at Nisbet and Jedfoot.

The line was operated under the Tyer's block telegraph system with a train staff and tickets. It became the last line in Scotland to be so signalled. At the intermediate stations the staff members were notified of trains, in later years, by telephone. The locomotive crews on the line were required to have in their possession the green coloured, wooden and brass staff, which bore the legend Roxburgh-Jedburgh. The staff is now in the safekeeping of the Scottish Railway Preservation Society (SRPS) at the museum at Bo'Ness having appeared in a railway auction in February 2000 (as recorded in the *Railway Magazine*). Occasionally one train was required to follow another along the line; in this case the crew would be given sight of the staff and issued with a written 'ticket' which would function as their authority to proceed. The second train would then carry the staff which would be handed to the signalman at the end of the line. The block instruments used in conjunction with the train staff were of the two-position type. For a time the passenger train leaving Roxburgh at 11.21 am would proceed with a ticket, whilst the following goods train would carry the staff to Jedburgh. The train staff was normally taken from one end of the branch to the other. However there were occasions when snow blocked the line, for example between Nisbet and Jedburgh. In this case the locomotive crew would be given the staff at Roxburgh as their authority to proceed. After reaching the temporary terminus of the line the crew would then return the staff to the Roxburgh signalman. David Stirling mentions that the SRPS holds a set of key tokens engraved Roxburgh Junction-Jedburgh and assumes that these would have come into use had the flooding not ultimately caused the cessation of passenger trains. It would not have made sense to change the arrangements solely for the remaining goods trains.

Roxburgh Junction was fully signalled and its signal box was brick-built with stone sills beneath the rather small windows. It had a slate roof. The wooden access steps, with brown-painted handrails, faced towards the Jedburgh branch. The name boards on each end of the box were lettered in white on a blue ground. The window frames were painted white. A boarded crossing was laid over the Jedburgh branch line. The signal box was normally open on weekdays from 6.25 am (an hour earlier on Tuesdays or on occasions when special trains were being operated) and 'switched out' at 9.27 pm. It had 48 levers. It closed on 8th August, 1964.

Jedburgh was also fully signalled and its 'box' opened at 6.10 am and closed at 9.30 pm on weekdays. Jedburgh signal box had between 15 and 20 levers. It was

Roxburgh Junction signal box on 11th August, 1963. *ARPT/J.M. Boyes*

Roxburgh Junction box on 11th August, 1963, showing the entrance steps and boarded crossing over the Jedburgh branch tracks. *ARPT/J.M. Boyes*

The interior of the Roxburgh signal box showing the single line block instrument for the Jedburgh branch. *ARPT/J.M. Boyes*

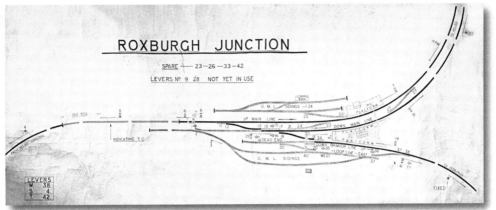

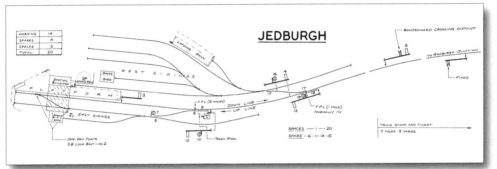

Signalling diagrams for Roxburgh Junction and Jedburgh.   *(Both) Bruce McCartney Collection*

This is a fine view of Jedburgh signal box with the inner home signal, protecting the platform (*right*), adjacent but partly hidden. Note the stepped platform for the signalman to receive the train staff, though in practice it was just as easy to lean out of the window. In contrast to Roxburgh Junction, the nameboard faces onto the tracks.   *Armstrong Railway Photographic Trust/Fleetwood Shawe*

The bar signal at Ford crossing, 1947.
LNER Magazine

The yard exit starter at Jedburgh.
ARPT/J.M.Boyes

Platform starting signal at Nisbet.   Up starter at Jedburgh showing   Liverpool Railway Signal Co.
balance weights and lamp hoist.   shunting signal at Roxburgh
Junction.

(All) Armstrong Railway Photographic Trust (ARPT)/J.M. Boyes

Lattice post upper quadrant starting signal at Jedburgh. *ARPT/Fleetwood Shawe*

Jedburgh advance starter and Bonjedward fixed at caution distant signals. *ARPT/J.M. Boyes*

Lattice post subsidiary signal at Roxburgh Junction. *ARPT/J.M. Boyes*

Two-direction fixed distant signals between Jedfoot and Nisbet. *ARPT/C.J.B. Sanderson*

Bracket signal for Jedburgh branch, with main-line repeater, at Roxburgh Junction. *ARPT/C.J.B. Sanderson*

Lattice post upper quadrant home signal at Jedburgh. *ARPT/J.M. Boyes*

a tall NBR box located near to the station throat by the slaughterhouse. In later years, at least, the upper, matchboarded part of the building was painted in a pleasant pale green colour with doors and window surrounds being in a much darker green. The window frames were white. The signal box nameboard, facing onto the tracks was, in later years, painted green with lettering picked out in white. The steps were painted in the same colour as the doors. Just to the south of the box was a small building used for storage of signal oil. Fortunately some photographs of both Roxburgh Junction and Jedburgh signal boxes and their signals exist. Other photographs survive showing some of the signalling items at the intermediate stations on the branch. Both Roxburgh and Jedburgh boxes were opened for Sunday trains as required. There were two regular signalmen at each place who worked either the morning or the evening shift. Jedburgh signal box closed on 8th August, 1964, being a block post until the end.

At the other stations there is mid-20th century photographic evidence of the signal frames on the station platforms. At Kirkbank the frame appears to be located in an open-fronted small hut, a replacement for the earlier building, towards the south end of the platform. Kirkbank closed to goods traffic in 1959 and the signals protecting the goods siding were removed. At Nisbet a similar structure appears in photographs; it is located further along the platform from the station building. Apparently this structure had a ground frame containing eight levers and two spaces. Five of the levers controlled the signals (home and distant in each direction plus the shunt signal controlling egress from the siding. There was one lever each for the gate lock, the points and the point lock). Jedfoot had a similar structure on its platform. This was located to the north of the station building and was, again, open fronted.

The various level crossings on the line, at Ormiston, Ford (between Nisbet and Bonjedward) and Bonjedward originally had full-time crossing keepers. The crossings were described as being 'partly protected'. Presumably this referred to the presence of the lever frames operated by the crossing keepers but not protection with track-circuiting and full signalling. Ford crossing, perhaps the others too, had a type of 'bar-shaped' signal, which could be rotated to show the position of the crossing gates to train crews. From an approaching train the continued closure of the gates would be indicated by the signal face being displayed, whilst if the crossing was clear the signal arm would be viewed end on (with the face parallel to the track) making it all but invisible. At Ford this signal was still in existence until about 1947.

The signals on the branch were mounted on lattice posts with finials. Most had lower quadrant arms though some, latterly, had replacement upper quadrant arms. Distant signals were latterly all of the 'fixed' variety with non-moving arms and with a yellow aspect permanently showing. There were some oddities. For example the home signal at Nisbet was mounted some distance above the warning distant signal for the next crossing along the line; the home signal was of the lower quadrant type whereas the distant signal was of the upper quadrant type (albeit 'fixed')! Near to Jedfoot there were two distant signals mounted on the same post, one for observance in each direction of travel. Some of the subsidiary or shunt signals were mounted on posts; others were on the ground at low level.

After the passenger service ceased there was a considerable reduction in staffing. Crossing keepers were no longer required; instead the fireman on each goods train would open the gates and the guard would close them after the train had passed over the crossing. At the three intermediate stations signalmen were performing the crossing keepers' role. At Jedburgh towards the end of the life of the branch the role of porter-signalman was created.

The permanent way

As mentioned in Colonel Yolland's report, at the time of opening of the branch, the rails were of short lengths of 16 and 20 ft in length. They were relatively light being of just 65 lb. per yard in weight. The sleepers were of larch laid on sand and gravel ballast of not less than 1 ft 9 in. in depth. The 'fine' nature of the ballast can be seen in some of the earliest photographs of the branch and Roxburgh Junction. This ballast proved to be unsuitable during wet periods and it was easily washed away during flooding. It was replaced by stone ballast of larger proportions than the original 'gravel'. Even this required replacement at times of exceptional erosion of the trackbed. In some of the cuttings the original ballast did not provide adequate drainage and, again, larger ballast was used for replacement. This reduced the need for the replacement of waterlogged sleepers.

Over the years the whole of the line, and eventually the tracks in the station yards, were relaid with much heavier bullhead rails of 60 ft in length, though shorter lengths of rail were still employed in some of the sidings. The rails were held in place in the rail chairs by oak keys placed on the outward-facing side of the rails as was usually the case.

Fortunately the memories of Jim Hall, a ganger on the branch, were recorded as part of the Scottish Borders Memory Bank, and they provide an excellent insight into the work associated with the permanent way and the trackside. A ganger is the person in charge of each of the trackwork teams. Jim started work when the branch was under the auspices of the LNER, continuing to work throughout the British Railways (BR) period of the line's history. He was in charge of the 'Jedburgh Gang', the team of four, including himself, which was responsible for the maintenance of the permanent way between milepost 51 and the end of the line at Jedburgh, a total distance of 5¼ miles. Of course the gang were also responsible for the sidings whose length must be added to the branch mileage. The sidings at Nisbet, Jedfoot and Jedburgh came under their jurisdiction. The remaining two miles of the branch and part of the St Boswells line through Roxburgh Junction was looked after by the Roxburgh Gang. Both gangs were responsible to a permanent way inspector who had his office in St Boswells. A total of 10 men made up his Newtown St Boswells permanent way maintenance section.

For what were the permanent way gangs responsible? First of all there were 'every day' all-year-round jobs, and then there were tasks related to the particular seasons of the year, with, finally, what may be called 'special tasks'.

The everyday work was the general maintenance of the track to ensure safe movement of the trains. This consisted of general observation, replacement of broken fishplates and the oak keys which held the rail in position, and the oiling of points. This was done five days per week until, with the withdrawal of passenger trains, when it was reduced to just two days per week. Other tasks for the gang included the regular checking of weighbridges, including the one at Nisbet, though fuller servicing was performed by an engineer from Avery's, which company had supplied the machine in the first place. The gang's responsibilities included the removal and rolling back of the top plate so as to allow inspection of the bearings.

The seasonal winter work included such tasks as clearing snow from points and salting them to ensure that the blades and other parts moved during periods of frost. Summer work could involve cutting back brushwood and long grass, attention to the boundary fences and hedges and weeding.

Special work often took place on Sundays when the Jedburgh Gang would join with the others in the maintenance group, for example to replace cracked or worn sections of rail. This could involve work not only on the Jedburgh branch but also much further away. Jim Hall recalls performing such tasks on the Peebles branch, at Miller Hill (between Dalkeith and Edinburgh) and on the East Coast main line. Often the work would commence on a Saturday evening and last through until late on Sunday, when the lines were less busy with traffic. This provided overtime, and extra remuneration, for Jim who had a young family to raise.

In severely inclement weather the maintenance gang made use of the lengthmen's bothies. There were six of these spaced out on the Nisbet to Jedburgh section, one of which was at the west end of the station yard at Nisbet.

(Jim Hall ended his railway career at Roxburgh on the Kelso line, having, for a time, been permanent way inspector at Peebles. Nisbet was his former 'base'. In addition to the demise of the Jedburgh line, the Peebles branch was also closed and the closure of the Selkirk line was imminent. Like many of his colleagues, Jim faced the inevitable. He left the railway and obtained a new position as bridge engineer for the Selkirk County Council Roads Department. Then, after the amalgamation of the counties, he worked for the new Borders District until his retirement in 1983.)

Milepost 56, Jedburgh.

NBR rail chair on the Jedburgh branch, 1963.
(Both) ARPT/J.M. Boyes

Chapter Eight

The passenger train services

The *Teviotdale Record* newspaper was first published shortly before the Jedburgh branch opened and it was happy to report on happenings on the line and to publish the passenger train timetables and any changes to the schedules. This newspaper, the NBR's passenger timetables and the working timetables form valuable sources when tracing the early days and evolution of the public train service on the line. Later both working and public timetables of the LNER and British Railways, plus editions of *Bradshaw Guides*, provide detailed indications of the passenger services. During relatively short periods of interruption to normal services, such as strikes or spells of inclement weather, special notices would usually be published and the public were kept informed by advertisements of the service changes in local newspapers.

The carriages

North British Railway Study Group (NBRSG) member, T. Dagg, writing in the group's journal, identified some information regarding the composition of the early Jedburgh branch train. It was formed of three carriages. Firstly there was a full brake carriage, then a composite (with first and second class accommodation) and then a brake third carriage. For occasions when extra accommodation was needed an additional third class carriage was stabled at Jedburgh. This would be used, for example, on fair days. All of the carriages were four-wheelers and they were all oil-lit. Oil lighting persisted on the branch until after World War I when a carriage with gas-lighting was sent down to the branch from Craigentinny (Edinburgh). The Jedburgh branch was one of the last lines to use gas lighting. It was the duty of the guards to raise and lower the gas lamps at the start of the night or day respectively. The General Appendices at the start of the 20th century each contained a note to the effect that footwarmers were available for first class passengers on the Jedburgh line and to Kelso, supplied by the station staff at Jedburgh. The station master was responsible for ensuring that those that had cooled were replaced. Cleaning with a lightly oiled rag was necessary after the warmers had been placed in the heating boiler.

Early in the history of the branch there were through carriages on some trains between Jedburgh and Edinburgh (via St Boswells). These through carriages were six-wheeled locker composites with, on occasions, a six-wheeled brake composite being attached. The locker was for the luggage of through passengers. Later on, the through carriage became a bogie coach. The carriage stock on the branch was under the supervision of the station master at Roxburgh Junction acting on the advice of his carriage & wagon man. If a carriage needed anything other than very minor repairs it was sent to Cowlairs Works, the outward and return journeys usually being within the consist of a goods train. Apparently in NBR days the upholstery in third class accommodation was red and it was blue in first class; there were no curtains.

A special notice was issued by the NBR in the passenger timetable for October 1914. It read:

> In consequence of the European War Crisis, the Train, Coach and Steamer Services shown in this Time Table may be altered or curtailed at any time without notice and the company will not be responsible for any loss, injury, damage or delay through any failure to afford the ordinary services or any modified services.

The consequent timetable changes for the branch are described later.

However, the special excursion trains, such as the trains run in connection with the Glasgow exhibitions or to and from the major rugby matches, required the provision of special rakes of carriages by the NBR and LNER, though where a special excursion train was joined at Roxburgh Junction then the branch train would take passengers from Jedburgh and the intermediate stations to join the main train. The stock for these trains was normally worked down from Edinburgh; the locomotives involved were employed on the special trains before working the empty stock back to Edinburgh.

Later, in LNER days, the carriage used on the branch was a brake composite though the through trains between Jedburgh and Tweedmouth brought a variety of carriage stock from the north-east of England (also Tweedmouth-based locomotives) to the line.

It has not been possible to trace any pictures of the Sunday School excursion trains to Tweedmouth so it is not known what carriages were used, either in NBR, LNER or early British Railways days, though there are references to the children bring transported 'ten to each compartment'. For the special 'railway enthusiast trains' in the late 1950s and 1960s British Railways Mark I corridor stock predominated, though one of the trains, which ran in July 1961, contained a couple of Gresley-designed, former LNER, vehicles. One of these specials probably formed the longest passenger train to be run on the branch, the carriages extending well beyond the platform at Jedburgh station, as the locomotives ran round their train.

A six-wheeled parcel van, built to passenger trains standards, was often part of the goods train in the final years of the branch, indeed, on occasions, when traffic was extremely light, this appears to have been the sole vehicle!

Passenger timetables

The inaugural passenger train service for the Jedburgh branch was published in both the *Teviotdale Record* and the *Kelso Chronicle*. There were four trains scheduled to run in each direction, running on Mondays to Saturdays only. There were no Sunday trains. *Rutherford's Guide* referred to omnibuses from the Spread Eagle Hotel and Harrow Inn attending all trains. Fares were 6d. or 3d. The timetable showed that the first morning passenger train from Jedburgh left at 6.40 am calling at all stations to Roxburgh. The second left at 9.10 am and the third morning train at 10.40 am. There was just one afternoon train at 5.10 pm. The first terminated at Roxburgh whereas the others reversed there and ran on to Kelso. There was no connection on towards Kelso from the first train. All trains carried first and second class passengers but the first of the day was advertised to

Jedburgh Railway timetable at opening.

carry people with fourth class, that is with Parliamentary class, tickets. The 9.10 am and 5.10 pm trains carried third class passengers but the 10.40 am was for first and second class ticket holders only. The trains took 27 minutes for the journey to Roxburgh, calling at Jedfoot Bridge three minutes after leaving Jedburgh, a further five minutes on to Nisbet and 10 minutes thence to Old Ormiston.

In the reverse direction the first train of the day was the 7.15 am from Roxburgh arriving at Jedburgh at 7.42, a Kelso to St Boswells train providing a connection into this train at Roxburgh. This first branch train carried first, second and fourth class ticketholders. The second train, starting at Kelso at 9.25, carried first, second and third class ticketholders and, having left Roxburgh at 9.46 am arrived at Jedburgh at 10.11. The third train, this time for just first and second class passengers, left Kelso at 1.41 pm, calling at all stations as was normal, arriving at Jedburgh at 2.12 pm. This train ran to these timings on Mondays to Thursdays but on Fridays its departure from Kelso was delayed until 2.10 pm with the result that it called at all stations 29 minutes later throughout. The final train of the day up the branch was the 6.50 pm departure from Kelso, catering for first, second and third class ticketholders, and calling at Roxburgh at 7.00 pm. Here it picked up through passenger traffic from Edinburgh and Hawick. Its arrival at Jedburgh was at 7.25 pm. An announcement in the Teviotdale newspaper, dated 17th April, 1857, from Thomas Rowbotham the NBR General Manager advised that the 9.10 am train from Jedburgh would be retimed to leave one hour earlier at 8.10 am carrying both passengers and livestock as far as Kelso.

By the end of May 1857 the trains were becoming so popular that the service was expanded to six in each direction with Jedburgh departures at 6.40, 9.10 am, 1.20, 2.50, 5.10 and 7.45 pm. The first two trains and the fourth terminated at Roxburgh whilst the others ran through to Kelso. Four of the trains provided connections for Hawick and Edinburgh whilst the 1.20 provided a good connection into a train for Tweedmouth and Berwick at Kelso. In the reverse direction there were also six trains leaving Roxburgh at 7.15, 9.46 am, 1.47, 3.20, 7.05 and 8.56 pm. Again four trains provided connections with trains from Edinburgh and Hawick.

Later the *Teviotdale Record* had even better news for passengers wanting through travel to Berwick. The first train from Jedburgh, the 6.40 am, 'now takes passengers direct to Berwick at parliamentary fares'. In addition passengers leaving Berwick by the first train were to be brought direct to Jedburgh arriving at 'ten minutes before eleven'. However, the same newspaper report went on to say that the 4.35 pm train from Edinburgh would be 'given up' and the train to Kelso at 7.45 pm would cease to run. The newspaper felt that these would not cause undue problems as there was a train from Edinburgh at 6.30 pm arriving at 9.23 and the 5.10 pm train would still convey passengers through to Kelso. At the same time it was reported that the charges for the carriage of goods of all kinds by passenger train has been considerably reduced. For example small parcels could be carried between any two stations on the line for the sum of 2*d.* For the rest of 1857 there were thus five passenger trains each way between Jedburgh and Roxburgh.

In May 1858 the same newspaper was pleased to announce that two extra trains would run between Jedburgh and Kelso. A train would leave Kelso for Jedburgh at 6.50 pm and leave Roxburgh at 7.00 pm on the arrival of the 4.35 pm from Edinburgh. Also a train would leave Jedburgh for Kelso at 7.45 pm. The former train would carry just first and second class passengers whilst the latter would accommodate third class passengers in addition. The announcement was made that on Saturdays there would be reduced price first, second and third class tickets issued to and from all stations between Jedburgh and Kelso, though the newspaper opined that the public would not be satisfied until return tickets were issued every day and for all stations on the whole NBR system.

By February 1872 the public timetable for passenger trains showed several changes, not the least being that Sunday trains would leave Roxburgh for Jedburgh at 10.19 am and 7.13 pm. Down trains (from Jedburgh) would operate at 7.35 am and 5.25 pm. On weekdays the pattern of departure was altered to produce departures from Jedburgh at 7.00, 9.45 am, 2.05, 4.40 and 7.05 pm. Return trains from Roxburgh would leave at 9.00, 11.50 am, 3.55, 5.58 and 9.02 pm. The *Southern Reporter* did not indicate which of these trains would run through to Kelso, nor did it mention connection times for St Boswells, Hawick or Edinburgh. However, its 31st October edition provided greater clarity indicating departures from St Boswells which would connect with, or provide through carriages for the Jedburgh branch trains provided that each of the trains ran strictly to time. Letters to local newspapers indicated that this was not always the case! All five of the down trains on the branch had good connections or through carriages onwards from Roxburgh to St Boswells. By 1875 the timetable showed five trains in each direction on the branch, also two return trains on Sundays. Connections at Kelso for Berwick trains were often unhelpful! There was just one change to the timetable from April 1876 with the former 7.10 am from Jedburgh being retimed to run a quarter of an hour earlier. The 1877 timetable, printed in the *Southern Reporter*, announced that the afternoon train from Roxburgh Junction [*sic*] would be leaving 11 minutes later (at 4.00 pm) and the early afternoon train from Jedburgh would leave at 2.25 pm rather than 2.00 pm. The 1879 timetable followed the same general pattern though individual train timings varied. The greatest change in timings was for the former 7.45 pm train which was retimed to leave Jedburgh earlier at 6.35 pm.

All trains after about 1882 carried passengers of first, second and third classes; the fourth class tickets, which had in any case been issued for only a couple of trains, were abolished.

The timetable for July 1885 appeared in the *Southern Reporter*. It showed a very similar pattern of trains to that in the late 1870s, though, as might be expected, there were some minor changes in departure and arrival times. The November 1887 timetable was identical. The similarly published timetable for the St Boswells, Kelso and Berwick showed that the Jedburgh branch trains, in each case, continued on to Kelso after reversal at Roxburgh. Passengers for Tweedmouth and Berwick faced waits of 40-50 minutes at Kelso.

By 1889 a rescheduling of the afternoon and early evening trains allowed an extra train in each direction to be inserted into the schedules. For example the 6.11 pm train from Roxburgh was replaced by trains leaving at 5.15 and 6.30 pm. The 6.40 pm from Jedburgh was replaced by trains at 6.05 and 7.00 pm to Roxburgh. The *Southern Reporter* indicated onward connections at Kelso for Tweedmouth and Berwick although some of the waiting times were of an hour's duration. Some rebuilding of Jedburgh station and its facilities were proposed soon after this, though the general feeling amongst both local dignitaries and members of the public was that it would have been preferable to build a brand new station closer to town.

By April 1891 the service reverted from six trains each way back to five, the timetable becoming very similar to that of the mid-1880s. This situation pertained until the mid-1890s though the *Southern Reporter* dated 27th June, 1895, indicated that the 3.52 pm train from Roxburgh would run 19 minutes later and that a new evening train would start at 7.40 pm. A new 'forenoon train' would leave Jedburgh at 10.40 am and an additional train for the evening would start at 7.58 pm, 'the trains leaving Jedburgh being thus increased from 5 to 7'.

The *Railway Magazine*, in its 'Pertinent Paragraphs' column of July 1898 noted that a morning connection had also been established between Hawick, Kelso, Jedburgh, Selkirk, Galashiels and Glasgow, with passengers being able to reach the 'Western Metropolis' by 10.10 am. However, by October of the same year the number of Jedburgh branch trains had reverted to five each way. Onward connection times for the Berwick line were still 'very generous', in most cases involving an hour's wait at Kelso, a situation that was to continue for some time.

At this time a through coach from Edinburgh to Jedburgh was attached to the 4.25 pm from Edinburgh, with the coach returning from Jedburgh to Edinburgh at 9.45 am the next day. The prices of tickets from Jedburgh to Edinburgh at this time were 9s. 5d. (first class single) and 15s. 9d. (first class return) with the corresponding third class tickets being priced at 4s. 8d. and 9s. 4d. A note in the 1902 NBR passenger timetable indicated that the through carriage from Edinburgh to Jedburgh would not be detained at St Boswells for the 3.00 pm from Carlisle if this were to be running late!

In July 1904 the *Railway Magazine* once again referred to the Jedburgh line in reporting that on the 'southern section' of the NBR a new train had been timetabled to leave Hawick at 8.20 am and convey traffic from the Kelso, Jedburgh, Selkirk, Melrose and Galashiels districts being scheduled to arrive at Edinburgh at 9.55 am.

KELSO AND JEDBURGH BRANCHES.

Up Trains. — 6 WEEK-DAYS / Sundays.

Stations and Sidings.	Distance from St Boswells	1 1stPortobello & Kelso	2 1stPortobello & Kelso	3 Pass. 1 3 Class.	4 Pass. 1 3 Class.	St Boswells Pilot	Stores Tues. p m / 7 Tues. 1 3	from Granton / 2ndPortobello & Kelso	8 Pass. 1 3 Class.	9 Pass. 1 3 Class.	10 Pass. 1 3 Class.	11 Pass. 1 3 Class.	Sun 1 Pass. 1 3 Class.	Sun 2 Pass. 1 3 Class.
Edinburgh dep.		Goods Tues. only.	Goods ex. Tues.	a.m. 6 20	9 17 Goods		Goods		p.m. 2 25	p.m. 4 25	6 0		p.m. 6 40	a.m. 7 50 / p.m. 4 40
Carlisle ,,		4 15	9 0 a.m.						1 12	3 20			5 50	4 20
—St Boswells Jn. dep	M. C.	5a15	7a15	8 28	11 4	11 10	12 37 / 2 25		3 40	5 50	7 15	8 40	9 45	6 55
—Maxton ... ,,	3 1	5 25	7 45	8 36	11 11	11 25	12 45 / 2 35		3 47	5 56	7 19	8 48	9 54	7 4
Rutherford ... ,,	5 43	5 33	7 33	8 43	11 17	11 35	12 52 / 2 45		3 53	6 1	7 23	8 55	10 1	7 11
—Roxburgh Jn. arr.	8 48	5 45	7 45	8 50	11 25	11 45	1 2 / 2 55		3 59	6 7	7 28	9 2	10 8	7 18
— Kelso ... dep.	11 46			8 30	11 10				3 50	5 50		8 45	9 50	7 0
— Roxburgh Jn. arr.	8 48			8 40	11 20				3 57	5 58		8 55	9 58	7 8
— Do. ... dep.	8 48			8 54	11 29	12 2			4 4	6 10	7 34	9 6	10 10	7 20
Kirkbank ,,	10 20			8 58	11 33	12 15			4 8	6 14		9 10	10 14	7 24
Nisbet ,,	12 65			9 5	11 40	12 35			4 13	6 19		9 17	10 21	7 31
Jedfoot Bridge ,,	14 1			9 10	11 45	1 0			4 18	6 23	7 45	9 22	10 27	7 37
— Jedburgh ... arr.	15 56			9 15	11 52	1 10			4 23	6 27	7 48	9 27	10 35	7 45
—Roxburgh Jn. dep.	8 48	6 0	7 50	8 53	11 28		1 4 / 3 35		4 2	6 10	7 30	9 5	10 10	7 27
—Kelso ... arr.	11 46	6 20	8 10	9 0	11 35		1 10 / 3 45		4 9	6 17	7 37	9 12	10 17	7 27

No. 5.—Leaves at Roxburgh all Wagons for Heiton Siding and Kelso, to be taken on by Kelso Train. Takes Wagons to and from Maxton, Rutherford, and Roxburgh, as well as to and from Stations on Jedburgh Branch. This train carries Road Wagons ticketed as follows:—"South Leith and Jedburgh Road Wagon," "St Boswells and Jedburgh Road Wagon," the Van Way-bills to be delivered to Station Master, Jedburgh.

No. 7.—Leaves its Jedburgh Branch wagons and Road Van Goods for Jedburgh Branch at St Boswells. Lifts at Roxburgh the Wagons left off by Jedburgh Train for Heiton and Kelso. Does not lift Wagons at Maxton or Rutherford, except for Heiton, Kelso, and the South. This train carries Road Wagons ticketed as follows:—"Edinburgh and KelsoRoad Wagon," "South Leith and Kelso Road Wagon," "Galashiels and Kelso Road Wagon," "St Boswells and Kelso Road Wagon," the Van Way-bills to be delivered to Station Master, Kelso.

No. 8.—When the 1-12 p.m. Express from Carlisle is running 40 minutes or more late, this Train must not be kept for it.

No. 9.—This Train must not be detained for 3-20 p.m. Express from Carlisle when the latter is late.

‡ No. 10.—Calls at Kirkbank and Nisbet when required only to set down Through Passengers arriving at St Boswells by the 6-0 p.m. Express ex Edinburgh. The Guard must ascertain before leaving Roxburgh whether or not there are any passengers in the Train for Kirkbank or Nisbet, and only order the Train to stop if there are any such passengers.

Through Carriages and Van are run from Edinburgh to Kelso by Nos. 4 and 9. A Through Carriage is run from Edinburgh to Jedburgh by No. 9.

Shunting at Kelso.—The Branch Engine is available for shunting Goods Traffic between 11-35 a.m. and 1-55 p.m.

Down Trains. — WEEK-DAYS / Sundays.

Stations and Sidings.	1 Pass. 1 3 Class	1stPortobello & Kelso 2 Cattle Tues.	1stPortobello & Kelso 3 Goods ex. Tues.	4 Pass. 1 3 Class.	Stores Tues. July 28.	6 Pass. 1 3 Class	7	8 Pass. Frid. only. 1 3 Cl.	St Boswells Pilot	9 / 10 Pass. 1 3 Class	2ndPortobello & Kelso 11 Pass. Goods	†12 Pass. 1 3 Class	13 Pass. 1 3 Class.	Sun 1 Pass. 1 3 Class.	Sun 2 Pass. 1 3 Class.
—Kelso ... dep.	a.m. 7 0	only. Tues. 7a15	Tues. 9a15	a.m. 10 5	p.m. 1 15	1 55		p.m. 2 30	Goods	5 0 / 5 10		p.m. 7 5	p.m. 8 5	a.m. 7 45	p.m. 5 55
Heiton ,,		7 25	9 25							5 20					
—Roxburgh Jn. arr.	7 7	7 30	9 30	10 12		2 2				5 25		7 11	8 11	7 52	6 2
— Jedburgh dep.	6 40			9 45		1 35			3 0	4 40		6 50	7 56	7 25	5 35
Jedfoot Bridge ,,	6 44			9 49		1 39			3 6	4 44		6 54		7 34	5 39
Nisbet ,,	6 49			9 54		1 44			3 12	4 48		6 58		7 34	5 44
Kirkbank ,,	6 57			10 2		1 52			3 22	4 57		7 3		7 42	5 52
— Roxburgh Jn. arr.	7 4			10 10		1 59			3 30	5 4		7 8	8 9	7 50	6 0
— Do. ... dep.	7 13			10 22		2 8				5 13			8 15	7 52	6 2
— Kelso ... arr.	7 20			10 30		2 15				5 20			8 22	8 2	6 12
—Roxburgh Jn. dep.	7 9	7 35	9 35	10 17	1 20	2 4	1 37	3 40		9 30 / 5	7 14	8 12	7 53	6 3
Rutherford ... ,,	7 16			10 24		2 11		3 50	5 16 / 5 40		7 21		8 0	6 10
—Maxton ... ,,	7 23	7 55	9 55	10 30	1 35	2 18	1 48	4 0	5 22 / 5 50		7 28		8 6	6 16
—St Boswells Jn. arr.	7 30	8 5	10 5	10 36	1 45	2 25	2 55	4 10	5 28 / 6 0		7 35	8 27	8 15	6 22
Carlisle ... arr.	10 20			12 42		5 21		5 21		8 32		12·24		12 4	
Edinburgh ,,	9 15			12 10		3 55		5 0		7 55		8 55		10 20	8 42

No. 1.—Does not work Goods Traffic to or from Nisbet or Kirkbank Stations.

No. 2.—Carries Live Stock for Haymarket from Kelso and other Stations on Branch, including that from Jedburgh Branch, to go forward from St Boswells by 5-30 a.m. ex Carlisle. Calls at Heiton Siding and Maxton only for Live Stock or Perishable Traffic.

No. 3.—On Mondays, July 6 and 20, this Train will start at 8-40 a.m., and will work Live Stock from all Stations on the Branch to St Boswells. It will go on immediately from St Boswells, but will not proceed northward from Galashiels sooner than its booked time.

No. 4.—Does not convey Empty Coaching Vehicles.

No. 9.—Carries a Road Wagon ticketed "Jedburgh and Edinburgh Road Wagon," the Van Way-bills to be delivered to Station Master, St Boswells, and also a Wagon labelled to South Leith, in which to place spare sheets at Intermediate Stations to St Boswells. On Mondays lifts Live Stock for Haymarket, which must be transferred at St Boswells to 3-52 p.m. Train from Earlston.

No. 11.—Carries a Road Wagon ticketed "Kelso and St Boswells Road Wagon," the Van Way-bills to be delivered to Station Master, St Boswells.

† No. 12.—Is a Mixed Train on Mondays only as between Kelso and St Boswells. On other days it is not a Mixed Train.

Through Carriages and Van are run from Kelso to Edinburgh by Nos. 4, 6, and 12.

A Through Carriage is run from Jedburgh to Edinburgh by No. 4.

The *Southern Reporter* of September 1908 showed a continuation of the weekday pattern of five trains each way between Jedburgh and Roxburgh with just two on Sundays. However, the first train of the day from Roxburgh was timetabled to run non-stop to Jedburgh taking just 15 minutes for the journey compared with the 20 minutes or so for the other stopping trains. The first train from Jedburgh, the 6.25 am, ceased to run through to Kelso. Instead it terminated at Roxburgh but a connection allowed Kelso passengers to reach their destination by changing on to a St Boswells to Kelso train. The 1910 *Bradshaw* timetable showed an identical pattern. Both Sunday trains continued to run throughout in both directions linking Jedburgh and Kelso, though there were no other Sunday trains on the Tweedmouth to St Boswells line to provide connections.

The miners' strike of 1912 had a dramatic effect on the branch timetable. In an attempt to reduce coal consumption the number of trains each way was reduced from five to two. The first down train left Jedburgh at 6.10 am, arriving at Roxburgh at 6.31. The only afternoon train left Jedburgh at 4.35 arriving at Roxburgh at 4.56. The corresponding up trains ran at 9.10 am and 6.10 pm from Roxburgh. Each train provided connections at Roxburgh with trains to/from Kelso, also St Boswells for Edinburgh.

The 1914 NBR working timetable shows that the service had returned to six passenger trains in each direction on weekdays with a single Sunday train. The 9.02 am and 9.20 pm from Roxburgh to Jedburgh were marked as 'mixed trains' though they were prohibited from lifting or leaving wagons at Jedfoot. Departures from Roxburgh were scheduled for 6.42 (non-stop to Jedburgh), 9.02, 11.45 am, 4.19, 6.18 and 9.20 pm. Each train apart from the 6.42 started at Kelso but ran purely as passenger trains to Roxburgh. The 6.42 am started at St Boswells at 6.12 and ran direct onto the branch at Roxburgh. Mails for Kelso (from Carlisle) were carried on this train. In the reverse direction passenger trains left at 6.10, 7.35, 9.45 am, 1.40, 4.46 and 7.05 pm. The 6.10 am and 4.46 pm were to run as mixed trains but were not allowed to work traffic to or from Nisbet and Kirkbank stations.

World War I later produced some further timetable changes. The early 1916 timetable, for example, showed just four trains each way on the branch on weekdays with the Sunday service being one train each way. Even this solitary Sunday return working stopped on 1st May, 1916. The *Railway Magazine* reported: 'on the Edinburgh, Peebles and Galashiels, and on the Selkirk, Kelso and Jedburgh branches, all the Sunday trains are deleted from the services'. This pattern continued into 1917 with four weekday trains each way between Jedburgh and Kelso though with an additional Roxburgh to Jedburgh working on Tuesdays, Thursdays and Saturdays.

In early 1920, before the start of the miners' strike, the timetable consisted of six trains in each direction with passenger trains leaving Roxburgh at 9.02, 11.51 am and 4.16 pm. All started from Kelso with the 9.02 am running as a mixed train but prohibited from leaving or lifting wagons at Jedfoot. Any livestock wagons were to be from Roxburgh to Jedburgh only. There were three later trains starting from Roxburgh at 5.10, 6.58 and 7.54 pm, the last of which ran as a mixed train. In the reverse direction trains left Jedburgh at 7.28 (mixed), 9.31

KELSO, ROXBURGH, and JEDBURGH.—North British.

Miles	Down.		Week Days. mrn	mrn	mrn	aft	aft	aft	Sundays. mrn	aft
	Kelso	dep.	6 45	8 37	1125	4 3	5 50	8 58	9 50	6 44
3	Roxburgh	arr.	6 52	8 47	1135	4 10	5 58	9 8	9 58	6 51
		dep.	6 58	9 2	1145	4 17	6 13	9 20	1010	7 4
4¾	Kirkbank		....	9 6	1149	4 21	6 17	9 24	1014	7 8
7¼	Nisbet		....	9 12	1155	4 27	6 23	9 30	1021	7 14
8½	Jedfoot Bridge		....	9 17	1159	4 31	6 27	9 35	1027	7 18
10	Jedburgh	arr.	7 13	9 23	12 5	4 37	6 33	9 41	1035	7 24

Miles	Up.		Week Days. mrn	mrn	mrn	aft	aft	aft	Sundays. mrn	aft
	Jedburgh	dep.	6 25	7 40	9 45	1 40	4 43	7 5	7 25	5 30
1½	Jedfoot Bridge		6 29	7 44	9 49	1 44	4 47	7 9	7 29	5 34
2¾	Nisbet		6 34	7 48	9 54	1 49	4 51	7 13	7 34	5 39
5¼	Kirkbank		6 42	7 54	10 2	1 57	5 0	7 18	7 41	5 46
7	Roxburgh (*see above*)	arr.	6 49	7 59	1010	2 4	5 7	7 23	7 46	5 50
		dep.	6 55	8 6	1022	2 13	5 16	7 32	7 53	5 58
10	Kelso 689	arr.	7 2	8 11	1030	2 20	5 23	7 39	8 0	6 5

ST. BOSWELLS, DUNS, RESTON, and BERWICK.—North British.

Miles	Down.		Week Days. a	mrn	mrn	aft	aft (Except Tuesdays and Saturdays.)	aft (Tuesdays and Saturdays.)	aft (Sats. only.)
	St. Boswells	dep.	6 35	8 40	1120	3 54	6 0	6 0	8 55
4½	Earlston		....	8 49	1129	4 3	6 12	6 12	9 4
10½	Gordon		....	9 1	1141	4 15	6 26	6 26	9 16
14½	Greenlaw		....	9 10	1150	4 24	6 37	6 51	9 25
18½	Marchmont		....	9 17	1157	4 31	6 47	7 1	9 32
22	Duns	arr.	7 14	9 24	12 4	4 38	6 56	7 10	9 39
		dep.	7 20	10 0	1230	5 25	....	....	
25¼	Edrom		7 28	10 7	1237	5 32	....	....	
26¾	Chirnside		7 32	1011	1241	5 36	....	....	
30¾	**Reston** * 794	arr.	7 41	1018	1248	5c43	....	....	
42	**Berwick**	"	8 9	1043	1 13	6 36	....	....	

Mls frm Reston.	Up.		Week Days. mrn	mrn	aft (Except Saturdays.)	aft (Sats. only.)	aft	aft	aft (Tues. only.)	aft (Sats. only.)
	Berwick	dep.	....	8 40	1245	1 0	3 35	5c25		
	Reston	"	....	9 19	1 12	1 27	4 15	6 15		
4	Chirnside		....	9 28	1 20	1 35	4 23	6 23		
5½	Edrom		....	9 33	1 24	1 39	4 27	6 27		
8¾	Duns	arr.	....	9 40	1 31	1 46	4 34	6 34		
		dep.	7 20	9 45	1 35	1 49	4 40	....	6 35	6 35
12¼	Marchmont		7 27	9 53	1 42	1 56	4 47	....	6 42	6 42
16¼	Greenlaw		7 36	10 3	1 51	2 5	4 56	....	6 50	6 51
20¼	Gordon		7 44	1012	1 59	2 13	5 4	....	....	6 59
26¼	Earlston [*and above*		7 58	1026	2 11	2 25	5 15	....	....	7 10
30¾	**St. Boswells 798, 799**	arr.	8 8	1036	2 21	2 35	5 25	....	....	7 20

a Conveys Passengers only from St. Boswells, Carlisle, and South thereof. *c* Change at Reston.

* Station for Coldingham and St. Abbs.

Bradshaw's Guide timetable 1910.
Author's Collection

Table 170 KELSO, ROXBURGH, and JEDBURGH

Miles			Week Days only mrn A	mrn A		aft S	aft	aft	aft	S A
—	Kelso	dep	8 40	11 21	..	1215	2 0	6 27	..	8 55
3	Roxburgh	arr	8 46	11 28	..	1220	2 5	6 32	..	9 0
—	167 Edinburgh (W)	dep	6 25	10 3	..	1210	2 20	4 15	5 45	7 4
—	169 St. Boswells	"	8 37	11 17	..	1 16	3 40	5 57	7 7	8 47
—	Roxburgh	dep	9 0	11 39	..	1 32	4 5	6 35	7 30	9 8
4¾	Kirkbank		9 5	11 43	..	..	4 9	6 39	7 34	9 12
7¼	Nisbet		9 12	11 49	..	1 39	4 15	6 45	7 40	9 18
8½	Jedfoot		9 16	11 53	..	..	4 19	6 49	7 44	9 22
10	Jedburgh	arr	9 21	11 58	..	1 44	4 24	6 54	7 49	9 27

Miles			Week Days only mrn A	mrn A		aft S	aft A	aft	aft	S A
—	Jedburgh	dep	7 15	9 57	..	12 6	1 48	5 50	7 6	8 15
1½	Jedfoot		7 20	10 1	..	..	1 52	5 54	7 10	8 19
2¾	Nisbet		7 24	10 4	..	1211	1 55	5 59	7 13	8 23
5¼	Kirkbank		7 32	1010	..	..	2 1	6 5	7 19	8 29
7	Roxburgh	arr	7 36	1014	..	1219	2 5	6 9	7 23	8 33
15½	169 St. Boswells	arr	7 57	1035	..	1234	2 24	6 50	8J12	9 50
56	167 Edinburgh (W.)	"	9 49	1155	..	1 46	3 41	8 54	..	..
—	Roxburgh	dep	7 47	1022	..	1 31	2 13	6 15	7 26	8 41
10	Kelso	arr	7 52	1027	..	1 36	2 18	6 20	7 31	8 46

A Thro Trains between Kelso and Jedburgh. **J** Arr. 8 24 aft on Sats. **S** or S Saturdays only.
For **OTHER TRAINS** between Kelso and Roxburgh, see Table 169

LNER passenger timetable July 1939-April 1940.
Author's Collection

am, 1.58, 4.42, 6.10 and 7.23 pm, with the mixed train prohibited from handling goods traffic from Nisbet or Kirkbank.

Any permanent return to 'normality' of train working on the branch was interfered with by the next miners' strike starting in late 1920. The NBR issued a notice entitled *'Suspension and Alteration of Passenger Train Services from and after 25/10/1920'*. On the Jedburgh branch this was limited to the discontinuation of the 6.10 pm from Jedburgh and the 6.58 pm from Roxburgh to Jedburgh.

The July 1922 *Bradshaw* showed a service of five trains between Kelso and Jedburgh with an additional evening train which started at Roxburgh. In the reverse direction there were also five trains from Jedburgh to Kelso with an additional working from Jedburgh to Roxburgh in late afternoon. The timings of the trains indicate that it was necessary for two locomotives to work the passenger service instead of one locomotive operating 'shuttles' along the line. However, by October 1922 the service had reverted to six trains in each direction. Trains left Roxburgh Junction [*sic*] at 9.03, 11.04 am and 4.09 pm. The first ran as a mixed train but all three started from Kelso. Later trains started from Roxburgh at 5.00, 6.50 and 7.43 pm, the last of these retimed slightly when running as a mixed train. Again Nisbet and Kirkbank goods traffic was not conveyed on this last train. From Jedburgh departures were at 7.21 (mixed), 9.30 am and 1.46 (all for Roxburgh and then Kelso), 4.34, 6.02 and 7.16 pm for Roxburgh Junction only. For some reason the 9.30 am train was not allowed to convey empty coaching stock!

The 1923 pattern was very similar with some small changes to departure and arrival times. The first and last trains from Roxburgh Junction to Jedburgh ran as mixed trains and two trains from Jedburgh fell into the same category though the 5.57 pm train (retimed from 6.02 pm), normally a passenger train only, ran on alternate Saturdays as 'mixed' with two minutes added to its journey time. The pattern extended into 1924, 1925 and 1926 with minor timing changes.

In September 1927 there were some changes to the pattern involving some 'Saturdays Only' trains. According to the *LNER Working Timetable* for September of that year trains with passenger accommodation left Roxburgh Junction at the following times: 8.57 (mixed from Kelso), 11.44 am (from Kelso; could run at 11.42 if van traffic was light), 1.28 (from Kelso; Saturdays only and stopping only at Nisbet on the branch), 3.38 (could run at 3.36 if van traffic was light), 4.40, 6.46, 7.35 (to run at 7.40 from Roxburgh if a 'mixed' train), 9.14 pm (Saturdays only from Kelso); to run at 9.20 if required to run 'mixed'). The eight trains timetabled for Saturdays constituted the busiest timetable ever for the branch. In the reverse direction trains left Jedburgh at 7.15 (mixed to Kelso), 9.46 am (to Kelso), 12.06 (Saturdays only to Roxburgh Junction), 1.55 (to Kelso), 4.15 (to Roxburgh), 5.50 to Roxburgh (to run 3-4 minutes later if running 'mixed' on alternate Saturdays), 7.10 to Roxburgh and 8.15 pm to Kelso (Saturdays only). The 9.46 am from Jedburgh was not allowed to convey empty coaching stock.

In the 1930s the *Hawick News and Border Chronicle* issued summaries of the passenger train service (between Hawick and Jedburgh) providing an additional source of timetable information. The 1930 and 1932 timetables showed six trains from Jedburgh and six in the reverse direction. Some of the connections to and from Hawick were timed differently on Saturdays. By 1938

Beyer, Peacock & Company-built NBR 0-4-2 No. 324 is seen attaching a horsebox onto the back of a train of clerestory carriages heading eastwards from Roxburgh Junction. This locomotive was built in 1861 and rebuilt in 1887 before its final withdrawal in 1912.   *Bill Lynn Collection*

A passenger train for Jedburgh waits for the signal to clear at Roxburgh Junction's branch platform in the charge of North British Railway 'G9' class 0-4-4T No. 9354. The train consists of a single brake composite coach.   *M. Halbert Collection*

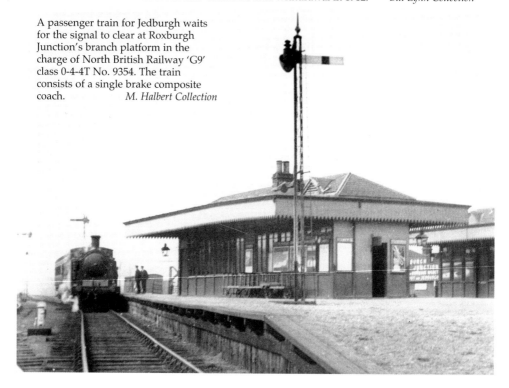

the newspaper was showing seven trains in each direction between the two towns with two of these in each direction providing Hawick connections on Saturdays only.

The year 1939 saw the start of World War II. The LNER issued an emergency working timetable which saw the Jedburgh to Roxburgh service initially reduced to four trains in each direction with the deletion of lunchtime trains. However, these trains were soon reinstated. In 1943 one of the trips along the branch which had terminated, after reversal at Roxburgh, at Kelso, was cut back to end its journey at Roxburgh Junction, this being the 9.57am. The return of this working, formerly starting at Kelso at 11.21, was amended to form an 11.56 am departure from Roxburgh arriving at Jedburgh at 12.15 pm. These changes were announced in the *Hawick News and Border Chronicle.*

A significant change affecting the branch was announced in *The Scotsman* of 2nd August, 1945. At this time the war in Europe had ended and the war in the Pacific was shortly to draw to a close. The LNER announced that it had made arrangements with a view to giving a morning service from Jedburgh to Berwick on weekdays starting on Monday 6th August. The 7.12 train from Jedburgh was retimed to leave at 7.00 am, calling at Jedfoot (7.04), Nisbet (7.07), Kirkbank (7.13) and Roxburgh Junction (7.24) from where it would run to Kelso arriving at 7.30, then providing an onward train at 7.50 for stations to Berwick. The motive power consequences resulting from this, and similar trains, are discussed in Chapter Fourteen. The October 1945 working timetable thus showed five trains each way on the line. Three trains for Jedburgh started at Kelso, the remaining two from Roxburgh Junction. In the down direction one ran from Jedburgh to Kelso, one through to Berwick and three from Jedburgh to Roxburgh Junction.

The following year, on 1st October the *Berwickshire News and Advertiser* reported a further improvement in the train service to Jedburgh, albeit on Saturdays only from 12th October. A train would leave St Boswells for Kelso at 9.00 pm giving a connection out of the 7.02 pm Edinburgh to Hawick and St Boswells. The train would then return to St Boswells. A new Saturdays-only train would leave Jedburgh for Roxburgh at 8.50 pm. This train would allow passengers to cross the platform at Roxburgh Junction to join the 9.00 pm from Kelso to St Boswells alternatively the train for Kelso. In addition the branch train would then return to Jedburgh, leaving Roxburgh at 9.45 pm, having picked up any passengers arriving at Roxburgh on the 9.35 pm Kelso to St Boswells or arriving from the St Boswells direction. Roxburgh Junction was thus very busy on a Saturday evening!

The floods of 1948 were to cause the complete cessation of passenger trains between Jedburgh and Roxburgh Junction and the diversion of London and Newcastle to Edinburgh trains over the Berwick-Kelso-St Boswells route meant that no convenient paths were available for local passenger trains between Kelso and St Boswells. The events linked with the cessation of the branch passenger service are dealt with elsewhere though one puzzling item remains. Why did the *Railway Gazette,* dated 27th August, 1948, state that the Roxburgh to Jedburgh passenger train service was resumed on 19th August?

North Eastern Railway Wilson Worsdell-designed 'D20' class 4-4-0 No. 2358 awaits departure from Jedburgh with the 5.20 pm train to Kelso. This was a Tweedmouth engine which would work back to its home depot with the NBR and NER train crews changing over at Norham station beyond Kelso.   *Bill Lynn Collection*

Roxburgh station with an unidentified 'V3' class 2-6-2T on a through St Boswells to Berwick train. The carriage is a single brake composite carriage, with first and third class seating which may, a few years earlier, have been employed on the Jedburgh branch.

Armstrong Railway Photographic Trust

The passenger facilities at the branch stations

The layout of the station facilities are shown on a LNER plan, entitled 'Station Arrangements at Jedburgh' dating from 1926. The station master's living accommodation was integral to the station buildings at Jedburgh and a small garden was included on the yard side of the building. The porters' room was a separate building to the south of the main building, almost level with the buffer stops of the platform road. The waiting room was at the south end of the station building, adjacent to the booking office. A linked wash room and WC were shown as a small building separated from the main building at its north end.

For many years the station building at Jedburgh showed few changes but by the late 1930s it was beginning to show its age. A 1939 document contains details of some proposed changes. The overall roof which linked the station platform and the shed was removed. A new verandah, some 66 ft long, was planned to provide passengers with some shelter. It was planned that it would project 6 ft from the wall of the station building. It was sloping and roofed with steel sheeting (with lead flashing at the upper end) and pine facing boards. Seven trusses would provide support. A glazed screen was fitted at the end of the new roof at the south end; a similar screen at the north end was shown on the plan to be unglazed. The screens projected 4 ft from the wall thus leaving a 2 ft roof overhang. After these changes the lower part of the walls of the station building, facing onto the platform, were painted in a shade of medium green with the entrance doors being a darker shade. The upper parts of the walls were painted in white, soon weathering to an off-white/pale grey colour.

Travellers on the line had barely time to get used to the new platform arrangements when the floods of 1948 brought about a cessation of the passenger train service, though no doubt the station staff appreciated the protection from the elements when loading or unloading parcels traffic in the 1950s and early 1960s!

At Kirkbank the station master's house was to the east of the line and next to the road, just on the north side of the single passenger platform. The station building with its slated roof was located on the platform and on its east side faced onto the approach drive. It is believed that for a time at least there was a grounded coach body located on the south side of the station building and next to this was located the small cubicle housing the urinal. There was a sawdust house at the southern end of the platform next to where the lever frame was located. The station building had a brick rear elevation with two large chimney supports. A sliding door led into the parcels accommodation. There were no windows on this side of the building. On the platform side the walls were matchboarded at 6 in. centres. A single door gave access into the waiting area. The station was illuminated by oil lamps. Two of these were attached to the station building; the other two were attached to the fence at the back of the station platform. The clock was mounted on the wall on the platform side. Originally the platform was timber-faced but some time, probably in LNER days, it was refaced in concrete. Also in LNER days the matchboarding was painted in a chocolate brown colour below and a shade of cream above (see the article by Mike Smith in the *NBRSG Journal* No. 105). The platform had several

A locomotive uses the run-round loop at Jedburgh station. Note the rails and water column still extant outside the shed. Also note the platform furniture, including a barrow with milk churns, and advertisements for Phoenix Insurance, tinned salmon and Brylcreem.

Bruce McCartney Collection

This rather poor photograph is included as it shows the front of the station master's house at Jedburgh and his small garden. The date is 14th April, 1963, just a few years before the line finally closed to all traffic. *R.M. Casserley by kind permission of Margaret Casserley*

flower borders with rose bushes and looked more attractive than the corresponding platform at Nisbet.

At Nisbet the platform and station building were located on the south-west side of the level crossing. The side of the small station master's house fronted onto the road. Behind this was the station building itself located at the north-east end of the platform. In the station building was the waiting room, the telegraph and general office from which tickets were purchased. There was also a small store room. Outside there was a single station name board towards the centre of the platform. The station building was built on a brick base but was matchboarded above. To the rear there was a small brick-built extension. There was a single chimneybreast. One end of the building abutted onto the station house. The south-west end of the building was windowless. The side facing onto the platform had three doors allowing access to the interior, with four windows in total which were extended upwards to the eaves. There were two plain panels between two of the windows and the adjacent doors and the station clock was mounted above one of these. One lamp was attached to the wall on the platform side of the building and one on the station house faced the tracks to illuminate the path to the platform from the side of the level crossing. Formerly there were three others mounted on posts along the rear platform fence. Toilet facilities were located to the rear of the station building adjacent to the store and consisted of a gentlemen's urinal and a dry closet. (The station master's house had a small garden with a hen run and 'drying green' for the domestic washing!)

This 19th century photograph shows the North British Railway's staff on the platform at Jedburgh station. The gentleman sitting on the barrow is likely to be the first Jedburgh station master, William Hartley, who was in charge at the station for about 40 years.

Jedburgh Museum and Jail

Jedfoot station is shown when it was stilled manned. Note the 'named' platform seat and the rodding for the pointwork leading from the ground frame located in the platform hut. The crossing gates protect the traffic on the Kelso to Jedburgh and Hawick road.

Jedburgh Historical Society

Jedfoot station building was shorter than that at Kirkbank. It was located towards the south end of the station platform which had a gravelled surface. On the yard side elevation there was a single window and the base of the single chimneybreast broke up the otherwise uniform matchboarding. The ends were plain but also matchboarded. On the platform side there were three entrance doors and four windows, all with heavy framing, with panels extending up to the eaves. The roof was slated. To the left (north) of the front of building was a small hut which contained the ground frame with a solitary lamp to one side. To the right was a small slate roofed store with a door and single window on the platform side. In later years the building and fences were painted white. The platform was timber faced on the passenger side but stone faced on the goods side. Towards the end of its life the small platform flower beds looked unkempt with weeds and wild flowers dominating.

This view of Roxburgh was taken in October 1954 from the platform used by Kelso-bound trains. Opposite is the platform for St Boswell trains with the Jedburgh platform hidden behind the platform buildings on the left-hand side. The cast-iron footbridge survived until the cessation of train services. Note the signal box where the Jedburgh line joins.

Armstrong Railway Photographic Trust/C.J.B. Sanderson

Chapter Nine

The goods train services

The Scottish Borders in the 19th century was not a major industrial region. The principal industry in the 19th century was agriculture, the fairly hilly nature of the town's surroundings making the rearing of lambs and sheep very important in the local economy. After the construction of the Jedburgh branch livestock was moved by rail from the town to other local markets ('marts'). T. Dagg, in an article in the *NBRSG Journal* mentions that on one occasion even a Highland Railway double-deck sheep van made an appearance at Jedburgh or Roxburgh for this traffic. Industries depending on wool developed with the manufacture of textiles, including the local tweed cloth, and glove-making being important exports from the town. Grain mills and the tanning industry were also found in Jedburgh. The coming of the railway also resulted in wagonloads of coal arriving from collieries at Scremerston, in Northumberland, and from the Scottish Lowland pits. Formerly the coal had arrived by cart via Yetholm. The *Teviotdale Record* in April 1859, however, made the comment that two loads which had arrived recently by cart had been sold locally at a lower price than the coal being brought in by rail! The local gas company works also received supplies of coal and there was much coal arriving for domestic use.

Other materials which were advertised for delivery at Jedburgh station in the local newspapers included 'superior quality' guano (Browns of Jedburgh), drain pipes, tiles and bricks (Shidlaw Brick & Tile Works) and lime and clay products (Shoreswood Coal & Lime Co.). This last company appointed Andrew Dunn as its local agent, who was based at Jedburgh station but able to arrange deliveries of wagonloads to Old Ormiston, Nisbet and Jedfoot station sidings. In addition the railway facilitated the delivery of agricultural machinery, seed potatoes, seeds, fertiliser, and both food and market goods, and also the dispatch of timber and potatoes. One rather specialist agricultural product was the large tonnage of dead rabbits caught by the many rabbit-trappers in the area. Regular dispatches were made to Glasgow, Newcastle-upon-Tyne, Leeds, Manchester and Birmingham.

Rutherford's Register and Directory of 1866 refers to Jedburgh station as being 'small and inconveniently placed in the outskirts, beyond Bongate and over half a mile from the market place'. The directory contained references to several businesses and traders having offices at the station. John Burn was described as a coal, lime and tile agent and contractor for delivery of railway goods in Jedburgh. Johnston & Co. (of Scremerston and Shoreswood collieries, Berwick-upon-Tweed) were also lime and manure agents. John Laidlaw was a coal agent and J.S. Turnbull was the agent for the Marquis of Lothian's coal, lime and tiles business.

In the 19th century Jedburgh's principal manufacturers of woollen goods were James Boyd & Son, manufacturers of blankets and tweed, based at New Bongate Mills. The Laidlaw Brothers also manufactured tweed at Allars Mill whilst John Hilson and Sons were manufacturers at Bongate and Canongate

A view of the traction engines in the yard of Ralph Dumma, the haulier and mill owner, who is not to be confused with a Ralph Dummer, who was another mill owner! Both appear in census records for the town.

Mary, Queen of Scots Museum, Jedburgh

The family of George Burn, one of the Jedburgh coal merchants whose lorries were loaded at the Jedburgh station yard.   *Jedburgh Historical Society*

William Burn was a local contractor, haulier and coal merchant who traded under the name of William Burn and Sons. His lorry, shown in the picture, is an early Seddon Mark 5 vehicle.

Fotki/Brian Edgar Collection

Mills. Ralph Dummer was also a local woollen mill owner. At the start of the 20th century David Cockburn operated at Canongate Mill.

William Farmer was a timber merchant based in the railway yard whilst Andrew Yellowlees cut timber at Bongate Saw Mills. The local coal agents, all of whom had offices in the station yard at the end of the 19th century, were Messrs George Burn, William Burn, James Carruthers, William Cowen, Walter Spence, William Spence and Robert Stewart. These delivered coal locally by horse-drawn carts, though later William Burn & Son had a fleet of large motor lorries and expanded into the haulage business as well as being coal merchants. Burn was the official agent for NBR and LNER deliveries to Jedburgh and its environs but many deliveries were made by the railway company's own vehicles.

A local firm which is likely to have visited the station yard was the firm of mill owners and hauliers, Dumma's, which had their own yard near to Jedburgh station. Ralph Dumma, the proprietor, operated several traction engines and Foden Tractors. His traction engines included Burrells Nos. 3343 (built in 1911), 2226 (of 1899) and 2464 (of 1902). No. 3343 bore the name 'Jetherts' [sic]. One of the company's roles was to transport roadstone on behalf of the county council, some of this stone emanating from the Carter Fell Quarry.

Some of the rail wagons appearing in the station yard sidings would have been owned by the rail companies, though there were three establishments based in Jedburgh, which had private owner wagons. The first of these was William Burn, mentioned above. In addition the Jedburgh Co-operative Society had wagons in its own livery as did the Jedburgh Gas Light Co. Ltd (later known as the Jedburgh Gas Co. until being vested in the Scottish Gas Board when nationalization of the gas industry took place in May 1949). Incoming coal, for example, is also likely to have arrived in liveried wagons from collieries in Scotland and Northumberland. Much of the rail traffic was handled in wooden-sided vans and open wagons, though later specialist wagons, such as acid-carrying tankers, made an appearance.

In the 20th century the largest industrial concern to be based in Jedburgh was officially opened in June 1929, namely the North British Artificial Silk Co. Ltd which manufactured artificial silk or rayon yarn. The company's name was changed to North British Rayon Ltd in 1931 but closed for business in July 1956.

Between 1929 and the mid-1950s, the North British Rayon Ltd works took delivery of almost all of its raw materials by rail, namely wood cellulose, caustic soda, carbon disulphide, and sulphuric acid. These were transported from the railhead to the works by lorry. The wood cellulose arrived in the form of sheets made from wood pulp. Caustic soda arrived in solid form in large drums. The carbon disulphide also arrived in drums for storage at the factory in under-water tanks. The sulphuric acid arrived in a concentrated form in specialist rail tank wagons, and was later diluted for use in the factory.

Briefly the process involved the wood pulp being soaked in caustic soda to loosen the fibres. After pressing the shreds were treated with carbon disulphide and more caustic soda. The fibres were thus translated into a syrupy mix called viscose. This was forced through fine jets into a sulphuric acid bath forming threads which were then 'caked'. Salt was also used in the process. Finally the threads were wound into hanks or cones.

One of the bi-products of this process was Glauber Salts dispatched from the factory in jute sacks. It could be used in the pharmaceutical industry as a laxative and in the paper, detergent and glass industries. Station master John Bennett has recorded the activity in the Jedburgh station yard. He was responsible for the provision of specialist cartage equipment and all the associated clerical work.

The sulphuric acid arrived in the owner's tank wagons. A trailer unit with a special tank and pump was used to transport the acid to the works. One driver handled this dangerous traffic. He was provided with clogs, gloves and goggles. Acid fumes permeated the whole atmosphere around the town, even more so in damp conditions. Bennett claimed that silver coins in pockets would turn black!

Salt was required in bulk and there were always one or two wagons in the siding for this traffic. The salt came from Runcorn in Cheshire. This was unloaded by hand shovels, though, if time were short, a mobile crane and scoop could be used.

The wood pulp arrived 'in shiploads' and caused a strain on resources such as the cartage strength when it arrived.

Good quality 'singles' coal arrived for the provision of power in the factory and between 700 and 800 tons arrived each week. Two 6-ton haulage tractors were detailed for this work and five or six trailers were available. The coal was unloaded from rail wagons to the trailers using the mobile crane and scoop. An extra man was always provided to assist the drivers in the unloading process. Four or five of the railway staff were detailed for handling the salt and coal traffic and were provided with clogs and industrial gloves.

Regular dispatches of the Glauber Salts were made by rail in addition to the factory's main product, the rayon yarn, which was sent out daily in wooden cases and railway containers. The 4.47 pm goods train from Jedburgh usually contained two or three vans, containing rayon, at the front of the train to facilitate their being transferred at Roxburgh to join the 6.20 pm evening goods train for St Boswells.

One of the railway's cartage units was permanently on hire to the rayon factory for the conveyance of rubbish to a local tip. There was constant concern from the local populace regarding overloaded coal trailers discharging coal onto the local roads and from the discharge of toxic waste into the Jed.

A common sight in Jedburgh was the articulated Scammell 'Scarab', usually loaded by George Forbes, and driven by Jock Haig, which made several return trips between Jedburgh station yard and the Rayon works every day. It carried coal to fire the boilers at the works. According to the book recording the history of the rayon works the consumption of coal in one week would be enough to run the 'Silver Jubilee' train 31 times from Edinburgh to London!

Other outgoing Jedburgh branch items included rabbits (by the ton), salmon from local rivers and agricultural produce such as wool, grain, potatoes and sugar beet. Incoming traffic could include fertiliser (including lime), coal, slates, explosives (for local quarries) and roadstone. Cattle and horses could be loaded and unloaded at Jedburgh (also Roxburgh) but only horses were accepted at the other stations on the branch.

Goods facilities at Jedburgh

The extensive station yard was used by various delivery firms and hauliers, supplementing the provision of these services by the NBR, the LNER and finally British Railways. Many of the independent firms maintained their own offices and staff at the station yard. Various changes in the layout of the sidings and yard took place during the life of the branch.

On approaching Jedburgh station in the years around 1860 the view for locomotive crew was of the line leading to the station platform with the run-round loop to the left (or east side). The locomotive facilities, namely the shed and turntable, were approached via turn-outs from the run-round loop. Locomotives would have used the platform road to run-round their goods train before shunting the wagons into the station yard with its sidings located to the west of the line. One siding was located on the west of the line to the north of the main yard. A point then created a turnout allowing access to the main sidings. Straight ahead a track led to the unloading dock where, for example, road carriages could be unloaded. The next track led to the goods shed whilst a turnout from this led to a single, long siding extending almost the length of the yard. Crossovers existed to allow wagons from the unloading bay to access the main platform road and to allow wagons from the goods shed to be hauled into the loading bay road. These crossovers each formed loops which could be used by a locomotive for running round a few wagons whilst shunting. There was no headshunt for the yard; all shunting movements would have required the locomotive to use the main line.

By the time of publication of the large scale maps of 1898 several changes had taken place, perhaps the most obvious of which was the removal of the locomotive turntable and the construction of the Station Saw Mills. (The map seems to indicate the existence of a short rail line within the saw mills though this has not been verified from other sources.) On the west side of the line, opposite the mills, a headshunt had been constructed allowing separation of shunting movements from any activity on the line to the station platform. A signalled crossover allowed access to and from the sidings. Within the station yard and leading off just south of the headshunt was the short siding for the cattle dock with an adjacent hut. The next much longer siding led to the coal staithes with a slightly shorter siding to the east of this but lying parallel to the coal siding. A small hut was located adjacent to this siding opposite the coal staithes. The next road led through the goods shed with the crossover in front allowing access to the shed from the line leading to the loading bank. At the loading bank a crane was provided. The former crossover from the loading bank line to the platform road had been removed further isolating the sidings from the platform facility. A weighbridge was provided at the main road entrance to the station yard. In the absence of a turntable it was now necessary for goods trains to run tender-first in one direction along the branch. The turntable site was the location of the new slaughterhouse. Archie Veitch had a cattle merchant's business in Jedburgh around this time and his wife was the owner of this slaughterhouse.

By 1918, when a new survey was made, the Station Saw Mills had been demolished but the track plan in the yard remained essentially the same. At

This is a general view of Jedburgh station and yard taken from the trackbed to the north. A variety of vans and open wagons are in the yard sidings and the smoke from a locomotive awaiting departure with its train can be seen in the passenger platform. The goods shed lies just to the right of centre and a loading dock is next to the siding on the right.

Bruce McCartney Collection

The stone-built goods shed with its slated roof and sliding doors, stands in the station yard at Jedburgh. By this time, in the early 1960s it had lost its own tracks but the three-ton crane still stands adjacent to the rear of the shed. Various delivery vehicles and trailers occupy the site.

Bruce McCartney Collection

some time a grounded coach body was installed to the north of the cattle dock siding which was a bothy for the use of the crews and yard staff.

A plan of the station, dated 1922, shows further changes. Firstly permission had been granted to the Shell Marketing Co. Ltd to have a 'stand pipe and oil pipe' on railway property. Permission for this, subject to certain terms and conditions, was granted by the General Manager of the NBR in a letter of 7th December, 1920. These pipes were to be placed at the end of the long headshunt from the locomotive shed. The end of this headshunt projected for a few yards beyond the line of the northern-most wall of the slaughterhouse. Once these pipes had been installed, permission was granted by the NBR General Manager (in a letter dated 29th March, 1922) for the construction of a stile over the railway's boundary fence to allow Shell staff to access the siding. The purpose of the exercise appears not to have been recorded but is likely to have been associated with the discharge of fuel or oil from rail tankers at this point.

The same map shows that various coal 'depots' had been created on the east side of one of the two yard sidings. In order, from north to south were located the Co-operative Society, G. Burn, R. Stewart and William Burn, all associated with local coal deliveries. The end of this siding is shown as having a bank rather than traditional buffer stops.

In addition the length of the passenger platform to the south of the overall station roof is marked as a 'cattle loading wharf'. The track at this point was normally used to access the crossover for a locomotive to run-round its train. Presumably cattle wagons had to be moved to allow this to happen. The same plan showed that access to the slaughterhouse was via a track which left the main road to the south of the station and yard and followed a route between the railway fence and the Jed.

In 1926 the LNER ceded a small area at the south end of the station (28 square yards) to the Roxburgh County Council and the Burgh of Jedburgh for a road improvement at the bridge over the Jed.

By the end of the 1920s the additional wagon traffic associated with the arrival of the rayon works, especially the unloading of the specialist tank wagons and those loaded with wood pulp and salt, created a pressure on space in the sidings at Jedburgh. Despite this there was no immediate change to the layout of the yard.

However, the track layout was altered in the mid-1930s according to a LNER plan dated 1936. The two sidings referred to above had a combined capacity of 41 wagons. The late 1930s modifications produced an increased capacity of 51 wagons, comprising two sidings each accommodating 13 wagons and a longer siding holding 25 wagons. To allow these changes the former depots or 'sheds' were to be removed to 'new sites' not specified on this plan. Other changes compared with what is evident from earlier plans included the small building adjacent to the signal box being labelled as an oil store. A small bothy was placed near to the old loading bank at the west of the yard. The loading bank adjacent to the station platform was fitted with a 3 ton crane and 'coal lets' occupied the area to the south of the locomotive shed. In addition a 'weighing machine' was placed on the loading bank south of the station platform, earlier referred to as the cattle loading wharf. At the south end of the yard several changes took place. Two of the sidings were cut back slightly allowing space for the railway's goods office and an office for George Blaikie & Co. To allow a new weighbridge to be built William Burn's office was moved to a position adjacent to the yard's western boundary. The station master's office was next to this. A 'proposed runway' is marked across the two shortened sidings. Its purpose becomes clear when another plan, dated 1937 is examined.

This period, towards the end of the 1930s, was clearly a time of much change for the Jedburgh station and its yard. The 1937 plan marks the line to the locomotive shed with a series of crosses, presumably indicating its being taken out of use. The inspection pit is still identified within the shed. Beyond the engine shed to the south the sheds at the 'coal lets' area are crossed through. Both the end of the platform road and the run-round road are marked as having sleeper buffers. The south end of the platform is still in use as a loading bank with its 3 ton crane marked; this area is described as having a stone wall edging to the platform though the rest of the passenger platform is identified as being 'sleeper-edged'.

The goods shed at Jedburgh was of stone construction and it was separated from the station platform by a siding. It had a 3 ton crane mounted on a loading bank also made of stone. It had wooden doors and a steeply pitched slate roof. Changes took place in the vicinity of the goods shed in the 1930s. The siding into the shed was cut back and a buffer stop was erected. The outer, north-facing door of the shed was usually closed and the building's use was changed to that of a garage for the 'mechanical horses' used for deliveries to the town and surroundings. A fuel tank and pump were erected in a recess created at the end of the loading bank next to the station platform, well out of reach of the arc of the crane jib as it swung round. The purpose of the 'runway' mentioned earlier is now clear. It provided a means of access towards the goods shed for the 'mechanical horses'. The line of rails leading to the goods shed was shown on the plan as being fitted with a 'choke' (or chock) preventing wagons from being pushed towards the closed shed door.

The area to the west of the passenger building is identified as a garden. In the yard the goods offices of the railway company and of George Blaikie are identified (the former shown as measuring 19 ft x 10 ft, the latter 14 ft x 7 ft). Three warehouses are marked on the plan to the east of the three sidings. They were identified as being occupied (from south to north) by William Burn & Son (200 sq. yds in area), the Co-operative Society (190 sq. yds) and George Blaikie & Co. (205 sq. yds). Various other small buildings were stores or a bothy for yard workers. In addition Burn's office was by the weighbridge as before; this is shown as measuring 15 ft 6 in. x 6 ft 10 in. Jim Hall recalls that in the 1940s two 'contract men' from a company called Mutter & Howie Ltd, operated out of Jedburgh station delivering merchandise to local shops. Mutter & Howie were a firm of carters, based in Midlothian, who appear to have gone out of business around 1946.

By the neck of the goods yard there was a 'straw shed' for the livestock wagons and near to this a ground shunt signal was located. The water crane was located between the run-round loop and the shed track. A note on a surviving plan mentions that a 'Porters messroom and foreman's office are to be put in.'

A few years before the closure of the line at least two changes were made to the track layout at Jedburgh. Firstly, the yard headshunt was removed with shunting between sidings having, once again, to be performed using the main line of the branch. However in the absence of passenger trains this did not cause any difficulties. Secondly, with the locomotive shed having lost its railway use when the passenger trains ceased, the rails to it were removed.

At the time of writing the main road realignment and improvements, plus the development of the station site, with its filling station, commercial and retail establishments, have removed all trace of the station yard, sidings and facilities.

It is worth mentioning that John Bennett, the former Jedburgh station master, recorded, in his small booklet entitled *Random Reflections of a Roving Railwayman* the names of some of his 'very happy' staff including John Brown (chief clerk in the goods department assisted by Ray Taylor and Jessie Liddle), Bob Michie (in the booking office), John Anderson (foreman) and Dave Cowe.

Goods facilities at the intermediate stations on the branch

Goods facilities were provided at each of the intermediate stations on the branch though these were somewhat restricted, loading banks being limited to two or three wagons and storage space being limited to a further five or six. When no locomotive was present some movement of wagons occurred using pinch-bars. Despite the limitations the branch stations were busy in their heyday with the 1920 branch takings, for example, being over £21,000.

Old Ormiston station, when built, had just a single siding with a headshunt with a three-bay 'lime drop' at the north end of the siding. There was a small loading bank at the south end of the headshunt siding but originally there was no crane. By the turn of the century at Kirkbank, as the station was now called, the bank had been cut back on the east side and another siding had been laid. The second siding became what was formerly part of the headshunt though the connection between the sidings and the branch was moved southwards in the Nisbet direction as a result. By this time a small crane had been provided on the west side of the first siding on the loading bank; this could be used to unload items from wagons placed in the adjacent siding only. A shunting signal later protected movements from the sidings onto the branch. To give some indication of the volume of traffic handled, this small station yard dispatched 11,748 head of cattle to the local markets in 1920. This was a formidable figure for such a small facility. In addition the sidings handled lime, other fertiliser and agricultural produce such as potatoes and straw. There were two sawdust huts for use on the floor of livestock wagons, and a weigh house ('weighing machine') for road vehicles. Office work was performed in the wooden building on the station platform. Adjacent to one of the sawdust houses in the yard was a small lamproom. Originally there was a small signal cabin at the south end of the platform which contained the frame for the signal levers. The home signals were later controlled from a covered ground frame on the south end of the platform. Later on the signalling was completely removed. A platelayers hut was located on the east side of the line midway between the station and the crossover from the sidings to the branch main line.

Nisbet was the next station towards Jedburgh. On one side of the river (to the south) was the Crailing estate which included five large farms in addition to the

Church and Manse. On the other side the station served a large area with many farms: Nisbet Hillhead, East and West Nisbet, Upper Nisbet and Ploughlands to name but a few. Initially Nisbet had a single siding complete with a headshunt almost as long as the siding itself. There was a loading bank of some 40 yards in length with a sloped road approach. A second siding was later laid adjacent to this loading bank. There was no crane provided but the loading bank had a store-shed for tools (including pinch bars for moving wagons when no locomotive was present), brushes and pails, plus sterilizing fluid for the floors of the cattle wagons. Until 1948 it also housed the hampers for the local rabbit catcher. A fence was located at the back of the bank. As at Kirkbank a small shunt signal was located adjacent to the crossover onto the branch line. There was also a sawdust house, the sawdust being for the floors of the cattle wagons to prevent the cattle slipping on the floors. There was a weigh house for road vehicles. The weighing machine was by Avery's and the building also functioned as the oil and lamp house. Also there was the old carriage body, mounted on bricks, with its entry to the rear.

Farm traffic associated with the Monteviot and Crailing Estates included outward wagonloads of potatoes, straw, wood and sugar beet whilst coal probably provided the largest import. Local resident Jim Hall recalled that when he was young, in the 1920s, the farms would perform much bulk-buying of provisions and barrels of herring, oatmeal and molasses. These would arrive at the station for collection. Later, of course, motor transport brought such items direct to the farms and country houses. When the sidings at Jedburgh were full it was not unknown for the up goods to leave a few wagons of empties or non-perishable traffic at Nisbet to be 'tripped' on to Jedburgh when siding space became available. The siding could hold upwards of 12 four-wheeled wagons.

Jedfoot Bridge, later Jedfoot, was built with a single siding on the east of the branch. This siding extended almost to the fence at the side of the adjacent road. The yard was referred to as a depot on contemporary plans. By the 1890s a second, shorter, siding had been built on the east side of the original one (as at Kirkbank) and the headshunt was removed. After this time any shunting was performed from the main line of the branch. A loading bank lay behind the passenger platform on the longer first siding and this had a loading gauge approximately level with the end of the platform. Two small coal storage facilities existed at the end of the longer siding in the 1920s at least and a weighbridge, plus a small office, was near to these at the edge of the railway property to the east of the sidings. It is believed that no crane was provided here. Coal and road van traffic was handled at Jedfoot, access to the yard being via a gate adjacent to the main road. Some other small buildings at the side of the yard may have been offices associated with this business. The signal cabin here controlled the station approaches, the level crossing and the points at the entrance to the yard sidings. As at Kirkbank and Nisbet there was no loop for trains to pass.

After the cessation of passenger trains a grade 1 porter looked after each of Kirkbank and Nisbet stations. They were responsible for the paperwork and accounting procedures associated with the goods traffic. At Jedfoot the sidings still received traffic though the paperwork for this station was dealt with by Jedburgh as the small yard office shed had been knocked down.

Goods timetables

It is fortunate that some of the working timetables for freight and goods trains for the branch have survived. In addition to information from these timetables the early timetables for both passenger and goods trains appeared in some local newspapers. It is possible, combining these sources, to put together a picture of the traffic on the line, though the overall picture is not as complete as it is for passenger trains.

The first surviving timetable referring to the goods services on the branch appears to be the North British Railway's working timetable of May 1863 which has been reprinted by the North British Railway Study Group. The times of the goods on the branch do not appear in the main tables. Instead a separate note reads as follows:

JEDBURGH BRANCH WORKINGS
NB The Trains will run over this Branch subject to Train Staff Regulations

The engine on this Branch is to work all the Goods Traffic between Station and Station, and also between the different Stations on the Branch and Roxburgh. By the trip at 8.50pm from Kelso, it will have to take forward all Goods for Jedburgh and Stations on the Jedburgh Branch; and by the trip 7.10pm from Jedburgh, it will take down direct to Kelso all Goods and Foreign Empty Wagons going to or beyond Kelso, which it may not have been able to remove to Roxburgh in the former trips during the day.

Unfortunately these 'former trips' are not shown in the timetable, though there were several gaps in the passenger timetable when these trips could have occurred.

The 1880 NBR working timetable, part of the National Railway Museum collection, gives a more complete picture. There are two goods trains timetabled to work on the branch. The first, described as an up train, left St Boswells at 11.00 am picking up or dropping off wagons at the sidings at Maxton and Rutherford before arriving at Roxburgh Junction at 11.55 am. The train carried road wagon traffic ticketed 'South Leith and Jedburgh Road Wagon' and 'St Boswells and Jedburgh Road Wagon', the van waybills were to be given to the agent at Jedburgh. The train remained in the sidings at Maxton for a passenger train to overtake. Wagons for Heiton siding and Kelso were to be left at Roxburgh Junction. It then left Roxburgh Junction at 12.10 pm calling at Kirkbank (12.25), Nisbet (12.50) and Jedfoot Bridge [*sic*] (1.20) before arriving at Jedburgh at 1.30 pm. In the event of this train being suspended a train, hauled by the St Boswells pilot engine, left St Boswells at 11.47 am, making the same stops, and working through to Jedburgh. It did not convey Heiton and Kelso traffic.

In the return direction the down goods left Jedburgh at 2.20 pm calling at Jedfoot Bridge (2.26), Nisbet (2.32), Kirkbank (2.42) arriving at Roxburgh Junction at 2.50 pm. After a 10 minute wait it called at Rutherford and Maxton before arriving at St Boswells at 3.30 pm. The accompanying note referred to the train being worked by the St Boswells pilot if the first morning goods had been suspended. The train carried the 'Jedburgh to St Boswells Road Wagon'.

In addition to the scheduled goods train some passenger trains ran as mixed trains. Whilst a timetable note prohibited the 6.45, 9.50 am and 6.35 pm trains from Jedburgh from carrying livestock, the afternoon trains may well have done so. The connecting train for St Boswells off the 2.15 from Jedburgh was 'intended to work goods and livestock traffic from Kelso and Roxburgh to St Boswells', according to a footnote.

The 'Loads of Engines' table in the 1896 working timetable was almost certainly academic for the Jedburgh branch. The permitted loads (in each direction) were:

Class of locomotive	Loaded goods wagons permitted
18 in. cylinder 6-wheeled coupled engines	50
1st class 6-wheeled coupled engines	45
2nd class 6-wheeled coupled engines	45
3rd class 6-wheeled coupled engines	40
1st class 4-wheeled coupled engines	45
2nd class 4-wheeled coupled engines	40
3rd class 4-wheeled couple engines	30

The 6-coupled engines were 0-6-0s whilst the 4-wheeled ones were likely to be 0-4-2 or 2-4-0 locomotives. No photographs exist showing such long trains on the branch.

The working timetable for 1st July, 1896 has also been reprinted by the North British Railway Study Group and the relevant parts, referring to the Kelso and Jedburgh branches is reproduced on page 74.

Note that in the up direction the 11.10 am goods from St Boswells to Jedburgh is now worked by the St Boswells pilot and that the following 2.25 pm goods drops off Jedburgh branch wagons and the road van at Roxburgh, presumably to be carried onwards to Jedburgh by the 9.06 pm mixed train.

In the down direction the 6.40 am and 4.40 pm from Jedburgh to Roxburgh can run as mixed trains in addition to the scheduled goods train at 3.00 pm, the return working for the St Boswells pilot engine, again calling at all stations on the Jedburgh branch.

The May 1914 working timetable shows the train schedule for the period just before the start of World War I. Essentially the service is very similar to that of 1896. In the up direction one daily goods leaves St Boswells at 11.43 am, still worked by the St Boswells pilot engine. It called at all stations to Jedburgh though at Jedfoot it only left road van traffic. Two trains could run 'mixed', namely the 9.02 am and 9.20 pm from Roxburgh to Jedburgh. In the down direction the goods left Jedburgh at 2.40 pm (providing 80 minutes for shunting and assembling the train, if it arrived on time) whilst the 6.10 am and 4.46 pm trains are shown to have run as 'mixed'. Down trains did not work goods traffic to Nisbet or Kirkbank stations, for, as with the up train at Jedfoot, the entrance to the sidings faced in the wrong direction. The practice was established, in the absence of run-round loops, that Kirkbank and Nisbet Jedfoot sidings would be served and shunted by up trains whilst down trains would serve Jedfoot.

The timetable published at the time of the miners' strike in 1920 showed that the goods train still started from St Boswells but at the slightly amended time of 11.45 am and then leaving Roxburgh Junction at 12.17 pm. Calls were then made at Kirkbank and Nisbet, but the Jedfoot visit at 1.10 pm was for road van goods only. Two up trains were described as 'mixed', the 9.02 am (8.40 from Kelso) and 7.54 pm from Jedburgh. The first of these did not lift or leave wagons at Jedfoot and did not convey livestock for intermediate stations, only from Roxburgh to Jedburgh. In the down direction the goods train path was identical to that of six years earlier whilst the 7.28 am was the only 'mixed' train but this, predictably, did not convey traffic for Nisbet and Kirkbank. The down goods contained a wagon for Leith which picked up spare wagon sheets from all intermediate stations to St Boswells. In the event of there being insufficient time to complete shunting at Jedburgh extra time was allowed for additional marshalling of the train at Roxburgh. On alternate Mondays the down goods conveyed live stock for Gorgie market, Edinburgh, on the 2.30 pm train from Jedburgh, which called at all of the branch stations. Apart from minor adjustments of a few minutes the 1922 and 1923 timetables showed a similar pattern and timings. At this time the goods traffic inspector for the branch was inspector Russell of St Boswells.

In 1923 the two mixed trains on the branch were the 7.21 am from Jedburgh to Kelso and the return 8.40 am from Kelso to Jedburgh whilst the May 1924 timetable showed an additional working. On Tuesdays only, and running when required, there was an 'engine and van' movement at 6.00 am from Jedburgh to Roxburgh Junction. The locomotive concerned was the Jedburgh branch passenger engine. On arrival at Roxburgh it picked up wagons of livestock which formed the 6.45 am train to Jedburgh arriving at 7.00 am in time for the locomotive to work the first passenger departure of the day at 7.12 am. The down goods could make a 'cross trip' from Roxburgh to Kelso to transport livestock if required though no additional time was allowed. Cattle for Gorgie market was to leave Jedburgh, Nisbet and Kirkbank on the 2.30 pm train from Jedburgh.

In 1925 the Tuesdays-only train from Jedburgh was described as a cattle train and worked additionally on Monday 4th May and alternate Mondays thereafter. Details of the stock had to be wired to the Jedburgh station master on the previous Saturday. This connected with the 6.30 am Kelso to St Boswells cattle train at Roxburgh. These trains ran in association with the St Boswells sales. The first and last passenger trains from Roxburgh to Jedburgh were 'mixed' whilst the first Jedburgh morning departure was also 'mixed'. On alternate Saturdays the 5.53 pm departure from Jedburgh also came into this category.

These special livestock trains did not appear in the 1926 or May 1927 timetables with the pattern having reverted to the up and down goods trains plus two up and one down 'mixed' and the afternoon 'mixed' on alternate Saturday afternoons. The first morning passenger train also conveyed cattle wagons for Gorgie market, these wagons being transferred to the Kelso to Gorgie train at Roxburgh Junction. An extra up train could run from Kelso to Jedburgh as a 'mixed' on Saturday evenings from the September 1927 timetable.

In 1931, in connection with the St Boswells sales, an engine, guard and van would leave St Boswells at 7.00 am arriving at Jedburgh at 8.00 am. It would return from Jedburgh at 8.15 am lifting livestock wherever required, reaching St Boswells at 9.25 am. On Mondays any livestock for Gorgie market would be taken by the 3.00 pm train from Jedburgh (and other branch stations) and then by the 7.10 pm special from St Boswells to Gorgie.

Six years later, in 1937, the timetable showed the Saturday goods train at 9.15 am from St Boswells calling at all stations and arriving at Jedburgh at 11.17 am. The 'usual' goods on other weekdays left St Boswells at 11.45 am, arriving at Jedburgh at 1.33 pm. A timetable note was affixed to both of these trains: 'Work back 3.00 pm, Jedburgh to St Boswells via Kelso'. The note attached to the 3.00 pm (which did not stop between Jedburgh and Roxburgh) was somewhat complicated (the original grammar is retained):

Calls where required to lift or RV [road van] purposes on Jedburgh branch. Stations to advise Jedburgh as early as possible. If number of stops require to be made, must be despatched from Jedburgh ahead of the booked time. This train after arrival Roxburgh Junction at 3.30 pm will make cross trip to Kelso with traffic, returning sufficiently early to take up working of 4.40 pm Roxburgh Junction to St Boswells.

In 1938 the first goods is shown as leaving Hawick at 8.25 am rather than starting at St Boswells and was marked 'Saturdays only'. The later goods, marked 'Saturdays Excepted' also started from Hawick. The corresponding down goods trains left Jedburgh at 2.10 (Saturdays) and 3.00 pm (other weekdays) with the same timetable note applied as in 1937 except that the destination of the train from Kelso was Hawick rather than St Boswells. The May 1939 timetable showed the same pattern albeit with timing alterations. Three up trains ran as 'mixed' whilst two ran in the opposite direction. The 'Emergency Timetable' published by the LNER on 4th December, 1939 showed no changes in respect of the goods workings on the branch. Furthermore the October 1943 working timetable was remarkably similar except that the goods trains reverted to starting from St Boswells and that on Saturdays the down goods left Jedburgh at 12.35 pm, reversing at Roxburgh (arrival 1.05 pm) on its way to Kelso, arriving at 1.52 pm. The Saturdays-excepted goods was to run 25 minutes earlier from Jedburgh if stops were required to service the sidings at branch stations.

By 1952 the passenger service on the branch had ceased and the working timetable showed goods trains only. In the up direction the goods now ran as a class 'K' (branch freight or freight stopping at intermediate stations). It left Kelso at 8.30 am and Roxburgh Junction at 9.00 calling at all stations on the branch. Over 2½ hours were allowed for shunting at Jedburgh before the down goods left at 12.30 pm, making a Jedfoot stop only at 12.45, before arriving at Roxburgh Junction at 1.10. It travelled onwards to St Boswells, arriving at 1.55 pm. A second up goods left Kelso at 3.40 pm (Saturdays excepted) and, after reversal at Roxburgh Junction, arrived at Jedburgh at 4.35. No intermediate calls were made on the branch. The train left for Roxburgh at 5.15 or 5.30 pm arriving at 5.45 or 6.00 pm (at different times of the year) before heading for St Boswells where it arrived at 6.40 pm. Between June and September this train called at Nisbet to lift hampers of dead rabbits!

It must be remembered that the rayon works was still open until 1952. After its closure the amount of goods traffic decreased significantly and the goods service was reduced, often, to just a single trip each day. In 1953 there were two paths for goods trains each way on the branch. The 8.30 am from Kelso shunted at the intermediate sidings before arriving at Jedburgh; it then returned at 12.30 pm arriving at Roxburgh at 1.10. The second pathway was from Kelso at 3.40 pm on

Mondays to Fridays, then leaving Roxburgh at 4.05 for Jedburgh, without calling at the intermediate sidings. This train then left Jedburgh at 5.15 pm stopping at Nisbet to pick up hampers of dead rabbits 'when required'. Trains ran on to St Boswells. In 1959 the working timetable showed the service as running to Jedburgh only 'when required', particularly to pick up horse box traffic.

A 'Trip and shunting engine notice' for 7th January, 1963 indicates that a 'J35' class 0-6-0 was normally rostered for the goods working to Kelso and Jedburgh. St Boswells engine shed had closed on 16th November, 1959, as reported in the *Railway Observer*, and so the 'J35' was one based at Hawick. The lococrew would start their shift at 8.35 am, their engine being already prepared by the shed staff. The locomotive then left Hawick at 8.50 am and ran light to St Boswells arriving at 9.15. Leaving at 9.39 am it called at Charlesfield military depot siding (when required) before it was allowed five minutes at Maxton. Heading east once more it arrived at Roxburgh Junction at 10.05 am. Then it headed towards Kelso where it would attach meat traffic to the 9.59 am passenger train from Tweedmouth to St Boswells if required. Leaving Kelso at 11.30 am it returned to Roxburgh Junction. The part of the notice related to the Jedburgh branch was marked 'QR', the letter R indicating that the train ran onto the branch only when required. The letter Q indicated that the train would run (as required) on Mondays, Wednesdays and Fridays. If running the goods would arrive at Jedburgh at 11.50 am with a half-hour allowed for any shunting before the return to Roxburgh.

JEDBURGH BRANCH

WEEKDAYS

UP TRAINS

Distance from Roxburgh Junction	No.	520	760
	Description		
	Class	K	K
	Departs from	Kelso 8.30 a.m.	Kelso 3.40 p.m.
M.C.		am	SX PM
1 52	Roxburgh Junction .. (S) ..	9 0	4 5 ...., ...
4 17	Kirkbank	9 20	.. .. ..
5 33	Nisbet	9 35	....
7 8	Jedfoot	9 45	.. .. ..
	Jedburgh ....(S)..	9 55	4 35 ....

DOWN TRAINS

Distance from Jedburgh	No.	525
	Description	
	Class	K
	Departs from	
M.C.		PM
1 55	Jedburgh ....(S)..	12 30 .....
2 71	Jedfoot	12 45 ....
5 36	Nisbet	....
7 8	Kirkbank	.. ..
	Roxburgh Junction ..(S)..	1 10 ....
	Arrives at	St. Boswells 1.55 p.m.
	Forward Times on Page	W 89

The British Railways working timetable for 1952 showing the surviving goods trains which ran as class 'K', that is, branch goods or ballast trains stopping at intermediate stations. One loco lamp was placed above the buffer on the driver's side. Note that Jedfoot was the only halt for the goods in the down direction. *Author's Collection*

Both of the crew look towards the photographer as the Jedburgh goods train is hauled over the Teviot river bridge between Nisbet and Jedfoot by Reid-designed class '35/5' 0-6-0 No. 64463, a Hawick-based locomotive. The sole vehicle, apart from the brakevan is the six-wheeled parcel van.   *Hugh Davies*

The platform starting signal has already cleared for 'J35/4'class 0-6-0 No. 64509, of Hawick depot, to pull away from Jedburgh with the goods train which, on this occasion, consists of several vans probably with the products of the rayon works, pus the usual six-wheel van marshalled in front of the brake van.   *Armstrong Railway Photographic Trust/E.E. Smith*

The brick-built part of the platform on the left was formerly regarded as a loading dock. On the right are the 'drops' for the coal to be distributed by the various local coal merchants. A solitary wooden-sided coal wagon stands opposite. *Bruce McCartney Collection*

Mark Goodier, the mobile crane driver enjoys a cigarette break. The crane, fitted with a grab, was used to load coal from the railway wagons into the two 6-ton Austin 'Loadstar' lorries which took the coal to the rayon works. The lorries were also used to transport sugar beet in season. *(Both) George Lumsden*

Under the TOPS system (introduced in the 1970s), now known as a class '08', 350 hp diesel-electric shunter No. D3380 hauls a mixed goods out of Roxburgh Junction in the direction of St Boswells on 4th September, 1963. *Armstrong Railway Photographic Trust/J.M. Boyes*

A 'B1' class 4-6-0 with a goods train awaits the clearing of the starting signal at the end of the Roxburgh Junction branch platform so that it can proceed towards St Boswells with its train containing bogie bolster wagons. Note the repainted platform edging and lamps, also the drinking fountain and platform flower bed. *Armstrong Railway Photographic Trust/Malcolm Dunnett*

Former LMS 'Jubilee' class 4-6-0 No. 45696 *Arethusa* was a Carlisle (Kingmoor) locomotive when it was rostered for the St Boswells goods to replace another failed locomotive. As usual the locomotive off this working 'filled in' on the Kelso and Jedburgh goods train, thus bringing a very unusual locomotive to the line. It was photographed shunting in Jedburgh yard in the morning of 29th May, 1964. *Jedburgh Historical Society/John Spencer Gilks*

The same locomotive was photographed later in the day passing Nisbet station and its level crossing with the return afternoon goods, a train consisting, on this occasion, mainly of mineral wagons. Note that the engine is coupled to a Fowler tender. *Armstrong Railway Photographic Trust/J.M. Boyes*

BR Standard class '4' 2-6-0 No. 76050 was hardly likely to be taxed by the weight of its Jedburgh goods train! It was photographed leaving Roxburgh Junction with a solitary coal-laden mineral wagon and brake van in tow. *Bruce McCartney Collection*

A '4MT' class 2-6-0 prepares to leave the platform road at Jedburgh with the daily goods. The train consists of several mineral wagons, and a solitary wooden-sided open wagon which, no doubt arrived laden with coal. A solitary van plus the brake van make up the rest of the train. *Bruce McCartney Collection*

When not required to make a trip to Jedburgh the locomotive could be utilized to make a special return run back from Kelso to St Boswells with 'surplus traffic'. On its final return to St Boswells the footplatemen and guard would leave any wagons in the sidings and the locomotive would return light engine back to Hawick, with a scheduled arrival of 4.35 pm. The crew then booked off at 4.50 pm having completed a day of just over eight hours.

Bruce McCartney recorded the branch goods as being 'diminutive' in 1960 and some photographs dating from the same era show just a single van forming the train. He does recollect an occasion when he was cycling down the hill from Bonjedward towards Jedfoot expecting a great freewheel along towards Mounthooly. He was to be disappointed as he had arrived as the crossing gates were across the road with the goods crossing in front of him! He remembers the day clearly; it was Friday 6th May, 1960, the wedding day of Princess Margaret! The locomotive hauling the train was a 'J36' class 0-6-0, probably from Hawick shed.

The experiences of a young Dick Marks are recorded in Bruce's book *Memories of Lost Border Railways*. Dick was a young schoolboy who befriended one of the St Boswells goods guards. Visits to the brake van and involvement in shunting manoeuvres thus became commonplace. He enjoyed rides to Jedfoot or Nisbet though leaving the train at the latter could involve a three mile walk back to Jedburgh. One of the interesting tasks for the guard on these trains was to take two milk churns of water to the cottage between Nisbet and Kirkbank ('Kirkbank crossing') for at that time this building had no running water; presumably the former well near the cottage could no longer provide water of the right quality. If not involved with activities associated with the brake van Dick became involved with the delivery of local parcels, emanating from the goods train, which were carried on an open trailer hauled by a three-wheeled Scammell unit to the town and its immediate environs.

At that time the crossing gates and signals at Jedfoot were still operated by staff from Jedburgh and it was necessary for a member of staff from Jedburgh to cycle to Jedfoot to open the gates and pull off the signals. Dick often accompanied him on his own bicycle. Until the closure of the passenger service there had been crossing keepers at Ormiston, Nisbet Gatehouse and Bonjedward in addition to road crossings at the stations. By the end of the goods service all crossing gates were operated by the train crews except at Jedfoot.

Another reminiscence comes from local career railwayman Bill Berridge. He recalls cycling out to Bonjedward Mill to help the crossing keeper. One day the engine came out from Jedburgh to pick up a wagon at Jedfoot. The driver was whistling for the crossing but the gates were closed and the crossing keeper wasn't there! Bill was not fazed by this for he simply opened the gates to let the locomotive pass through. He describes this incident as his first experience of railway work … at the age of 14!

No doubt there were similar experiences by young persons in many railway backwaters, not solely in the Borders region. These would be impossible with today's Health & Safety requirements!

Chapter Ten

Excursions and special trains

Jedburgh Railway and North British Days

It was on the 4th August, 1856 that the first 'cheap' excursion train ran on the Jedburgh line in connection with the St James' Fair. The event was reported in the *Jedforest and Teviotdale Record* in the following week's edition. The train left Jedburgh at mid-day for Roxburgh and Kelso and more than 100 persons travelled on the train. Half of the passengers left the train at Roxburgh to visit the remains of Roxburgh Castle and to walk along the banks of the Teviot, before visiting the fair. A second train left at 2.00 pm and was also well patronized. Most of the participants in the excursion returned on the evening train scheduled to depart at 8.00 pm from Kelso but which was held for an hour to let other excursion trains depart for the 'North', one of which had a huge train consisting of 36 carriages and requiring two engines at its head! Kelso had rather limited platform space, which would have made dealing with a train of this size, and its large number of passengers, rather difficult. A huge crowd had assembled at Jedburgh to see the arrival of the returning special train and to accompany the passengers on the one mile walk to the town centre. The general feeling was that the event had been a great success.

On the 14th May, 1857 the same newspaper reported on the celebration of Queen Victoria's birthday. Nearly 80 people travelled on the first service train destined for Kelso or Edinburgh; others were anglers taking advantage of their day off from work. Many businesses in Jedburgh had decided to close giving their staff a day for recreation. Further excursion tickets were available for the 'common riding' event.

It was the North British Railway, the operator of the line, rather than the Jedburgh Railway, which advertised another cheap return excursion train from Jedburgh and Roxburgh to Edinburgh for New Year's Day 1858. The advertisement was actually dated 11th December, 1857 but appeared in the Christmas Day edition of the *Kelso Chronicle*. The cost was 4s. 6d. return in first class and 3s. in what the advertisement described as 'covered carriages'. Children under 12 could travel at half price whilst those under three years of age travelled free. The fare was 6d. cheaper for each class from Kelso and Roxburgh. The train was scheduled to leave Jedburgh at 7.15 am, 35 minutes after the first service train of the day, and was advertised to arrive in Edinburgh at about 10.00 am. It was arranged that the Jedburgh Brass Band would travel on the train. The return was at 7.30 pm from Edinburgh. Participants in the outward journey could, if they wish, overnight in Edinburgh and return on one of two trains on the following day on payment of a supplement of 50 per cent of the excursion fare.

Jedburgh is well-known for its annual Games, held in the summer months. As well as traditional Scottish sports such as caber-tossing, other competitions have involved wrestling, quoit throwing, velocipede (cycle) racing and running.

Over the years the Games attracted well-known participants from all over Scotland and the North of England. Just three years after the opening of the Jedburgh line the *Teviotdale Record*, in its report of the Games, referred to the arrival, between nine and twelve o'clock, of excursion trains from neighbouring towns. The 'Harrow Hotel' horse-drawn bus met the passengers from these trains and conveyed those that didn't want to walk to the showground. A few years later, in 1865, the same newspaper referred to the procession to the event being joined by people travelling by the train at 10.00 am. Other references to the arrival of spectators arriving by train are found in the 1860s and 1870s with the 1878 newspaper reporting: 'As the morning crept on, the trains brought a large number of excursionists'. The event continued with varying levels of success into the 20th century but reports of arrivals by train diminished. In 1928 there was a reference to buses arriving in the town with spectators, reflecting a change in local public transport preferences.

Returning to the branch line's early years, *The Scotsman* newspaper, dated 13th September, 1860, contained an advertisement for a 'Grand Excursion' from Edinburgh to Galashiels and Jedburgh. The special train was to leave Edinburgh at 7.00 am and return from Jedburgh station at 5.00 pm on 15th September. The return fares from Edinburgh to Jedburgh were 4s. first class and 2s. in 'covered carriages'. The fare to Galashiels was 6d. cheaper in each case. No mention is made in the advertisement of tickets being available for intermediate stations between Jedburgh and Galashiels.

The Jedforest Band's website contains a brief description of what was described as 'the town's annual summer trip by rail to Edinburgh', implying that this had taken place on at least one previous occasion. Over 600 people took part. The train left at about 6.00 am and returned to Jedburgh after 10.00 pm in the evening, both journeys being described as 'without incident'. Being accompanied by the Jedforest Instrumental Band the trip attracted much attention and in Edinburgh crowds followed them as they marched through the streets. The reveille (at Jedburgh) was described as being not-so-acceptable 'as fifes and drums are anything but helps to somnolence at four o'clock in the morning'!

In 1864 the *Teviotdale Record* of 16th July indicated that the NBR was planning to run a trip from Jedburgh to St Boswells Fair leaving at just after four o'clock in the morning. Passengers would be allowed to leave the train close to the showground rather than detraining at Maxton or Newtown St Boswells.

On the 12th July, 1865, Jedburgh played host to a party, some 1,000 strong, consisting of the warehousemen, porters and carters of the port of Leith together with their wives, families and others. They arrived at Jedburgh station at about 11.00 am. They marched in procession with their various insignias and flags to the Market Place where they dispersed. They were accompanied by brass and flute bands and pipers. At about 2.00 pm they assembled once more and proceeded to Ferniehurst Castle where they engaged in a dance upon the bowling green. They were accompanied back to the station by the Jedforest Instrumental Band and a large crowd of townspeople. Their train back to Leith left just after six o'clock in the evening. There was an account of the proceedings in the *Southern Reporter* newspaper.

The same edition of the newspaper reported on another event involving the Jedforest Instrumental Band which took place just two days later. The band left Jedburgh by train on their annual excursion. The destination was Galashiels and in their visit, lasting several hours, they visited Abbotsford, the former home of Sir Walter Scott. On returning to Galashiels in the evening they played through the principal streets of Galashiels in company with the Galashiels Town Band. Their train left for Jedburgh at 8.09 pm and it was reported that they all seemed well pleased with their visit.

The New Year's Day special excursion from the Borders to Edinburgh became an annual event though the pattern of some of the arrangements evolved over time. The advertisement appearing in the *Kelso Chronicle* of Friday 28th December, 1866, for example, showed the train as leaving Kelso at 6.45 am then calling at Roxburgh, St Boswells, Melrose and Galashiels on its way north. For passengers from Jedburgh, it was necessary to travel by 'ordinary train' leaving at 6.05 am to join the main train at Roxburgh. The NBR advised the public that the sale of tickets would cease at 9.00 pm on 31st December to allow the company to make sufficient arrangements. On this occasion there was a limited number of tickets available for return by 'covered carriage' in any train (excepting the fastest) up to and including the 24th January for which the return ticket would cost 5s. 6d.

One very special train which passed through the platforms at Roxburgh but did not visit the Jedburgh branch was that for the visit of Queen Victoria to the Borders in August 1867. She was accompanied by her daughter, Princess Helena with her husband Prince Christian of Schleswig-Holstein. Princesses Louise and

RECEPTION OF THE QUEEN IN THE MARKET-SQUARE, JEDBURGH.

Queen Victoria's carriage enters the Market Square at Jedburgh on the occasion of her visit to the Borders in August 1867.   *Illustrated London News/Author's Collection*

Beatrice and Prince Leopold were also on the train. A special notice, which is part of the Buccleuch Papers in Edinburgh, was issued by the NBR Manager's Office on 15th of that month. On 21st August the Royal Train was to leave Carlisle at 7.12 am hauled by two NBR locomotives having taken over the train from the London & North Western Railway engines. It was to take water at Riccarton Junction between 8.17 and 8.22 am. (This would seem a brief time period for both locomotives to take water.) It was to pass through Hawick station at 8.48 am before arriving at St Boswells at 9.12 am. Reversing direction with a change of engines in the platforms it was required to leave at 9.17 am. Observing a 20 mph speed restriction at Kelso Junction, St Boswells, it then progressed through Roxburgh without a stop until scheduled to arrive at Kelso at 9.40 am. From there the Queen was taken by carriage to Floors Castle where she spent a couple of nights as the guest of the Duke and Duchess of Roxburghe. A fireworks display was held in her honour. After resting on the morning of Thursday 22nd August, the Queen visited Melrose and Abbotsford after lunch. She returned to Kelso via Newtown, St Boswells, and Newstead. Crowds turned out to see her carriage pass by. After a further night at Floors the Queen set out by carriage before lunch on Friday 23rd. Her destination was the town of Jedburgh which was specially decorated and garlanded for the day. Her route was via Heiton and Eckford. Large crowds turned out to welcome her, according to the Teviotdale newspaper and the *Illustrated London News.* So Jedburgh welcomed its Queen but Jedburgh station did not welcome the Royal Train!

After her return to Kelso the Queen's train was originally scheduled to leave Kelso at 10.30 pm, travelling via Kelso, St Boswells and Eskbank to Edinburgh, where Caledonian Railway locomotives would take over to take the train on to Larbert. A late change in the running timetable meant that on the day the train left Kelso at 11.15 pm, passing through Roxburgh, then St Boswells at 11.38 pm. A brief stop was made to take water at Eskbank, between 12.45 and 12.55 am. The train was to pass at just 4 mph through Waverley station at 1.16 am before scheduled arrival at Larbert at 2.26 am (55 minutes later than the original plan). Here the Caledonian locomotives left the train. Its ultimate destination was Balmoral. This was the first Royal Train to traverse the newly-opened line of the Great North of Scotland Railway to Ballater and would have shortened, very considerably, the carriage ride at the end of the Queen's journey.

On 15th July, 1870 a special train was organized to carry the body of the late Marquis of Lothian from his London residence to Jedfoot station. Later in the day a hearse conveyed his coffin to St John's Episcopal Church in Jedburgh. The following morning a special choral communion service was held for the relatives and friends of the Marquis. The service was attended by the Provost, the magistrates, the procurators and the town council plus tenantry from the Lothian Estates and many persons from the local neighbourhood.

The occasion of the Jedburgh Annual Holiday was used by the NBR to provide an excursion train in 1870. On Friday 12th August this special train left Jedburgh at the early hour of 5.45 am for Edinburgh. On this occasion the Jed-Forest Instrumental Band accompanied the passengers on the train. After a long day in Edinburgh the return train left at 7.00 pm. The *Kelso Chronicle* reported that a large number of people took advantage of the train.

A special excursion ticket (available using ordinary service trains) was valid over the New Year Holiday at the end of 1871. The adult fare from Jedburgh to Edinburgh and back was 6s. return third class. Passengers could travel outwards on either 31st December of 1st January and return at any time up to and including the 4th January. A half-fare ticket was available for children aged 3-11.

Special trains of a very different sort were also run along the Jedburgh branch. The livestock markets (or 'marts') in the area were, as expected in a primarily agricultural sheep-rearing area, very large. *The Scotsman*, for example, contained an advertisement which was placed by Messrs John Swan & Co. in its edition of 13th July, 1874. A special stock train was scheduled to leave Jedburgh at 7.30 am to arrive in time for the start of the sale at 11.00 am in Edinburgh.

In 1888 the Glasgow Exhibition was held by the banks of the Kelvin. On Saturday 8th September the NBR provided a special excursion at cheap fares for the residents of the Jedburgh district to visit the exhibition. The mills and other businesses and trade establishments arranged a holiday for that day and some 378 passengers entrained at Jedburgh station. Other passengers joined the train at Jedfoot, Nisbet and Kirkbank raising the total number to upwards of 400 persons. The hour of departure from Jedburgh was 5.30 am and Glasgow was reached a few minutes before 10.00 am. The weather for the day was very favourable and the excursionists had a good day. Their return train left Glasgow at 8.10 pm arriving back at Jedburgh station at 12.15 am early the following morning. As was allowed by the special ticket a considerable number of the participants extended their stay in Glasgow until the following Monday, returning home on ordinary service trains. The excursion was reported in the *Jedburgh Gazette* of 15th September.

For 16th June, 1889 the Edinburgh Merchant Maiden Hospital Co., a body involved in charitable and educational matters, had organized an excursion to Jedburgh. They left Edinburgh by special train in the morning, together with their foundationers, and on arrival at Jedfoot they went to Monteviot having been invited by the Marquis of Lothian. After enjoying the beautiful grounds for a couple of hours they had lunch and then left for Jedburgh where they visited the abbey ruins. They then travelled up the Jed Valley to Ferniehurst which was in the process of renovation by Lord Lothian. Later the members dined in the Spread Eagle Hotel under the presidency of Bailie McDonald, the Provost of Jedburgh, whilst the foundationers, numbering about 90 persons, dined in the Corn Exchange. There was favourable weather for the whole day.

Sporting occasions were also served by the provision of special trains. For example, the Border Bowling Tournament was held on the two greens of the Langholm Bowling Club beginning on Thursday 18th June, 1891 and finishing on the following day. Fortunately the weather was very favourable and a number of passengers availed themselves of a special train from Jedburgh (also from Galashiels) which arrived at Langholm at half past nine in good time for the start of play at 10.00 am. *The Carlisle Patriot* newspaper included full details of the tournament and the special train.

Friday 18th May, 1893 saw the occasion of the visit to Teviotdale of the Edinburgh Borderer's Union. Their excursion, as reported in the local press, started from Edinburgh Waverley and took them to Nisbet from where they visited Penielheugh monument, the residence of the Marquis of Lothian at Mounteviot [sic] and the village of Ancrum before dining in the Corn Exchange at Jedburgh. They also visited Jedburgh Abbey, Queen Mary's House and Ferniehurst Castle. It was not recorded as to whether they had travelled by service train (with several changes en route) or by a specially chartered train.

What was described as a 'monster' excursion took place on Saturday 6th August, 1896. It was described in the following week's *Jedburgh Gazette* and recalled over 40 years later in an article entitled 'Old time excursion' in the *Gazette* of 12th August, 1938. No fewer than 744 travelled on this excursion which started from Jedburgh station: 535 from Jedburgh, 32 from Jedfoot, 82 from Nisbet, 75 from Kirkbank and 20 from Roxburgh. Jedforest Instrumental Band marched from the Market Place at 5.15 am to the station followed shortly by the Boys Brigade Band. The huge gathering at the station was swiftly loaded onto the special train ready for the scheduled departure at 5.45 am. In the event it departed just five minutes late. The weather was bright and fortunately the good conditions persisted throughout the rest of the day. The neighbouring stations loaded their passengers and the train set off for what was hoped would be a continuous journey to Craigendoran on the north bank of the Firth of Clyde. In practice a few stoppages were experienced but the train pulled in to Craigendoran station exactly on time at 9.45 am. The excursionists were transferred to the adjacent pier to embark on the steamer *Lucy Ashton*. In a very short time she was steaming down the Clyde under extremely placid conditions with both the Isle of Bute and the mainland bathed in sunshine. The destination of the cruise was Rothesay but the voyage to this port was prolonged by a sail in the Kyles of Bute to Tichnabruaich (now Tighnabruaich) from where the steamer returned to Rothesay. Other steamers, yachts and small sailing craft were passed en route as the participants were entertained with music provided alternately by the Jedforest Instrumental and Boys Brigade bands. Rothesay was reached at 12.30 pm where a hearty greeting was given to the excursionists who were left to 'find enjoyment according to their pleasure' until near five o'clock in the afternoon. Visits were paid to the castle and other places of interest in the town; some inspected an old convict ship that lay next to the pier, some visited Mount Stuart the home of the Marquis of Bute whilst others listened to the music of the Rothesay Pipe Band. The instructions were to be on board the *Lucy Ashton* by 10 minutes to five o'clock and shortly before that time the Boys Brigade Band marched down Victoria Street to the steamer playing selections of music. By 5.00 pm (the scheduled departure time) most were safely on board and at 5.07 pm the gangways were thrown off and the steamer sailed away from the pier. Whilst parting salutes were given with raised hands and the waving of handkerchiefs the bands played 'Jethart's here!' The captain varied his route back to Craigendoran from that followed in the morning for the excursionists' enjoyment. At Craigendoran station the train was waiting and, after loading, a prompt departure was made. The train arrived safely back at Jedburgh at 11 o'clock, the general opinion being that the holiday excursion had been admirably arranged and carried out. Nearly 750 persons went home very happy. The organizing committee had consisted of several Jedburgh dignitaries: Provost Sword, Bailie

The paddle steamer SS *Lucy Ashton* has just unloaded its passengers at Craigendoran Pier on the River Clyde. This was the vessel that provided excursionists from Jedburgh with their river cruise to Rothesay in 1896.   *Author's Collection*

In 1899 there was a summer holiday rail excursion from Jedburgh to Balloch Pier on Loch Lomond. The party travelled on a paddle steamer to Inversaid where they disembarked at the pier close to the hotel for an afternoon of varied activities: walks, games, listening to the band and picnics.   *Author's Collection*

Miller, ex-Provost Laidlaw, J. Lindsay Hilson and R. Jack. At a meeting of this committee a few days later the members were pleased to receive comments from the station agent at Craigendoran and one of the officers of the steamer as to the respectable appearance of the excursionists. It had been a memorable day.

The *Jedburgh Gazette* of 29th July, 1899 advertised an excursion for the Jedburgh summer holiday on 5th August. The excursion was to take place by train to Loch Lomond, with the destination station being Balloch pier. It was planned that an excursion by steamer would take place along the Loch to Inversnaid. The train was planned to leave Jedburgh at 5.45 am using the same 'railway pathway' as the 1896 event. Stops were to be made to pick up passengers at Jedfoot, Nisbet, Kirkbank and Roxburgh. The expected arrival time at Loch Lomond was 9.45 am and the steamer should reach Inversnaid at 11.15 am. The start from Inversnaid on the return journey was planned for 4.15 pm with the expected arrival time at Jedburgh being 9.20 pm.

The bugle call was sounded in Jedburgh at 4.45 am to wake up the participants and shortly afterwards the Jedforest Instrumental Band played lively airs as they marched from the Market Place to the station. The train departed at 5.45 am and picked up large additions at every station on the branch. En route there was a slight holdup before reaching the station at St Boswells and Balloch was eventually reached a few minutes after 10.00 am, slightly later than planned. (Note: the *Gazette* report quoted 'noon' for the arrival; this was clearly incorrect in view of the timings mentioned later.) The excursionists then embarked upon the steamer *Empress* which had been placed at their service for the afternoon. The steam up the loch was said to be a delightful experience and *Empress* arrived at Inversnaid pier at 11.50 am. The band had done excellent service during the cruise along the loch. On landing, some of the party took lunch at the nearby Blair's Hotel. Others visited the Inversnaid Burn, with its impressive waterfalls. Yet others visited the ancient fort, which had been erected nearby to overcome the threat from the McGregors. Some walked to inspect Rob Roy's cave, two miles north of Inversnaid, a location described by the author of the article as a place of seclusion and security.

Eventually it was time to return to the open area in front of the hotel where Mr Jack, of Bongate, Alnwick, took a picture of the party. A gentleman who had served his apprenticeship at Jedburgh and had travelled from Rothesay to meet the party was heard to remark: 'Jethart's here today!' The party re-embarked upon the steamer which had been tied up at Inversnaid for most of the day, and were able to partake of refreshments. The homeward journey began in weather which had become somewhat overcast and Balloch was reached, despite some choppy water, after an hour and a quarter. Soon the excursionists were seated in their railway carriages and a start was made on the return journey. Some parts of the journey were, apparently, made at great speed. There were a few unplanned stoppages but the train, having dropped off some passengers at Roxburgh and the branch stations, arrived at Jedburgh about an hour late at 10.20 pm. The walk from the station to the town was enlivened by the band who must have been tired after giving excellent performances during the long day. The exact number taking part was 376, of whom 206 entered the train at Jedburgh, 26 at Jedfoot, 59 at Nisbet, 64 at Kirkbank and 21 at Roxburgh.

INDUSTRIAL HALL AND PALACE OF HISTORY, SCOTTISH EXHIBITION, GLASGOW 1911.

In 1911 there was a special rail excursion train from Jedburgh to Glasgow for the Scottish Exhibition of National History, Art and Industry with its special pavilions, held in the Kelvingrove Park. The special train arrived back at Jedburgh at midnight, providing a very late journey along the branch.   *(Both) Author's Collection*

ART GALLERY AND CONCERT HALL, SCOTTISH EXHIBITION, GLASGOW 1911.

Rugby Union football has been a popular sport in the Borders for many years. The Saturday of 20th February, 1904 was the occasion of the Gala team visiting Jedburgh to take on the Jedforest team in the 'Border Championship'. Both teams were positioned near the top of the league table which appeared in the *Edinburgh Evening News*. Despite the inclement weather (involving arrangements to clear snow from the pitch if required) the NBR arranged a special train from Galashiels to arrive at Jedburgh in time for the start of the match, returning, after the match, once the spectators had had time to walk the short distance from the sports ground to Jedburgh station. Such special trains for rugby spectators were common in the Borders and continued after the World War: on Saturday 15th October, 1921, for example, a special train left Hawick at 1.40 pm in connection with the Jedforest v. Hawick match which kicked-off at 3.30 pm. The train returned from Jedburgh at 5.40 pm after the match had ended. The return fare was 3s. 6d. Seven years later, in 1928, it was reported by the *Hawick News* that just 24 persons travelled to Jedburgh on the special train arranged to take spectators to a Jed-Forest v. Hawick rugby match.

The arrangements for the annual excursion linked with the Jedburgh holiday encountered some difficulties in July 1903. In previous years Jedburgh had always requested a special excursion train to a specific destination of their choice. This year the NBR had said that they could not meet this request. The Provost of Jedburgh, Mr Hilson, and the treasurer, Mr Main, travelled to the railway's head office in Edinburgh and came back with an offer from the company to run an excursion train to Edinburgh but with tickets being available for onward travel to Loch Lomond, Rothesay and other nearby places. The special train would return to Jedburgh the same night. This offer was taken to a public meeting and it was resolved that the offer be accepted, the dissatisfaction caused by the previous refusal having been 'very considerably mollified'. This matter was even considered to be newsworthy by the *Edinburgh Evening News*.

Special livestock trains continued to run along the Jedburgh branch for the Hawick markets. The livestock market held at Hawick was one of the largest in the Borders. On Wednesday 29th and Thursday 30th August, 1906 some 27,000 lambs were presented there at the two-day auction sale. Several special livestock trains were arranged including one from Jedburgh scheduled to leave at 8.00 am. A second train from Berwick was to pick up stock on the line via Greenlaw on its way to Hawick. On 17th September a livestock train left Jedburgh at the same time taking stock for a one-day mart at Hawick; on this occasion 12,000 lambs were to be auctioned. Such trains had become a regular occurrence, not always with the same Jedburgh departure time. On 4th August, 1909 a train left Jedburgh at 5.45 am carrying stock for the Hawick Mart; 15,000 lambs were to be offered on that day. The advertisements for the marts and the trains were placed in *The Scotsman*, indicating their more-than-local importance.

Jedburgh held its October general holiday on Monday 2nd October, 1911. At an early hour a well-filled special excursion train left from Jedburgh station for Glasgow. The railway arrangements were made with the view of giving the excursionists a full day at the Glasgow Exhibition, with the return train not arriving at Jedburgh until midnight. The participants included a large number of local farmworkers, the fares for some of them, in a generous gesture, being

ARMY RESERVE VOLUNTEERS LEAVE FOR THE FRONT,

Jedburgh station saw much military traffic in World War I. It was used as a 'reserve' railhead for the training camps at Otterburn and Redesdale in Northumberland, and was the station of departure for both reservists and volunteers from the local area. Here reservists are being 'seen off' by youths and adults. *Jedburgh Historical Society*

Otterburn Camp, until the start of the war known as 'Ad fines' camp, was an army training area located 'over the Border'. When stations in Northumberland could not cope the station at Jedburgh became the army's railhead with units passing over Carter Bar by road vehicle or, occasionally, on foot. *Author's Collection*

R.A. CAMP, OTTERBURN

2

paid by their employers. 'Jeddart in Glasgow' was the newspaper headline in the *Southern Reporter* of 5th October! The 1911 exhibition was held in the Kelvingrove Park. It was entitled the Scottish Exhibition of National History, Art & Industry. The proceeds were to fund a chair of Scottish History & Literature at the University of Glasgow.

Records of special trains, using Jedburgh in World War I, especially those for the military, did not appear in the local newspapers of the time. However, surviving photographs and other records show that enlisted men from the area left Jedburgh by special train exchanging the local fields for the fields of war.

It was the usual procedure over a period of many years, from World War I to the 1960s for many soldiers to be brought to the training camps at Otterburn and Redesdale, over the border in Northumberland, by motor transport having arrived by special troop trains at the stations of Woodburn or Knowesgate. These former NBR stations, with limited facilities, were located on the former line between Reedsmouth [*sic*] and Scots Gap stations. Long troop trains, usually double-headed, would make their way up the single-tracked Border Counties line from the junction with the Tyne Valley line near to Hexham. For example on Saturday 15th July, 1922 five troop trains ran over the line:

Stoke to Knowesgate via Carlisle (carrying part of the 61st Brigade)
Oldbury to Knowesgate via Carlisle (carrying part of the 61st Brigade)
Derby to Knowesgate via Carlisle (carrying 62nd Brigade)
Knowesgate to Barry Links via Riccarton Jn (carrying part of the 54th Medium Brigade)
Knowesgate to York via Morpeth (carrying part of the 54th Brigade)

However, on this day, because of the large amount of military traffic, the station at Jedburgh was used as an additional railhead. Three trains, numbered 75-77, conveyed the 75th Brigade, Royal Field Artillery, from Aberdeen, Dundee and Perth to Jedburgh. Similar situations like this occurred on other dates. The trains conveyed the men, their baggage and horses.

The distances by road from Woodburn and Knowesgate stations to Redesdale Camp were about 10 miles and 13 miles respectively, whilst the route from Jedburgh, involving the crossing of the road summit at Carter Bar was closer to 20 miles. Standing instructions required the empty carriage stock of troop trains arriving at Jedburgh to be returned immediately to St Boswells.

LNER days

As in NBR days, livestock trains continued to be an important revenue earning activity for the branch. On 11th September, 1925 a sale of rams was organized for Kelso; a special train was arranged for the Jedburgh branch. A sale at St Boswells three days later produced a special train from Jedburgh at 6.40 am calling at the other branch stations to pick up wagons of stock as required. A second similar train left Jedburgh at 8.00 am. On 17th September there was another sale at St Boswells mart with just one special livestock train scheduled from Jedburgh, to leave at 7.50 am making the same station calls. The empty stock for all of these trains was worked to Jedburgh from Hawick. A

L·N·E·R

ONE-DAY EXCURSION TICKETS

WILL BE ISSUED FROM

JEDBURGH

ON

Monday, 3rd October 1297

BY ANY TRAIN ALL DAY

AS UNDER:—

TO	RETURN FARES.	
	First Class.	Third Class.
	S. D.	S. D.
Aberdour	....	7 6
Burntisland	....	7 6
Carlisle	...	7 6
Dunfermline (Lower) ...	...	7 6
Edinburgh (Waverley)	11 8	6 0
Falkirk (Grahamston) ...	...	8 0
Galashiels	4 9	2 6
Glasgow (Queen Street)	...	8 6
Gullane	...	7 0
Hawick	...	3 0
Innerleithen	...	3 6
Kelso	2 1	1 3
Kirkcaldy	...	8 0
Linlithgow	...	7 6
Melrose	4 0	2 5
Musselburgh	...	6 0
Peebles	...	4 6
Pinkhill (for Zoo) ...	...	6 0
St Boswells	3 2	1 11
Selkirk	6 0	3 0
Stirling	...	8 6
Walkerburn	....	3 6

A Special train will leave Edinburgh (Waverley) at 8-0 p.m., Galashiels at 8-55 p.m., Melrose at 9-3 p.m., and St Boswells at 9-12 p.m. for Kelso, and a connecting service will be given from Roxburgh to Jedburgh.

The Tickets are valid for Return on Day of Issue only by any train except :—

3-46 p.m. Express, Carlisle to Edinburgh.
5-52 p.m. Express, Edinburgh to Carlisle.

HUGH PATON & SONS, LTD., Printers, Edinburgh.

livestock sale took place at Hawick on the 18th September and trains ran in the same 'pathways' but were reversed at St Boswells for Hawick.

On the passenger side, in 1925 the LNER advertised cheap tickets in the *Jedburgh Gazette* for the sports day at Melrose on Easter Saturday. This event would include a rugby tournament and some races for athletes. The tickets were to be charged at 2s. 5d. third class return from Jedburgh, with slightly lower prices from Jedfoot and Nisbet. The tickets would be available for an outward journey at 12.30 or 1.46 pm trains (the former being an 'extra'). The scheduled return journey from Melrose was to be at 8.45 pm. A change at Roxburgh Junction was necessary and the branch train worked from Jedburgh at 9.00 pm to provide a departure from Roxburgh for the returning excursionists at 9.23 pm.

The Jedburgh branch was still the destination for excursionists from the more industrial regions to the north and for local sporting events but more usually it was excursions emanating from the branch that took place. However, after the Grouping of the railways the LNER advertised special day and half-day tickets for visits to Kelso, Jedburgh and other local towns. In June 1925, for example, a special train ran from Kelso to Jedburgh, leaving at 1.00 pm and picking up at Roxburgh, Kirkbank, Nisbet and Jedfoot, in connection with the annual Border Games at Jedburgh; it arrived at its destination at 1.34 pm. Another example was on 21st May, 1927 when special half-day tickets were available from Falkirk to Jedburgh at a cost of five shillings. The outward journey was to commence at 11.30 am with return from Jedburgh on the train leaving at 7.10 pm.

Monday 3rd October was an occasion when 'one-day excursion tickets' were issued from a variety of stations, including Carlisle, Edinburgh (Waverley), Glasgow (Queen Street), Falkirk (Grahamston), Kirkaldy, Stirling and Gullane to Jedburgh. A special train left Waverley at 8.00 am, though the advertising poster, printed by Patons of Edinburgh, showed 'pm' in error. In addition the year appeared as 1297, not 1927. The train ran through to Kelso with a connecting service from there to Jedburgh.

Advertisements for the excursions from Jedburgh, Jedfoot and sometimes the other stations on the branch were often carried in the *Jedburgh Gazette* as the LNER tried to stimulate traffic in the late 1920s and 1930s.

On 20th May, 1928 a special half-day excursion ran from Jedburgh (11.45 am), Jedfoot (11.49) and Nisbet (11.52) to Tweedmouth for the sum of 3s. from each station with seats being available for reservation in advance. The time of the return did not appear in the advertisement but may have been included on the special handbill available from the stations.

Also in 1928 the LNER advertised cheap rail facilities in connection with the trades holidays. On the 3rd, 4th and 6th August third class period excursion tickets were available from Jedburgh and Jedfoot to all stations in Scotland (to which there were through fares). On 6th, 7th and 8th one-day excursion tickets were available to numerous resorts in Scotland and on 4th only there were period excursion tickets for 8 and 15 days to the destinations of Newcastle, Tynemouth, Whitley Bay and Scarborough. On 23rd September of the same year there was a very special half-day excursion from Jedburgh, Jedfoot and Nisbet to Edinburgh, Dundee, Montrose, Stonehaven and Aberdeen with a restaurant car being attached to the train. Seats on the train, which started from Jedburgh at 11.05 am, could be reserved in advance from all of the starting stations.

The following year on 7th September there were cheap excursion tickets to Edinburgh Waverley from Jedburgh (6s.), Jedfoot and Nisbet (5s. 6d.) in connection with the Scottish Command Torchlight Tattoo. There was a special late night train put on to return participants leaving Waverley at midnight. The same advertisement referred to a special Sunday train from the same stations to Edinburgh (4s.), Dunfermline, Alloa and Stirling (5s.).

In June 1930 Sunday excursions were run to Kelso and Tweedmouth (on three occasions) and on the remaining Sunday two special trains, leaving Jedburgh ran to Edinburgh, Dunfermline, Alloa and Stirling, or Newcastle, Tynemouth and Whitley Bay, leaving Jedburgh at 10.00 and 11.00 am respectively. Tickets were also available from Nisbet for both of these trains. Similar excursions were run to the same destinations on a Sunday in July.

Local rugby tournaments were also associated with special excursion ticket prices. For example 7-a-side competitions were often held at the start or end of the normal 15-a-side season. On Saturday 12th September, 1931 cheap excursion tickets were issued at Jedburgh for travel to watch the 'Sevens' at Kelso, whilst much later in the decade, in 1938, the LNER issued cheap tickets for train travel from Jedburgh, Jedfoot and Nisbet to watch the 'Sevens' at Galashiels (2nd April) and Melrose (9th April).

The LNER and London, Midland & Scottish (LMS) railways jointly advertised cheap day excursions from Edinburgh for Monday 18th April, 1932. Jedburgh was included in the list of possible destinations with the return third class fare being six shillings, children 3-11 travelling at half price. Passengers travelled on ordinary service trains with appropriate changes.

July 1936 saw the usual Sunday School picnic train running from Jedburgh to Tweedmouth (for Spittal) though the contingent from Fairnington was conveyed by bus.

On Saturday 31st October, 1936 there was a rugby match between 'Jed Arts' and the team from Duns in the final of the East of Scotland Qualifying Cup. The match was played at Galashiels stadium at Netherdale. A special train was run from Jedburgh to Galashiels in connection with the match and some 50 supporters travelled from Jedburgh on the train. However, this was perhaps a sign of the changing times for six loads of supporters travelled by bus and a number of others used private cars. Apparently the crowd was about 1,200 with a bigger following from Jedburgh than from Duns.

A mammoth exodus of children from Roxburghshire was forecast when a special train, organized by Mr Bennet of Jedburgh, was planned to leave for London on 1st July, 1937 (reported in the *Southern Reporter*). The children would have a full day in London on 2nd July with the special train returning them to Roxburghshire on 3rd July. The children were be from 13 years of age upwards and parents would be asked to provide 22s. 6d. which would cover all of the trip's costs. Some 350 children from Roxburghshire alone had signed up for the trip and it was forecast that another 400 from Selkirkshire would take part. One teacher would travel for every 10 pupils and it was recommended that two qualified nurses should accompany the party.

On 1st May, 1938 the LNER advertised a special train, with buffet car, leaving Jedburgh at 11.05 am taking its passengers to Edinburgh (fare 4s. 2d.), Falkirk or Glasgow (5s. 6d.). The train did not stop at the other stations on the branch. Full details of the train's timings were available from Jedburgh station.

In 1938 the Empire Exhibition was held in Glasgow. Exhibition pavilions were erected on site including the Palace of Engineering & Industry and the prominent Tait Tower (or 'Tower of the Empire'). An international football competition was held in conjunction with the exhibition. Despite 1938 having one of the wettest summers on record some 12 million visitors were recorded. Amongst these were visitors from Jedburgh, Jedfoot and Nisbet who availed themselves of the day excursion tickets to either Ibrox or Bellahouston Park stations. These tickets were on sale for travel on any train on Saturdays and early closing days between 3rd May and 29th October. The return fare from all stations was 10s. 6d.

Another source of excursion traffic from Jedburgh was the annual trip and picnic outing organized by the United Sunday Schools of the town, of which there were six members. Each year a 'general superintendent' was elected to be in charge of the organization of the trip. The destination was invariably Spittal on the coast south of Tweedmouth. The first trip ran in 1925.

The organization of the 1926 trip was reported in the *Berwickshire News and General Advertiser* of 25th May. Kenneth McKenzie of the Boston-Blackfriars School had been elected as general superintendent. The departure times were agreed and 10 children were to be allocated to each compartment of the train. The charge was to be 5s. for reach adult and 2s. for each child inclusive of the cost of tea. Children who did not attend Sunday school would be provided with tea free of charge but would have to pay their own train fare. The Jedforest Instrumental Band was to accompany the trip with their expenses paid. Messrs William Burn had agreed to transport the tea urns and provisions to the picnic grounds and the delivery van of Mr McIntosh, the grocer, was also available if needed! Insurance against accident had been arranged and two halls engaged, in case of inclement weather. The following year the trip involved close on 1,000 travelling by train. A 'goodly number' travelled by charabanc in addition. The newspaper referred to the trip as the 'Bairns' Festival'. The 1927 trip was not as successful as the two previous years as a downpour occurred whilst the party was at Spittal and most of the afternoon was spent 'under cover'.

In 1935 the chosen day for the outing was 22nd June when some 500 children, plus some 'big folks', assembled at the station for a day out at Spittal, still a popular destination at the time. The weather was glorious and the youngsters had a wonderful time bathing and having donkey rides on the beach. Lemonade and pies, plus a sandwich tea, were provided for their refreshment. In case of inclement weather three halls were once again engaged at Spittal. Once again the haulier William Burn, of Jedburgh, provided free transport for the provisions for the event. The special train in 1935 returned from Tweedmouth station and reached Jedburgh via Kelso and Roxburgh at eight o'clock in the evening. The *Southern Reporter* recorded that most of the shops in Jedburgh were closed for the day. 'Every possible effort was made to ensure

One of the lorries in William Burn & Son's fleet. The presence of so many children next to the vehicle may indicate that this photograph was taken on the occasion of a Jedburgh Sunday School outing when Burns transported the refreshments for the children from Jedburgh to Spittal.   *Jedburgh Historical Society*

For many years Spittal, with its promenade, sandy beach and facilities to cope with a large influx of visitors, mainly children, was the chosen destination for the Jedburgh Sunday Schools' outing. Children were walked, 'in crocodile', from and to Tweedmouth station, the destination of the special train from Jedburgh.   *Author's Collection*

success and an enjoyable outing.' Jedburgh (or 'Jethart') was said to look like a ghost town on the day of the outing as hardly anyone was seen there.

These Sunday school special trains started in LNER days but continued after nationalization. It has been possible to obtain a copy of an article, written by Jimmy Cook, the former secretary of the Jedburgh Callants Club, in the 2009 *Jed Festival Magazine*. An edited version of the article is reproduced here:

The United Sunday Schools Spittal Trip

It was the biggest day in Jethart – oot o' Jethart!!
You couldn't get up early enough to get your new sandals and blazer on and then head down to the parish church hall to meet up with your pals and form up in ranks of whatever Sunday School you belonged to.

The Jedforest Silver Band headed the procession with the Sunday school flags in front of the children.

En route to the railway station the excitement mounted with the anticipation of getting on the train. Once there, ranks were maintained and entraining was well organised and supervised.

So many carriages were for the pupils and the rest for the families who had walked either alongside the procession or behind it! Shopkeepers and business people who didn't relish walking to the station could book a seat on 'Matha' Moore's bus and arrive at Spittal about the same time as the train.

In those days, between the two wars, there were no corridor carriages or toilets but surprisingly everyone seemed to manage alright – I think! With so many allocated to each compartment there were locked doors at each side. By the time we arrived at Spittal station there were various accounts of smuts in the eye from sticking you head out of the window - in spite of being told not to, and the odd sick case mostly through excitement.

Off the train ranks were formed up again and, with the band playing, we marched down to the parish hall in Spittal. Once settled, everyone got a pie and a small bottle of lemonade to keep them going until joining their family for a picnic later on, either on the beach or promenade.

(Jimmy then relates the various activities during the day performed by the children and the adults.) He continues:

Arriving home in the evening, tired but mostly happy, a day away from Jethart was certainly not a day wasted. During the war the Sunday School picnic had to be held locally, sometimes at Hartrigge or Riverside Park. After the war the trip to Spittal was revived but the train was never used again [sic]. It was buses and coaches, so it was never quite the same as the earlier days of the train.

Of course by the time our own families were the Sunday School pupils, the coach run to Spittal was still just as exciting because most of the post-war kids had never experienced a train journey or the procession to the railway station.

By train, or finally by bus, these outings took place for about 50 years, providing a memorable day out for thousands of children.

A publication by Berwick-upon-Tweed Borough Council dated 2004, entitled 'Spittal Point Development Brief', referred to Spittal as being 'the spa resort of the region'. It mentioned that the church and Sunday School outings, not only from Jedburgh, but also Hawick, Kelso, Selkirk and Galashiels, as being 'very much in evidence'. It even stated that the closure of the Kelso branch railway had prompted the decline of Spittal village as a holiday resort.

Local needs and conditions seem to receive little consideration nowadays either in the train or the bus worlds, and one feels that cold and dispassionate rows of figures on a form mean far more to our transport rulers than mere human considerations or the satisfactory serving of the public.

Despite a protest to British Railways by the town council, the decision was made that the outing should go ahead with the use of buses throughout, thus setting a precedent for some future years. It appears that BR declined to offer a 'picnic train' in 1953 and that the 'bussing' of the adults and children continued. In many ways the advertisement for the 'Picnic to Spittal' in the *Gazette* for June 1954 was another sad one. At 9.00 am the children were to assemble in the Grammar School playground at which buses would be loaded for the trip to Spittal. Five adults and 45 children were allocated to each bus, with five Sunday Schools taking part. The outward journey was scheduled for 9.30 am and the return departure at 6.30 pm. Adults other than the superintendents and teachers were required to make their own way to Spittal.

In the late 1950s and early 1960s, even before the publication of the infamous 'Beeching Report' proposing closure of the Border lines, groups of enthusiasts realized that the era of branch lines and steam locomotives, especially some of the older pre-Grouping ones, was coming to an end. Before it was too late, rail tours of the surviving lines were organized, usually with special motive power. Jedburgh was visited on three occasions, despite the apparent ban on passenger trains associated with the Sunday Schools' outing.

The first rail tour involving the Jedburgh branch took place on 4th April, 1959. It ran under the name of the 'Scott Country Railtour' and was arranged by the Branch Line Society. It consisted of three carriages (with a brake coach at each end) hauled by 'D34' class 4-4-0 No. 62471 *Glen Falloch*, provided by the locomotive depot at St Margaret's in Edinburgh. This locomotive was a veteran and had less than 12 months' further service before being withdrawn at the end of March 1960. Starting at Galashiels the train initially visited the Selkirk branch. After returning to Galashiels and then travelling on to St Boswells it took the route to Greenlaw before a further reversal, passing once again through St Boswells and Roxburgh Junction to traverse the line to Jedburgh. After running round its train at Jedburgh *Glen Falloch* worked tender-first via Roxburgh Junction and St Boswells with the train terminating at Galashiels. On the Jedburgh branch the well-patronized train was photographed carrying class 'B' (stopping train) headlamps whereas many such tours were accorded class 'A' status!

A second rail tour visited the Jedburgh branch just over two years later. This train was organized by the West Riding branch of the Railway Correspondence & Travel Society and was entitled the 'Borders Rail Tour'. The date was 9th July, 1961. The train originated at Leeds City station and arrived in the Borders via Carlisle and Hawick with locomotives being changed at both of these stations. The train left Hawick just before half past one in the afternoon. The locomotives provided for this leg of the journey were class 'D34' No. 256 *Glen Douglas* (formerly numbered 62469 before its restoration into NBR livery), and class 'J35' 0-6-0 No. 64624. *Glen Douglas* was, at that time, based at Dawsholm shed (64D) whilst 64624 was a St Margaret's engine (64A).

The entire 'Scott Country Railtour', 'D34' class 4-4-0 No. 62471 *Glen Falloch* and three Mark I carriages including a guard's compartment at each end of the train, is seen in this side-on view taken on the Jedburgh branch on 4th April, 1959. It ran with class 'B' (stopping train) headlamps. On the return journey to Roxburgh Junction the engine would work tender-first.   *S.C. Crook*

The Branch Line Society's rail tour, with its three Mark I coaches and No. 62471 *Glen Falloch* at the head, has arrived in the branch platform at Roxburgh Junction after running from St Boswells and passing Maxton and Rutherford. With the tour participants back on the train it will head up the branch towards Jedburgh. Note the North British Railway lattice signal post with finial and the passengers mainly in suits or sports jackets.   *M. Halbert Collection*

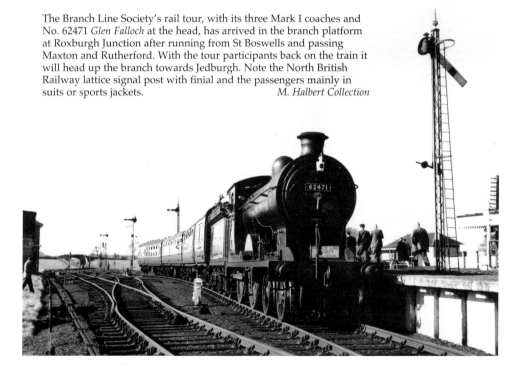

The Branch Line Society's special train hauled by No. 62471 *Glen Falloch*, an engine specially provided by St Margaret's depot in Edinburgh, passes Kirkbank station whose sidings are completely devoid of wagons. Several visiting photographers have used the embankment as a vantage point from which to take their photographs. *Bruce McCartney Collection*

A pause was made by the 'Scott Country Railtour' at Nisbet station where many participants availed themselves of the opportunity of taking photographs of their train. *Jim Sedgwick*

Some of the local inhabitants stand in the goods yard at Nisbet station to watch *Glen Falloch* start to haul its three-coach load on towards Jedfoot and Jedburgh. The line would see only two more passenger trains after this one.   *Jim Sedgwick*

On 9th, July 1961 the two locomotives head 'The Borders Railtour' along the branch towards Jedburgh. The pilot engine is *Glen Douglas*, in its 'restored' state as No. 256, whilst the train engine is 'J37' class No. 64624 of St Margaret's depot, both of which have been cleaned for the occasion.   *Armstrong Railway Photographic Trust/F.W. 'Bill' Hampson*

The special train was too long to allow all of the carriages to be accommodated in the Jedburgh platform and yet allow the two locomotives to run round the train for the return journey. The pilot, No. 256, was detached at the station approach allowing the 'J37' to pull the train into the station on its own. Here the staff is surrendered to the signalman.

Armstrong Railway Photographic Trust

Here, *Glen Douglas*, still carrying the class 'A' headlamps and the '1X43' reporting number, awaits the arrival of No. 62424 from the run-round loop so that they can be reattached (with the 'J37' leading) for the tender-first return journey back to Roxburgh Junction where a further run-round will provide extra work for the fireman. *Armstrong Railway Photographic Trust*

Despite having had only 10 minutes scheduled for the Jedburgh stop there was sufficient time for the participants to dismount from the train to take souvenir photographs and to chat with the locomotive crews. Note the Gresley brake coach at the end of the consist.
Armstrong Railway Photographic Trust

'B1' class 4-6-0 No. 61324 was a St Margaret's-based locomotive when it was used to haul the 'Scottish Rambler No. 2' Railtour though it spent part of its life at Darlington. Unlike the previous two tours, the train arrived at Roxburgh Junction from the east. Here, the locomotive and five carriages, with a buffet in the middle and brake coach at each end, run slowly over the Teviot viaduct to enter Roxburgh Junction station.   *Armstrong Railway Photographic Trust*

The special train, consisting of 10 carriages, made its way from Hawick, via St Boswells, to Greenlaw where it reversed. After travelling through St Boswells for a second time the train turned off the Waverley Route at Kelso Junction making its way via Roxburgh Junction (scheduled passing time 3.25 pm) before arriving at Jedburgh, with *Glen Douglas* leading, at 3.48 pm. It carried class 'A' headlamps and a board showing the train reporting number of 1X43. Just 12 minutes were allowed for the locomotives to separately run-round their train at Jedburgh before the cavalcade returned to Roxburgh Junction, tender-first with No. 64624 at the head, for a planned arrival time of 4.25 pm. Another 10 minutes were allowed for the locomotives to run-round their train once more before the train headed eastwards towards Kelso, Coldstream and Tweedmouth. Here Peppercorn 'A1' class 4-6-2 No. 60143 *Sir Walter Scott* took over the train for the run southwards over the East Coast main line. With its 10 carriages, mainly of Mark I stock, this must have been one of the longest trains ever to have traversed the Jedburgh branch!

The third and final rail tour, entitled the 'Scottish Rambler No. 2', traversed the Jedburgh branch on 14th April, 1963. On this occasion the event was jointly organized by the Branch Line Society and the Stephenson Locomotive Society. It was a tour over the four days of the Easter weekend and it was on the third day that the tour visited Jedburgh. On this day the train, consisting of five Mark I carriages including a refreshment coach, had started in Edinburgh's Waverley station being hauled along many of the Border lines by 'B1' class 4-6-0 No. 61324 allocated to St Margaret's depot in Edinburgh. The train approached Roxburgh from the direction of Coldstream and Kelso, having already visited the lines to Duns and Wooler (using Tweedmouth's class '2MT' 2-6-0 No. 46474 on the Wooler section). On arrival at Roxburgh the locomotive ran round its train for a tender-first trip to Jedburgh before running round the train and heading

'B1' class 4-6-0 No. 61324, used on the railtour on 14th April, 1963, had obviously received some attention from the locomotive cleaners and was looking quite photogenic even when running tender-first. Here the train is near to Jedfoot station. *Bruce McCartney Collection*

On 14th April, 1963 'B1' class 4-6-0 No. 61324 has used the run-round loop at Jedburgh and is now on the opposite end of its five-coach train and is facing northwards for its run back to Roxburgh Junction and on to St Boswells. None of the 'locals', apart from the photographer, seem to be present to witness the departure of Jedburgh's last passenger train.
Armstrong Railway Photographic Trust

chimney first back to Roxburgh. It carried class 'A' headlamps. After passing Roxburgh Junction it headed westwards towards St Boswells before making a return trip to Greenlaw. On its return to St Boswells the train continued towards Hawick where the 'B1' handed over to Grelsey 'A3' class 4-6-2 No. 60041 *Salmon Trout* for the journey on to Carlisle Citadel station via Riccarton Junction.

It is quite possible that more photographs were taken on the Jedburgh line during the visits by these three special trains than in all the other years of the line's existence added together!

These were the last occasions when paying passengers were to be conveyed over the line to Jedburgh though it is known that some 'unofficial' journeys were made later in the guard's van of the branch goods … not quite excursion trains but 'special' to the participants nevertheless!

On its return journey to Roxburgh Junction the 'B1', now running right-way-round with class 'A' headlamps, passes the deserted station at Nisbet. Note the rodding from the ground frame in the small wooden covering on the station platform. *Jedburgh Historical Society*

Chapter Eleven

Branch diary: Inauguration to Grouping

The Jedburgh Railway days

Whilst details of the history, infrastructure and trains, provide a good insight into the nature of a railway line, much of its character derives from its day-to-day happenings and its relations with its communities. Details of the various trivia and minutiae derived from personal memories, from newspaper reports and from contemporary advertisements contribute greatly to the overall picture. In the next three chapters such sources will be used to recreate some of the Jedburgh line's character, though more serious railway accidents and incidents have been grouped together in a later chapter.

The *Caledonian Mercury's* December 1856 report of the meeting to discuss the proposed link between the Jedburgh branch and the Border Counties Railway has already been discussed and won't be repeated here.

The *Kelso Chronicle* of 12th February, 1857 contained an advertisement for the let of a local mansion house called 'Lintalee', located to the south of Jedburgh close to the turnpike road. As well as advertising the desirability of the house with its six bedrooms and its extensive garden there was a specific mention of the proximity of the new railway line with its 'communication north and south three times a day' even though it was a couple of miles from the railway, on the other side of town!

No doubt the operators of the horse-drawn carriages taking passengers from the Jedburgh town centre to the station were delighted at the conversion of the High Street, and the road leading to the station, from a 'rough causeway over which carts and carriages rattled', into a 'thorough good' macadamized road. This conversion, reported in the *Kelso Chronicle* of 9th October, 1857, was described as being 'almost complete'.

On Friday 30th September, 1859 the *Kelso Chronicle* published the half-year accounts for the Jedburgh Railway which showed that in the period up to 31st July the line had carried 21,193 passengers producing a revenue of £758 7s. 7d. Goods receipts in the same period were £897. Both passenger and goods receipts had exceeded those of the previous year. After the deduction of working expenses, interest and taxes, plus salaries and miscellaneous other items the balance (exclusive of unpaid dividends) was almost £410. The Directors of the company proposed a dividend of 2½ per cent to shareholders. Although this was not quite as high as in previous years the Directors still felt that the line would ultimately prove to be a sound and lucrative investment. George Rutherford commented on the nuisance caused by the burning of coal rather than coke on the line. It was suggested that the Directors might communicate regarding this matter with the NBR.

On 7th November of that year the Directors met in an extraordinary meeting at the Spread Eagle Hotel. The article in the following day's *Caledonian Mercury* reported on the meeting which was to consider the proposal by the Chairman of the NBR for the amalgamation of the Jedburgh Railway with the North British company. The NBR was willing to guarantee a dividend of 3½ per cent for three years, and 4 per cent in perpetuity for Jedburgh shareholders. In response the Jedburgh Railway Directors had proposed that 4½ per cent should be guaranteed for five years and 5 per cent in perpetuity. A long conversation took place with some Directors feeling that the offers by the North British Railway were very fair but others were not content. George Rutherford, the Sheriff-Clerk moved that the offer of the NBR not be agreed to. Mr Riddell moved an amendment to decline to the principle of amalgamation on the North British terms but that the Directors should endeavour to make the best bargain they could with the company. A further two hours' discussion ensued but in the end the amendment was carried by 38 votes to 24. The shareholders were called and the amendment was carried by a vote of 117 to 72.

Another meeting of the Jedburgh Railway Co. took place at the Spread Eagle Hotel on 5th December, 1859, again reported in the *Caledonian Mercury*. The company Chairman, Mr Ord, presided. The heads of the proposed agreement between the NBR and the Jedburgh Railway were discussed. These were complex and included the taking over of the Jedburgh company's liabilities and obligations, the dividends to be paid (as originally proposed by the NBR), rates for carriage of minerals, and the prohibition of new works during the amalgamation period. Mr Ord said that he now, on careful consideration, advised shareholders to accept the offer made by the NBR and moved that the agreement be approved of. The motion was seconded. A protracted discussion followed in which Mr Rutherford said that the securities offered were insufficient. Finally the heads of agreement were agreed to with only Mr Rutherford dissenting.

On 10th November, 1860 the Directors met once again for the half-yearly meeting when the presented accounts showed that the line's revenue had increased over the previous half-year to £1,738 19s. 11d., being £83 13s. 4d. more than the corresponding period of the previous year. The meeting was told that the Bill for the amalgamation of the North British and Jedburgh railways had received the Royal Assent on 31st July of that year. As the duties of the Jedburgh company Directors were coming to an end they thanked the shareholders for their support. They were pleased to hand over to the NBR under such favourable circumstances. The *Southern Reporter* contained details of the meeting. The matters and affairs of the Jedburgh Railway Company thus passed into the history books!

North British Railway days

The winter of 1860-61 was quite a harsh one and there was a heavy snowfall in early January 1861. The *Kelso Chronicle* of 18th January reported that the ice, which had coated all of the local rivers, including the Teviot, had broken up and that the rivers were swollen. Although some large blocks of ice had been deposited in the haughs forming the Teviot's flood plain, there was no damage to the timber bridge which carried the railway over the river near to Nisbet station. Other bridges, further downstream had not been so lucky!

On 15th March, 1861 the station master at Jedfoot, George Borthwick, married Mary Slater, the daughter of a local farm steward. Mary was some 10 years older than George, who had become station master at the young age of 20.

Since October 1856 there had been 'rumblings' about whether the Jedburgh Railway should carry passengers and mails on a Sunday. Mr Ord, the Jedburgh Railway Chairman had expressed the view that if Sunday trains were put on and they did not pay then they would be taken off again (*Southern Reporter:* March 1862). Shareholders had wanted such trains but there was opposition to trains on the Sabbath. The general population of Jedburgh were inclined to use Sunday trains whilst those outside the town, living in more rural parts, were in opposition. Eventually the introduction of Sunday trains was sanctioned and two services were introduced; from Jedburgh there were trains at 7.15 am and 5.30 pm with return workings from Kelso at 9.50 am and 7.00 pm though the local newspapers were silent on the question of how many people used these trains and for what purpose, bearing in mind their timings.

There was a remarkable, if not unique, happening at Jedburgh station on 26th April, 1864 when a railway engine was impounded by a Sheriff Officer! It appears that the NBR had resisted a claim for payment of the full amount for the 'Poor Rates' as intimated to them by the collector, on the grounds that the railway station was situated outside the Burgh of Jedburgh. The local authority contended, with some success, that Poor Rates were payable in respect of each parish and the station was within the parochial boundary. The parish council took the matter to the Sheriff Court and obtained a decree against the railway company. So it happened, according to a much later edition of the *Jedburgh Gazette*, that a Sheriff Officer, armed with the requisite warrant, proceeded to the station and on the arrival of a train he 'poinded' (old word in Scots Law: 'take the property of' or 'impound') the engine, much, so it was said, to the dismay of the railway officials. However, this drastic action had the required effect and the rates were paid up shortly afterwards. The station master (or agent) at the time was, of course, William Hartley.

Yet another meeting to plan a new railway was held at Yetholm on 22nd October, 1864. The meeting considered the possibility of constructing a line (to be known as the Bowmont & Cale Railway) from either Ormiston (the first choice) or Nisbet station on the Jedburgh branch to Milfield on the Central Northumberland line (as yet incomplete). The line would diverge from the Jedburgh line at Ormiston, cross the Teviot, and then pass via Eckford, Wester and Easter Blinkbonny and Marlfield, to Morebattle, thence via the south side of Yetholm Loch to Town Yetholm and down the Vale of Bowmont, Shotton and Pawston to Langholm Bridge, thence via Howtel and Mindrum to Milfield. The line would measure 18 miles 1 furlong and the projected cost was £99,000 with a siding constructed to serve every farm on the route. The meeting was told that another line had been proposed and surveyed. This would leave the present projected line at Morebattle, following the Cessford Burn, continuing past Craigshiel and Wooden Burn to meet the existing line at Ormiston or Nisbet. However, the steep gradient at Wooden Burn would make the line impracticable. This line had been planned to satisfy the tenants of the Duke of Buccleugh and the Marquis of Lothian. Of course, neither line came to fruition.

The consequences of further bad weather formed the substance of a report in the *Glasgow Herald* of 1st June, 1865. Their Jedburgh correspondent detailed the state of the waters of the River Teviot. The river had broken its banks and the haughs near Crailing were under several feet of water. At the railway bridge near Nisbet the water was near to the top of the structure though fortunately it stayed firm.

The *Railway News* was the source of information for the *Kelso Chronicle* which reported, on 6th October, 1865, under the headline 'A New South of Scotland Line', that a new railway was planned to link the south-west and south-east of Scotland. The line would start at Lockerbie and proceed to cross the watershed of the Borthwick stream to join the valley of the Teviot, forming a junction with the NBR at Hawick. From thence it would continue its course along the south bank of the Teviot, then crossing over to form a junction with the Jedburgh branch near to Nisbet. It would finally terminate at a junction with the North Eastern Railway at Kelso. The proposed line, to be about 60 miles in length, would enable the Caledonian Railway to 'obtain full command of all transit from the south-east to the south-west of Scotland'. At that time the policies of the NBR had made an enemy of the NER and the Caledonian felt it would be warmly welcomed in the area. This line was also destined not to become a reality.

Two men, Messrs Mahon and McLevy, found themselves in court in December 1872, according to the *Jedburgh Gazette* of 21st December, charged with the poaching of rabbits. They had been seen by a local constable walking along the road near Bonjedward with a sack containing a ferret. They were somewhat dirty and dishevelled. Earlier George Borthwick, the station agent at Jedfoot, had accepted a parcel from the same two men but they had not paid for it. It was consigned to a Mr Pirie, a game dealer at Jedburgh. Borthwick said that the men were dirty and looked as though they had been out all night. They had a dog with them and the shank of an adze. They made off in the direction of Jedburgh. Walter Yale, who delivered parcels from Jedburgh station on behalf of the NBR, said that he had delivered the parcel to Mrs Pirie: 'Here's a bag from Jedfoot containing rabbits'. She paid the 4*d.* carriage charge to Yale. The Bench found the charge of poaching proven and both Mahon and McLevy were ordered to pay £1 10*s.* including court costs. As an alternative they were offered 14 days in jail. The superintendent cast some doubt on the honesty of Pirie in the matter.

A letter to *The Scotsman* published on 31st December. 1874 referred to a journey which someone, who signed himself 'Passenger' (from Jedburgh) had made in the Borders. The letter-writer said that on the evening of 28th December he had been a passenger between Kelso and Jedburgh. His train arrived at Roxburgh Junction where it was necessary to wait for the arrival of the train from Edinburgh. It was somewhat late but eventually it arrived and departed onwards to Kelso. He and his fellow passengers expected their own train to start … but no! They learned that their own train must wait for a truck of sheep, or cattle of some sort, which was coming from St Boswells by goods train. 'For nearly an hour we had to parade the platform in the snow, and anyone acquainted with the station will know how much this is the reverse of pleasant.' The porters allowed the Jedburgh passengers to share their fire and did their best to make them comfortable. The ultimate arrival of the passengers at Jedburgh was 11 o'clock, the scheduled arrival being 9.50 pm. The letter-writer commented that some delays are inevitable but being delayed by the convenience of goods and cattle was another question.

The Glasgow Herald and The Scotsman newspapers of Monday 4th January, 1875 reported on another case of bad weather affecting the Jedburgh and Teviotdale area. Very heavy snowfalls, lasting for three days, plus drifting, caused the complete blockage of the line between Kirkbank and Nisbet. On Friday 1st January the 3.30 pm train to Jedburgh from Roxburgh had come to a stand at Nisbet and was only extricated two days later on the Sunday morning. Later a Jedburgh to Nisbet shuttle service was introduced. Similar problems were experienced on the St Boswell's to Kelso to Berwick line; the evening Berwick train became stuck in the snow some 500 yards below Kelso station, only being released after four hours work. The level of water in the Teviot was expected to rise as the thaw set in.

Perhaps as a result of this repeated inclement weather which had caused flooding in various years in the 1860s and 1870s the NBR made an announcement that they intended to replace the timber bridge over the Teviot, between Jedfoot and Nisbet, with an iron bridge which would better resist the spells of high water and rapid currents in the river following snow thaw and heavy rainfall. The Southern Reporter of 15th April, 1875 contained a reference to this intention.

Comments were reported in the Southern Reporter of 21st November, 1878 concerning various grievances connected with both the passenger and goods services on the Jedburgh branch. Complaints were made about the lack of proper attention to the service of trains and also to the miserable condition of the third-class carriages used at that time on the line. Mr Walker, Manager of the NBR promised to look into the matters with his earnest attention!

One pleasant report involved the daughter of the Jedburgh station master, Mr William Hartley. On the 5th December, 1880 Kate (Catherine) Hartley, William's third daughter, was married to John Esdon, a marine engineer of Stirling in Scotland. The marriage took place at St John's Episcopal Church in the town.

A railway proposed in 1881 could have had some consequences for the Jedburgh and Kelso lines. Back In 1846 Parliament had passed an Act stating that all future railways in the United Kingdom should be of standard gauge; Irish Railways could be built using the 5 ft 3 in. gauge. However, some exceptions had been allowed and narrow gauge lines were created in several places. The engineers George A. & Cornelius Lundie were based in London but had connections in South Wales (to the Rhymney Railway) and in Northumberland. They had offices in Cardiff and Westminster, London. They had noticed the concern for public railways in central Northumberland and the Scottish Borders expressed both in print and at public meetings. The Lundies published a Prospectus, on 1st July, 1881, for a narrow gauge railway. The line of railway proposed was from the NBR at Rothbury in Northumberland (opened in 1862) via Thropton, Lorbottle, Whittingham, Glanton, Wooperton, Lilburn, Middleton, Wooler, Akeld, Kirknewton, Kilham, Pawston, Yetholm, Primside, Morebattle and Kalemouth to join the NBR's line at Heiton at the south end of the Roxburgh viaduct. A length of mixed gauge track would take the line into Roxburgh station. The distance of the line from Rothbury to Heiton was 47 miles. Being of narrow gauge it was considered that by using curves and steep, but short, gradients it would be able to serve more villages but at the price of lower speeds, lighter loads and trans-shipment problems at the ends of the line. The line would permit through communication from Newcastle to Kelso, and, notwithstanding the break of gauge, and traffic 'to and from all parts of the NBR Company's Galashiels, Jedburgh and Kelso lines south of Edinburgh'. Nothing more was heard of this scheme, although it will be noted that the proposed length of that line between Whittingham, Wooler and Kirknewton was used when the NER constructed its line from Alnwick to Cornhill-on-Tweed several years later. Neil Mackichan in his book entitled *The Northumberland Central Railway* mentioned that well-known author Cecil J. Allen had stated that the NBR had intentions to extend the Northumberland Central Railway to Jedburgh, though, apparently, no evidence was cited for this.

Apart from reports of accidents (dealt with elsewhere) there were no further newspaper reports relating to the Jedburgh branch until 1885 when the *Dundee Advertiser* of 7th July reported 'A case affecting cattle dealers and railway companies'. The case was described as being of considerable importance as regards the conveyance of cattle by rail. William Davidson, of Woodhead, Jedburgh, raised an action in the Roxburghshire Sheriff Court against the NBR for the sum of £66 for loss alleged to have been sustained by him by delay in transmission of 16 Irish store cattle and six shorthorns in November 1884. Davidson had purchased the cattle at Hallow Fair in Edinburgh on 12th November. He had them trucked on time at Haymarket station in the forenoon, in time, he expected, for them to reach Jedburgh by the last train the same evening. They did not, however, reach their destination that night, but arrived with the first train the next morning in a fatigued and low condition. They did not wholly recover from that condition for a whole month. For the defendants, the NBR stated that all cattle were sent at the owner's risk and under special contract. At the large markets the traffic was naturally greatly increased but the company did all it could to deal with the special work. It was further stated that the Jedburgh branch was only a single line, worked on the staff system. The normal last train, carrying the staff, had left Roxburgh Junction before the cattle arrived there. Thus the cattle had to remain at Roxburgh until the next morning. Sheriff Russell of Jedburgh gave his judgement and found in favour of the cattle dealer. He found the NBR liable and they had to pay Davidson £44 plus the court costs.

An incident of fare evasion was reported in the *Southern Reporter* of 6th December, 1885. A labourer pleaded guilty to travelling on the NBR between Kelso and Jedburgh without a ticket on 2nd October of that year. He appeared before Sheriff Russell in court at Jedburgh on 26th November where he was fined 2s. 6d. with 27s. 6d. expenses added. He was given the alternative of six days in prison but was granted a month in which to pay the fine.

Sent from Jedburgh station to Mr Harvey, the agent at Belses station, on 3rd August, 1885, was a 'North British memorandum' which read (using the original spelling, capitalization and punctuation):

Dear Sir,
Lady Lothian has sent word to ask you to send on some Boxed Luggage left by her at your Station on Saturday night to Nisbet. She also left in the carriage (She thinks) a Bundle of Ruggs with cricket bats inside.
If received by you send here by return advertising when done.

Signed J. Dingwall

Another item reads:

Dear Sir,
Please have a waggon [*sic*] for me tomorrow morning (Saturday) to put on a ton of potatoes for Mrs Scott.
Yours truly,
A. Lyle

A third, this time a telegraph message, reads:

From: Mr. Tait, Nisbet Station
To: Mr. Harvey, Belses Station
If you have any Parcels at your Station for Lord Lothian, Monteviot, send on to Jedfoot first train.
Signed: Tait

(John Tait was the station master at Nisbet station at that time, having formerly worked at Stow station as a railway porter. He lived in the Nisbet station house with his wife and family. Subsequent census records show that he had at least two further wives who lived with him at the station house.)

Fortunately similar delightful items of documents, letters and other ephemera have survived from the 1880s and are preserved in various Scottish archives, such as the Hub at Hawick, relating to parcels, bills, unpaid bills, tiles sent in error, beds, coals, timber, carriage of lambs and sheep, and even manure. One very sad surviving letter contains details of the provision of a special composite carriage by Jedburgh station for the conveyance of a lady 'who is out of her mind' from Belses station to a hospital in Edinburgh.

Returning to newspaper reports, the *Jedburgh Gazette* commented, in April 1887, on several incidents which had taken place on several of the local rail lines, including the Jedburgh branch. Offenders from Galashiels and other places on the railway had been, when convicted at the court in Jedburgh and sentenced to a fine or alternative imprisonment, fallen on an easy method of getting their fares paid. Though they had intended to pay their fines, they refused to do so until they were on their way, by train, to Edinburgh Prison. In the course of the railway journey they paid the fine to the accompanying police officer in charge, and stepped out of the train at the station of the town where they resided, having had their railway fare paid by the country. This practice was described as 'Dodging with the police authorities'.

On the 6th October, 1887 the *Southern Reporter* mentioned that one of the NBR's engineers, in connection with an extension of the Jedburgh line, had made a survey of the ground. The newspaper believed that should the scheme be carried out it would commence at the milestone below the present station and be brought up Bankheadhaugh, where the Jed would be bridged, then proceed through Old Bongate to the nursery near the Townfoot Bridge. The paper added that this revived the question of whether it was desirable to have a railway up the valley of the Jed and thence down Reed Water to Newcastle.

However, the *Southern Reporter* of 3rd November and the *Hawick Advertiser* of 5th November, 1887 both reported that the NBR Directors had decided not to extend the Jedburgh line into the town. It was considered that the cost of this extension, believed to be about £2,000, would not be justified with the limited increased profits expected if it were carried out. It was therefore expected that a new Jedburgh station would be built on the site of the present one.

The *Roxburghshire Gazette* reported 10 months later that there was considerable disquiet from local residents expressed at a meeting in the Corn Exchange, both as regards the location of the station and the facilities offered. The station was described as being no better than a cattle shed, with no general waiting room, a ladies room opening off the booking office which was unfit for purpose, and a lack of gentlemen's facilities. The train service was also criticized with the extended waiting time at Roxburgh necessitated by the timings of late afternoon trains. A resolution was passed calling on the NBR to improve the accommodation and facilities. A deputation including the Provost, various councillors and bailies was formed to liaise with the company's Directors. After the Directors received the communication of information the company Directors and the Jedburgh committee were to arrange a meeting. However, the results were not satisfactory as the NBR's proposals to remodel the station at Jedburgh were not considered acceptable.

On 5th April, 1888 the *Southern Reporter* briefly referred to a breach of the peace which took place at Jedburgh station. No further details were included. Adam Scott, a millworker, of Jedburgh, pleaded guilty as charged and he was fined 7s. 6d. by Sheriff Spiers, with the alternative of three days in jail.

On 25th November, 1890 a Hawick millworker named John Jackson, was found lodging in a first class railway carriage at Jedburgh station. He was charged and appeared in court before a Justice of the Peace being found guilty of this illegal act. He was offered a fine of 10s. or the alternative of seven days in prison. According to the report in the *Southern Reporter* he paid the fine.

A meeting was held at Jedburgh Corn Exchange on the afternoon of Tuesday 17th August, 1890 and was reported in the following day's *Edinburgh Evening News*. Provost Boyd had presided. The meeting was to protest against erecting the new railway station on the present site. A Mr Andrew Whitelock Mein, a landed proprietor and farmer, of Scraesburgh, told the meeting that the NBR proposed to remodel the present station 'on a scale of almost princely magnificence' at a cost of about £3,000 or £4,000. It would be more desirable to get the company to extend the railway into town. The additional money to fund this could be raised by shares sold in the district if the company agreed a reasonable dividend. He said that the cost could not be more than £10,000 or £12,000. The route that Mein favoured was by way of Headrigg, across the Jed at Hartriggenlodge and into the grounds at Queen Mary's House. A Mr Barrie, Mr Mein and the Chairman suggested other routes which might be submitted to the company. Councillor Oliver Hilson suggested that a telegram be sent to the NBR asking them to delay the acceptance of estimates until they had considered a communication from the present meeting. This was agreed. A certain Mr McDougall moved that the company be invited to bring the railway into Jedburgh. This was seconded by Mr Mein and agreed to unanimously. Mr Simson expressed the thought that the railway should be brought up to the Headrigg. The Chairman did not see why everything should hinge on the North British. It might be possible to approach another company that could bring a line over the Carter (Carter Bar, to the south of Jedburgh). Ex-Provost W. Hilson favoured the idea. He considered that it was a heinous proposal to build a station three-quarters of a mile from Jedburgh, and a great disgrace to the NBR. It gave a blow to any chance of Jedburgh extending its bounds. A committee was formed to wait on the decision of the NBR Directors. In the event the Directors declined to accede to the demands of the committee; the latter were empowered to approach the NER perhaps to investigate whether they would consider building a line over Carter Bar. There was to be no extension of the railway into the town resulting from these events.

Under the headline 'Jedburgh and the new railway scheme' the *Edinburgh Evening News* reported on a meeting held in Jedburgh on the evening of Tuesday 18th October, 1892. The ratepayers' meeting was well attended and was held primarily in connection with the forthcoming municipal elections. However, Bailie Young initiated a discussion regarding the proposed new railway between Manchester, Newcastle and Glasgow. If Jedburgh were to be left out of the scheme it would be a serious loss. Provost Boyd said that it had long been a dream of his to see a railway across the Scottish Border. From information he had gathered he was certain that the Jedburgh route was the best, and if a strong effort was made it would receive the best consideration. Its adoption would 'bring Jedburgh to the front'. There was plenty of money and first-rate men at the back of the movement. Bailie Laidlaw hoped that Jedburgh would be placed on the main line. Councillor Oliver Hilson said that communities such as theirs should give the promoters all the support they could. The opinions expressed by the various speakers were heartily endorsed by those present. A few years back in 1889, a Jedburgh resident had actually proposed a new line from Darlington, via Hexham, Liddesdale, Jedburgh, St Boswells and Lauder to Edinburgh!

The *Edinburgh Evening News*, on Thursday 18th May, 1893, and *The Scotsman*, published on the following day, reported that the Edinburgh Borderers' Union had visited the town of Jedburgh and Teviotdale on the 18th. The party had travelled by train to Nisbet station, from whence they drove to the Marquis of Lothian's Monteviot House (to view the gardens), Penielheugh Monument, and the village of Ancrum. At Jedburgh they dined in the Corn Exchange under the presidency of John Telfer. The afternoon was spent visiting Jedburgh Abbey, Queen Mary's House, Ferniehurst Castle and other places of interest. The newspaper recorded that the weather was sunny and pleasant. It was certainly a well-filled day.

Study of *Slater's Directory* for 1893 provides some useful information regarding trades conducted at Jedburgh at this time. Various coal agents operated from Jedburgh railway station: George Burn, William Burn, William

Cowen, Walter Spence, William Spence and Robert Stewart. Various manufacturers sent out their products by rail including James Boyd & Son (tweed and blanket manufacturers of New Bongate Mills), John Hilson and Sons (of Canongate Mills), John and William Hilson (of Bongate Mill), the Laidlaw Brothers (tweed manufacturers of Allars Mill) and Scott & Co. (hosiery manufacturers of Old Bridge End). William Farmer was a timber merchant also based at the station.

The weather was once again an important topic for the press in June 1894. The persistent heavy rain had caused the Tweed and its tributaries to develop a high flood. The large haughs near Crailing were covered in water to a depth of several feet and the tops of the hedgerows were visible as green streaks. An observer noted that the water was near to the top of the Teviot rail bridge, though no damage to the structure was reported on this occasion. A device called the 'Tweedometer' recorded a rise of five feet in the water level just below the confluence of the Teviot and Tweed, near Kelso. However, the increased volume of water had enabled some salmon to reach the upper reaches of the rivers. The *Glasgow Herald* of Saturday 16th June mentioned that on the Teviot, close to the Nisbet railway bridge, a Mr Robert Reid of Jedburgh, fishing with a minnow as bait, caught a salmon weighing 8 lb.

On Saturday 27th December, 1894 Jedfoot station wired to Edinburgh to say that there was flooding between the up home and distant signals. The permanent way was undermined and the track had become unsafe. The last train to pass safely had been the 11.40 am passenger service from Roxburgh Junction. Repairs were carried out by 4.30 pm the same day and the line was reopened on the Monday morning. However, on the 30th December a hurricane force wind with rain blew down the Teviot valley from the west as well as much of the south of Scotland. This was recorded in the *Edinburgh Evening News*. Jedburgh was still suffering from the effects of the rainfall of previous days and various roads were flooded near to the station. A little to the north of Jedfoot station, opposite the confluence of the Jed and the Teviot the line became undermined at several points over a length of about 50 yards. At one point the rails and sleepers were suspended 3 ft above a torrent of water. The cattle train from Gorgie to Jedburgh was cancelled as was the first train from Jedburgh, the 7.12 am 'mixed'. Passengers and parcels were carried to Roxburgh by a horse bus supplied by Moore's of Jedburgh. Later the bus linked Nisbet with Jedburgh and a shuttle service of trains connected Nisbet with Roxburgh. Fortunately the level of water fell rapidly and the repair gang were able to get to work and make good the damage. Their speedy efforts allowed the full train service to be resumed in the afternoon of the following day, the 1.46 pm Jedburgh to Roxburgh being the first train to travel cautiously over the repaired track. The service was short-lived as the track was once again washed out for some 30 yards on 1st January, 1895. Once again a bus service had to be introduced until track repairs were effected.

The *Jedburgh Gazette* of 21st May, 1898 contained an interesting letter to the editor which read as follows:

In Jedburgh there is one thing greatly needed – that is a tramway car, to run to meet the trains to and from the railway station, starting from the Lothian Park, a distance of one mile, fare 1*d*. each way. I hope our Town Council will put their heads together and ask the railway company to carry out this much-needed convenience.'

Of course, naught came of this proposal.

The *Southern Reporter* of 1st December, 1898 reported on several cases brought before Sheriff Baillie at the Sheriff Court in Jedburgh. One of these had involved a Jedburgh man, James Haig, of no fixed occupation. Haig was found guilty of committing a breach of the peace at Jedburgh railway station and was given the option of a fine of £1 or seven days in detention.

Yet another proposed railway scheme was discussed at the Jedburgh Town Council meeting on Monday 10th June, 1899. The scheme was entitled 'The Hawick and Jedburgh Light Railway'. Bailie Hilson said that landowners on the proposed route of the light railway had been contacted and that Captain Palmer Douglas of Cavers had replied that the line would be of incalculable value. He said that every reasonable facility would be given to allowing the line to pass through the Cavers Estate if the other landowners looked at it in a public-spirited manner. Bailie Hilson thought that the line would soon be a reality! Councillor Veitch, however, said that that Caver's reply was the only reply which was favourable to the scheme. The meeting was reported in the *Edinburgh Evening News* of 11th July.

Sheriff Court activity was once again reported in the *Southern Reporter*, this time on 7th November, 1900. The court was in session on 31st October with, once again, Sheriff Baillie presiding. One of the cases brought before him concerned two Irish labourers, John Welsh and Thomas Welsh, who had had a stand-up fight at Jedburgh railway station whilst being drunk. For this disorderly conduct they were fined 10s. each with the alternative of six days imprisonment. Their choice was not reported.

Another example of members of the public lodging in a railway carriage took place in December 1900. John Potter and Thomas Smith, both itinerant 'tramp-labourers', were charged with lodging in a railway carriage at Jedburgh station without permission. They appeared before the Justice of the Peace Court on Monday 3rd December. Both were found guilty by Provost Sword and fined 10s. (with the alternative of seven days in prison). The *Southern Reporter* reported that the Provost had said that the practice had become a great nuisance.

The name of Bailie Hilson cropped up again in the *Edinburgh Evening News* of 10th September, 1902. The report was of a meeting of the Jedburgh Town Council. Bailie Hilson referred to the recent alterations concerning the Border train service. He stated that Jedburgh had joined with Kelso to help them get a better service of mails in the morning. Kelso had got that but he had written to Mr Jackson of the post office to ask if Jedburgh could be included in the new arrangement. Jackson had replied that he regretted that the new arrangements could not include Jedburgh. Under the new arrangements passengers from London to Jedburgh had to wait at Roxburgh Junction for two hours in the morning. It seemed, to him at least, to be a rather niggardly policy. Bailie Hilson said that by helping Kelso Jedburgh had landed itself in a worse situation than they were in formerly. 'It seems that the post office is simply blocking the way'. They hadn't got an up-to-date system for getting the mails at all. Bailie Hilson replied that in justice to the

Beyer, Peacock & Co.-built 0-4-2 No. 324 was posed, with its crew and others in front of Jedburgh signal box sometime before 1903 when it was renumbered in the duplicate list as No. 1065. Sister engines Nos. 328 and 329 were also observed at Roxburgh Junction and on the Jedburgh branch. *Bill Lynn Collection*

This blue-enamelled NBR trespass sign survived at least until 1963. It is not known whether it survives in a museum or private collection or whether it was scrapped when the Jedburgh line closed. *Armstrong Railway Photographic Trust/J.M. Boyes*

NORTH BRITISH RAILWAY.

WARNING TO TRESPASSERS

Pursuant to the North British Railway Act. 1894.

The NORTH BRITISH RAILWAY COMPANY hereby give Notice to all persons not to trespass upon any of the Railways, Stations, Works, Lands, and Property belonging to or worked by the Company.

And Notice is hereby further given that any person who shall trespass upon any of the Railways of or worked by the North British Railway Company shall without having received any personal or other warning than this Notice, forfeit and pay by way of penalty any sum not exceeding Forty Shillings for every such offence.

)   **J. CONACHER,**
                                              GENERAL MANAGER

EDINBURGH, October 1894.

post office people the railway company were extortionate in their terms. The matter was referred to a committee for further consideration.

Two threatening events took place at the station during the next few years. On 25th September, 1903 a labourer, James Hill, of no fixed abode, was committed to prison for one month for a violent act when he attempted to stab, with a painter's knife, a booking clerk, Walter Yates. He was intoxicated at the time and caused a great disturbance on the station platform. The *Southern Reporter* stated that his outrageous conduct had caused a sensation at the station. However a very similar event took place less than 18 months later at the same venue. Joseph McCadden, a labourer, had been drunk when he created a similar disturbance. He went along the platform brandishing a huge knife in a threatening manner. The *Edinburgh Evening News* and the *Southern Reporter* stated that he was convicted at Jedburgh Sheriff Court on 16th February, 1905 and sent to prison for seven days.

The severe and protracted snow storms of late December 1906 cause some havoc in Teviotdale and other surrounding areas. Jedburgh received a further foot of snow on top of the foot of snow that was already lying on the ground. Twenty-eight degrees of frost (Fahrenheit) was recorded at nearby Hawick. The *Edinburgh Evening News* of 29th December referred to the telegraph as being the only means of communication between Jedburgh and the outside world. The railway line was completely blocked at Nisbet by a drift, which, according to the *Southern Reporter* of 3rd January, was 1½ miles in length with a depth of 12 feet. A complete train was embedded in a drift at Rutherford between Roxburgh and St Boswells. Workmen had been busily engaged since the previous day and it was expected to be another day before the snow blockage was cleared. However, this was to prove very optimistic as the same newspaper in its 31st December edition reported that the lines to Kelso, Jedburgh, also the branches to Lauder and Bervie were still blocked. The NBR had large squads of men clearing the lines but the blocks were very serious and traffic was still suspended on the lines mentioned. It was some days before the snow was fully cleared and a full train service could be resumed on the local lines.

This picture depicts a train in the snow at Roxburgh station in the harsh winter starting in December of 1906. At the end of his month the snow was so deep, and temperatures so low, that Jedburgh was totally isolated apart from the railway telegraph.

Jedburgh Historical Society

The track gang are about to start releasing the Jedburgh train from the grip of the huge snow drifts using nothing more than shovels and their physical strength. The snow is clearly several feet deep. *Jedburgh Historical Society*

Here a 'J31' class 0-6-0 and its train have been freed from the snow, with the track gang looking proud of their efforts! This is likely to be the same gang that appeared in the previous picture as both photographs were taken in December of 1906. *Bill Lynn Collection*

The *Southern Reporter* contained a brief note, on 9th January, 1908, to the fact that Robert Rutherford, for many years a driver on the Berwickshire goods train, had been promoted to passenger train driver on the Jedburgh to Roxburgh Junction line. He was a resident of Newtown, which village congratulated him on his promotion.

Ex-Provost Oliver Hilson had written to the NBR on 18th July, 1910 concerning the journey by the 7.05 pm train from Jedburgh to Kelso and thence to Berwick. 'Only one minute is allowed at Kelso for transfer between the two trains and this is a source of anxiety on the part of passengers travelling from Jedburgh.' He suggested that the Jedburgh train might leave five minutes earlier and the NER train for Berwick five minutes later giving a margin of 10 minutes at Kelso station. He also drew the attention of the NBR to the price of the 'so-called' tourist ticket between Jedburgh and Berwick which costs 5s. and showed no reduction on the combined return fares of the two companies. The reply he received appeared in the *Berwick Advertiser* of Friday 22nd July. On behalf of the company D. Deuchars replied that it would not be suitable to alter the 7.05 pm train from Jedburgh to Kelso. He had been in touch with the NER who told him that they could not make the onward connection, the 7.40 pm from Kelso to Berwick, any later. He added that with regard to the price of a tourist ticket between Jedburgh and Berwick, if the price of that ticket were reduced it might interfere with other tourist fares. He regretted therefore that the NBR could not see its way to making any alteration to the price. He pointed out that the advantage of the tourist ticket is that a passenger can break the journey anywhere en route, which cannot be done with ordinary tickets. Hilson's reply, also published in the *Berwick Advertiser*, expressed disappointment with Deuchars' letter and expressed the view that neither company (i.e. the NBR and NER) really desires to meet the reasonable wants of the travelling public. The exchange of communications appears not to have continued further.

Not surprisingly the National Coal Strike of 1912, which began in faraway Derbyshire, had an effect on the Borders railways. The *Jedburgh Gazette* (8th March) reported that the greatest inconvenience to the public was the curtailment of the local railway services. On the local NBR branches the discontinued trains were the 1.40 pm from Jedburgh to Kelso and St Boswells, the 2.00 pm from Kelso to St Boswells, the 3.57 pm from St Boswells to Jedburgh and Kelso, the 8.53 pm from St Boswells to Jedburgh and Kelso, and the connecting trains at 4.03 and 9.00 pm from Kelso to Jedburgh. In summary, Jedburgh had one outgoing and two incoming trains withdrawn. The local newspaper reckoned that this would occasion serious inconvenience to passengers. There were also restrictions to the acceptance of goods for conveyance by rail. The newspaper cited the refusal, on Monday 4th March, of the railway to accept five cart loads of wood at Jedburgh station. The delivery of mails was also affected. On 14th March the *Southern Reporter* stated that the only trains scheduled to leave Jedburgh would be the 6.10 am and 4.35 pm. The only trains leaving St Boswells for Kelso and Jedburgh would leave at 8.30 am and 5.55 pm. All Sunday passenger trains were cancelled on the Borders branches. *The Scotsman* of 25th March, 1912 contained an announcement from the Scottish railway companies that ordinary passenger and goods trains would be subject to discontinuation or alteration. Unnecessary journeys were to be discouraged by the discontinuation of all excursion and weekend tickets to English stations.

Once the strike had ended train services were gradually returned to something like the pre-strike timetable.

The *Southern Reporter* of 13th August, 1914, just nine days after Britain declared war on Germany, contained an article describing what was happening in Jedburgh. Reference was made to the numbers enlisting in the various branches of the imperial forces, in particular the Army Service Corps, the Army and Naval Reserves and the Territorials. 'Every man has responded to the urgent call to duty and they had an enthusiastic send-off, hundreds of persons accompanying them to the railway station'.

On 9th September that year the NBR, jointly with the Glasgow & South-Western Railway issued an 'Important notice' that as a consequence of the 'European War Crisis' their ordinary passenger and goods trains would be subject to 'Material Alteration or Discontinuance without notice.'

It was not long before the first local war casualty was reported. The *Southern Reporter* dated 1st October, 1914 recorded the death in action of Private Robert Storrie of Bonjedward, aged 29, who was serving in the King's Own Scottish Borderers. When a youth he was employed as a clerk at Jedburgh railway station. He had then enlisted and served with his regiment in India and Egypt. Later he had rejoined the NBR as a clerk at Leith Walk station. As a reservist he was called up when hostilities started and it is believed that he fell in the first battle at Mons. He left a widow who also hailed from Bonjedward.

Storrie's regiment performed a route march in late February 1915 to stimulate interest in recruiting. They arrived by train and began their march at Kirkbank

A World War I photograph showing troops embarking on a train of short carriages from Jedburgh station with, once again, a good turnout of local youths to witness the event. In the foreground the soldiers are occupying a third class carriage; first class compartments were reserved for officers. *Stenlake Publishing Collection*

station. They proceeded to Morebattle where they were provided with lunch. They then marched on to Yetholm for tea and cigarettes, before proceeding to Kelso where they were entertained by local ladies in the Corn Exchange. The men subsequently left by train for Galashiels via St Boswells. The account of the march appeared in the *Jedburgh Gazette* of 26th February.

The announcement of the death of William Steward, the Jedburgh station master, appeared in the *Hawick News and Border Chronicle* of Friday 31st March, 1915. A fuller appreciation was in the *Southern Reporter* of 6th April. Steward, described as the 'agent' for the NBR at Jedburgh, died in the station house after an illness of only a few days duration. The (unnamed) complaint had only appeared a week previously and he had been receiving medical treatment. He was just 36 years of age and had been appointed to the agency at Jedburgh some five years previously having been agent at Hawthornden and before that a railway clerk in Lanarkshire. Described as a capable and trustworthy servant of the railway, with the highest character and integrity, he had a valuable and intimate knowledge of railway workings. He was exceedingly popular with the public. He had a strong religious conviction and identified with the Home Mission and the YMCA. His widow and two children survived him.

The death of another railwayman with Jedburgh connections was announced in the *Hawick News and Border Chronicle* of 30th April, 1915. George Cunningham was born in 1842. In 1857 he entered into the service of the NBR and acted as a clerk at Jedburgh station. Later he was transferred to the office of the general superintendent at Waverley station in Edinburgh where he worked for 22 years. In August 1884 he was appointed as superintendent of the NBR's Western District. He totalled 58 years' service in the North British Railway. He died at Cupar in Fife.

Violence at Jedburgh station recurred in July 1915 when the *Southern Reporter* once again (on 22nd July) described an unpleasant incident. David Moffit, a groom who resided at Alnham, near Whittingham in Northumberland, was accused of having assaulted Alexander Richardson, a railway signalman, who was resident in Bongate, Jedburgh. Moffit was alleged to have struck Richardson a blow on the face with his clenched fist causing 'an effusion of blood'. In addition he was charged with conducting himself in a disorderly manner and committing a breach of the peace. Having pleaded guilty Sheriff Baillie fined Moffit 15s. with the alternative of spending seven days in prison.

The editions of the *Southern Reporter*, dated 9th and 16th August, 1917, made reference to the trades, shopkeepers and factory holidays in Jedburgh. Those employed in the town's mills had been granted extended holidays. In spite of the wartime restrictions on travelling facilities the business at Jedburgh railway station on the holiday Saturday and Monday had been brisk and had shown a marked increase on that for the corresponding period of the last two years. The trains were filled with holidaymakers bound mostly for Spittal on the Northumberland coast.

On the 13th August the *Edinburgh Evening News* announced that Robert Dickson was posted as 'missing'. Before enlisting for military service he was employed as a porter at Jedburgh railway station.

The announcement of another wartime death of a former railway employee at Jedburgh station appeared in the *Hawick News and Border Chronicle* of 1st February, 1918. Sapper William Archibald was drowned when a British vessel was sunk in the Mediterranean in December 1917. Prior to his enlistment he was employed by the NBR as a cleaner at Jedburgh. He was just 20 years old and lived in Hawick. The *Railway Magazine* of February 1918 reported that Matthew S. Strang was taking up the position of district superintendent of the NBR in Glasgow. He had started his career on the NBR and, after passing through different grades, he had held the station agency (station master) positions at Jedburgh, Inverkeithing and Perth.

It was in February 1918 that the Canadian Forestry Corps (CFC) arrived at Jedburgh. Many of the British foresters had enlisted for war service and the British War Cabinet had requested assistance from the Canadian Government in providing foresters for the cutting down of timber for military purposes and for pit props. The CFC records show that 139 Company was based at Lantonhill, near Bonjedward, north of Jedburgh, from February to November 1918. No. 127 Company was based at Birkenside to the south-east of the town from October 1918 to January 1919. According to the Jedburgh Town Council Minutes, 139 Company laid a 3 ft gauge railway along the length of the 'Oxnam Water Road' making the road impassable to ordinary traffic. The purpose of the line was to transport the cut timber but there is insufficient evidence to trace the precise route. Was the timber subsequently transferred to road vehicles or was it transported along the Jedburgh line? In the National Archive there is a Minute of Agreement between the Timber Supply Department and the town council for the building of a loading stage beside the branch railway, also the provision of an area for a timber yard but so as not to block access to the slaughter house at Jedburgh. This allows the identification of the area involved but doesn't indicate whether the yard and line were ever built and operated to link up with the branch line. There is another reference to the probable shipment of timber along the narrow gauge line to Jedfoot Bridge station. There is one final reference to the timber railway. In October 1918 a Private McLaughlin (Service No. 1003104) was killed when he was building a stack of timber. The stack collapsed and he was crushed to death. He was taken to the Bonjedward camp on the railway. He is buried in the Jedburgh (Castlewood) Cemetery and his grave is marked with a 3 ft 6 in. freestone cross. Some timber cutting also occurred to the south of the town; it may be that small railways were constructed there also. Being lightly laid and temporary structures they have not left any remains.

On 4th October, 1919 *The Scotsman* ran an article which said that as the current railway strike progressed the NBR had been able to reinstate many trains as the railwaymen's intentions of bringing the railway network to a standstill were being thwarted by numerous volunteers coming forward to perform in all branches of railway work. In addition members of the army had been deployed. The Earl of Elgin was specifically mentioned as he had had acted as fireman on a train from Waverley to Perth and return. The strike was a national one staring at midnight on 26th September and being settled at 4.15 pm on 5th October.

A mention was made in the article that there was a train service on the Jedburgh branch and on to Kelso, along with the lines to Duns and Selkirk. The Jedburgh service was run by an old driver named Robert Rutherford (*see page 147*), resident of Melrose, in his late 60s, who did not believe in strikes, Pat

Nolan, the fireman, and Johnny Cullen, the guard, who had a large family and could not afford to go on strike. As the signalmen at Roxburgh Junction were on strike the station master at Roxburgh, Tommy Dagg, manned the signal box. What followed is described later in Chapter Sixteen.

Dagg, incidentally, used to make fun of the then Kelso station master, Sam Wilson. Wilson liked to wear his blue serge uniform complete with a gold-braided peaked cap but Dagg considered this to be rather pompous. Dagg's platform announcements were thus along the lines of 'This is Roxburgh. All change for Kirkbank, Nisbet, Jedfoot and Jedburgh. Keep your seats for the Holy Land (Kelso!) and watch out for the man with the egg on his hat'. Dagg is known to have been fond of a dram!

From around this time, as recorded in *Auld Roxburgh*, there is a story of a 15 wagon cattle train which was left standing on the Jedburgh line at Roxburgh Junction. The train 'ran away' and didn't stop until it reached what was known as 'the blackberry cutting' a mile away. Fortunately there was no accident.

The *Berwickshire News and General Advertiser* of 30th November, 1920 announced that Mr Shaw, an inspector at Berwick station, had been promoted to the position of station master at Jedburgh. He was presented with a gold 'Albert' chain and pendant by some of his colleagues on the occasion of his promotion and Mrs Shaw was presented with an umbrella. Mr Stewart, the current Berwick station master, commented that Mr Shaw had always been civil, obliging and courteous, and willing to oblige others by his experience on the railway. He told Shaw that there were advantages in becoming station master at Jedburgh in that, compared with Berwick, there were no night trains and there was no chance of him being called out of his bed. Mr Shaw had been at Berwick for some 12 years, first as chief clerk, thereafter as night assistant and ultimately as inspector.

The Railways Act of 1921 took effect on 1st January, 1923 when the 120 or so railway companies were merged into four large groups. Originally the Minister of Transport, Sir Eric Geddes, had been minded to reorganize the railways of Britain into four English groups and two Scottish groups. Pressure groups, such as the Central Council of Railway Shareholders, encourage the Government to think again. Their Secretary, A.J. Fleming, wrote to newspapers, including the *Southern Reporter*, detailing the reasons why. The letter appeared in the 3rd February edition.

He wrote that Scottish railways had shouldered a large financial burden during the war and it would make much better financial sense if the Scottish companies could be combined with English companies. Furthermore combination with English companies would ensure that trains on the Anglo-Scottish main lines would be under the auspices of a single company.

In the end the Act which brought about the railway Grouping proposed just four groups with part of the Scottish system becoming incorporated into the London, Midland & Scottish Railway and the rest becoming part of the London & North Eastern Railway. The former North British Railway, including the Jedburgh line, became a part of the latter. Once this was settled it became possible for the final payment of dividends to NBR shareholders to take place.

Chapter Twelve

Branch diary: Grouping to Nationalization

After Grouping had taken place the day-to-day operations on the Jedburgh line, now part of the LNER, continued much as before with the same type of reports appearing in the press.

The *Hawick News and Border Chronicle* of 9th May, 1924 contained a display advertisement for the Fifth Border Musical Festival with the main events to be held in the Volunteer Hall at Galashiels on 16th May, at the Town Hall Hawick from 17th to 21st May and in the Playhouse at Galashiels from 22nd to 24th May. Other events were held in St Andrew's Church Hall, Hawick and the Technical College Hall at Galashiels. The advertisement announced the availability of cheap railway fares in connection with the event: day return tickets were available from local stations, including those on the Jedburgh branch, for the price of a normal single fare. The absence of a very late return train would have limited Jedburgh visitors to matinee performances!

Inclement weather reared its head again during January 1925. The New Year storm was particularly bad according to the *Southern Reporter*. Rain, which commenced on the morning of New Year's Day, had fallen continuously for days afterwards and the River Jed carried a huge volume of water, such as had not been seen for many years. The road near to Jedburgh railway station had been flooded and the railway track was undermined at Jedfoot. For the third time in a few days the 7.15 am train was suspended. As soon as the water receded sufficiently from the rails a large squad of workmen quickly made good the damage by dumping ballast into the broken embankment; the ballast had been supplied in sufficient quantities days earlier in case of emergencies such as this. As soon as the water permitted, then a full service resumed.

The *Berwickshire News and General Advertiser* for 12th May that year reported that Thomas Brown, of Duns station, had been appointed as the assistant booking clerk at Jedburgh station to replace Robert Black, recently transferred to Broomlee station in Peebleshire. Thomas was the son of Mr. John Brown who was a Jedburgh postman. Also in May the *Jedburgh Gazette* reported the decision of the Roxburghshire County Council to accept the tender of Sir William Arrol and Company to rebuild the road bridge at Jedburgh station.

The *Southern Reporter* of 2nd July reported on the successful annual Sunday School picnic trip to Spittal. The train with the children had left at 10.00 am and returned to Jedburgh at 8.30 pm. Charabancs and cars had taken the participants to the station. In some years, as described in Chapter Ten, the children had marched from the Market Place to the station behind the Jedforest Instrumental Band. Most businesses had closed, as usual, and the town had a deserted appearance.

On the 9th July there was an amazing story in the *Dundee Evening Telegraph*. A farmer in an outlying part of Peeblesshire offered a dog to his nephew in Roxburghshire. The nephew collected the dog in person. He was driven to Peebles station where he caught a train to Galashiels, changing again at

St Boswells and travelling up the Jedburgh branch as far as Nisbet with the dog. He returned to his farm at Crailing. Man and dog had travelled some 50-60 miles. After a couple of days the dog disappeared. A week later he received a letter from his uncle to say that the collie, footsore and worn out, had arrived at his old home! There was a happy ending to the story as the dog was allowed to stay with his first owner in Peebleshire.

Later the same year, on 6th August, the *Southern Reporter* contained details of the marriage of William Scott, the signalman at Jedburgh. A small ceremony was held at Jedburgh station at which William Shaw, the station master, said a few words and presented Scott with a handsome clock. Scott suitably replied.

The problem of persons lodging illegally on railway property came to the fore once again in 1925. Archibald Frater, a labourer residing, or lately residing, in Canongate, Jedburgh, was charged with lodging in a shed within the goods yard at Jedburgh station without the permission of the legal occupiers, George Blaikie & Sons, the coal merchants. He appeared in the Justice of the Peace Court before Justice W. Wells Mabon. Frater pleaded guilty and, according to the *Southern Reporter* of 27th August, was fined 5s., alternatively to serve five days in prison. He was given eight days in which to pay the fine.

The *Jedburgh Gazette* contained an item in its 14th May, 1926 edition concerning the General Strike and its effect on the town. It reported that the advice of the calling off of the strike was received by wireless in Jedburgh on Wednesday 12th May at about 1.15 pm, and a few minutes later the important news appeared on the window of the *Gazette* Office. A large crowd had gathered here and expressions of gratification at the welcome news were heard on all sides.

> The position at Jedburgh station yesterday (i.e. Thursday 13th May) was the same as it had been during the week, and no definite information is to hand regarding the resumption of the train service. There is a probability that there may be a restricted service at the weekend, but no official intimation has yet been made.

In the same item it was noted that all the existing coal restrictions would remain in force.

Six days later, the *Southern Reporter* contained an article relating to the ending of the strike entitled 'Situation on the Borders'. It stated that although bus services were running smoothly, train services were far from normal. Jedburgh's isolation from the world by way of the railway came to an end on Saturday (i.e. 15th May), when there were three outgoing and three incoming passenger trains. In the 60 years of its existence there had been on no former occasion so complete a stoppage of the Jedburgh branch of the railway.

The *Linlithgowshire Gazette* of 24th September reported that the train service on the Jedburgh branch had had to be suspended after a large thunderstorm towards the end of September 1926. The railway line was inundated at several points between Jedburgh and Nisbet, following a 'pitiless, incessant deluge' with no trains running between these points. Eight feet of floodwater were measured at Kelso bridge. A tree trunk carried in the flood damaged a service bridge near to Jedburgh station and the nearby haughlands at the side of the Jed were totally submerged beneath rushing water. The train service from Jedburgh station was totally suspended between Jedburgh and Nisbet and passengers were transported by motor bus from Jedburgh to catch their train on to Roxburgh at Nisbet station though a roundabout route was necessary as the main road north out of Jedburgh was closed. The *Hawick News and Border Chronicle* reported that within Jedburgh it was necessary for a four mile detour to be made when travelling from the town to the station. Other train services in the Borders were also affected. Services south of Riccarton on the Waverley route were diverted via Bellingham, Hexham and the Border Counties line as a result of a landslip blocking the line main line.

In November 1926 local newspapers reported that the same section of line was affected once more. The Teviot was in high flood and in the Crailing and Nisbet areas hundreds of acres of grassland were under water. Near the junction of the Jed and the Teviot, not far from Jedfoot station, a considerable section of the railway was submerged. The train service had to be suspended once more and throughout the day both passengers and mails were transported by motor bus between Jedburgh and Nisbet. Nisbet station was just above the water level so a shuttle train service linked Nisbet with Roxburgh.

A Jedburgh farmer, Andrew William McConnell appeared in Hawick Sheriff Court on 27th February, 1929 charged with travelling on the LNER without a valid rail ticket and wilfully obstructing a ticket collector in the course of his duty. He was defended by a Jedburgh solicitor, D. Sturrock, and pleaded not guilty. *The Hawick News and Border Chronicle,* published two days later, indicated that the farmer was found to be guilty and ordered to pay a fine of 5s. with an additional 10s. court expenses.

William Shaw, the station master of Jedburgh and Jedfoot stations, received some good news in September 1931 (*Southern Reporter* of 24th September). In the list of awards for best kept stations just issued by the LNER, Jedfoot station had been given a prize of £3 having been placed in the second class.

A large jointly-issued advertisement on behalf of the LNER and LMS appeared in the 9th April, 1932 edition of the *Edinburgh Evening News*. It was posted to publicize cheap day excursion tickets to be issued jointly by the two railways from the Edinburgh stations. Jedburgh was included in the list of destination stations, the return third class fare being set at 6s. It is interesting to note that whereas there were regular LNER railway advertisements promoting excursion travel to and from the coastal towns served by the railway, including North Berwick and Eyemouth, very few advertised cheap travel to the Jedburgh line.

An accident blocked the road entrance to Jedburgh railway station for a short time on 23rd March, 1933 according to the *Southern Reporter* published a week later. A car belonging to a Mr Moore, a 'motor hirer', but driven by a Mr Brodie, was turning into the station when it was caused to swerve by another passing car. The car made contact with one of the station gate post causing the front of the vehicle to become badly damaged. Luckily no-one was hurt. Moore also operated several motor coaches.

William Shaw, whose name has already featured several times in this account, had been appointed station master at Jedburgh in 1920. The *Southern Reporter* of 1st February, 1934 recorded that he had been promoted to a similar post at Shore Road station in Stirling. Prior to coming to Jedburgh Shaw had been an inspector at Berwick, though the newspaper incorrectly referred to his post as being assistant station master there. During his tenure at Jedburgh he had become very popular and made many friends and the newspaper said that when he left he would carry with him the best wishes of all.

The ceremony to wish him farewell was fully described in the same newspaper dated 15th March, 1934. He was the guest of a company of about 60 ladies and gentlemen, representative of the town and district, at the Spread Eagle Hotel in Jedburgh, under the Chairmanship of Provost Wells Mabon. Shaw was presented with a testimonial and gifts in appreciation of his services to the trading community and the travelling public generally. There was also a presentation to Mrs Shaw. Lt-Colonel Jackson of Glendouglas made the presentation on behalf of 130 subscribers whilst John Ewart presented gifts on behalf of the station staff. John Ewart, himself, was also scheduled to leave Jedburgh about a year after this event. Ewart had been chief clerk in the goods department at Jedburgh for some five years when he was promoted to a post at Hawick to replace Thomas Stanford who had, in turn, been promoted to the position of agent at Stobs station on the Waverley route (*Hawick News and Border Chronicle* 18th October, 1935). On 1st March the *Southern Reporter* announced that Mr Dickson, the station master at Eyemouth, had been appointed to succeed Mr Shaw.

The *Railway Magazine* in October 1935 had received a letter from a person who signed himself 'Precursor' to the effect that there were several stations on the LNER lines in Scotland that were in the hands of 'Stationmistresses'. He named Kirkbank on the Jedburgh branch together with Lundin Links, Rosslynlee and Deadwater, this last station being on the Border Counties line.

The *Southern Reporter* (of 26th March, 1936) referred to some 48 persons having travelled by train from Jedburgh on the previous Friday evening to see a rugby match at Twickenham. England beat the Scottish team in the Calcutta Cup 9–8 in a close match.

The Scotsman of 28th July, 1937 and the *Berwickshire News and General Advertiser* of 3rd August reported on the death of a man at Jedfoot railway station. Thomas Russell, described as a 'hallman' of Halliburton House, Coupar Angus, Perthshire, had been spending a holiday at Jedfoot. Mr Russell, who had been visiting his brother, Alexander Russell, of Bonjedward near Jedburgh, was leaving to visit his sister (one report says his married daughter) who was residing at Nisbet a few miles down the line. He had just said goodbye to his brother on Jedfoot station platform and he stooped down to pick up his suitcase prior to boarding the train. At this point he collapsed. He was attended by a nurse who happened to be travelling on the train but, despite her ministrations, was found to be dead within a few minutes. The *Berwickshire News* reported that he was 57 years of age (and unmarried) and had worked in his present position for nine years. Earlier he had worked at Newton Don, Kelso, and also at the Duke of Roxburgh's residence, Floors Castle. He was a native of the Kelso and in the Great War had served with the Highland Light Infantry.

A gruesome discovery was made by a workman who was unloading coal in the yard at Jedburgh station at the start of February 1938. According to the

The programme for the March 1936 rugby international. Some 48 Jedburgh rugby fans availed themselves of cheap tickets and travelled down to London on Friday 20th March. They returned on the Sunday, no doubt disappointed that Scotland had lost by a single point! *Rugby Football Union*

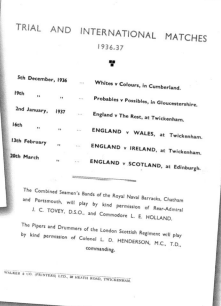

Hawick News and Chronicle the workman discovered a human hand, severed at the wrist, amongst the coal. There was no follow-up article to throw more light on this terrible event. However the coal had come from Newtongrange Colliery and it was believed that an accident must have occurred there.

On 7th February, 1938 a motor lorry driver, John Robinson, of Hill Farm, Seaton, Workington, Cumberland, drove his lorry through the level crossing gates at Jedfoot railway station. He was subsequently accused of dangerous driving. Apparently it was in broad daylight that he passed a stationary car before the crossing and crashed through the gates which had been closed across the road to allow a train to pass. His vehicle stopped in the middle of the 'four-foot' way thus blocking the rails. A witness, George Turnbull, who was in charge at Jedfoot station, stated that he was about to reopen the gates after the passage of the train when he heard the sound of a heavy vehicle approaching from the Jedburgh direction at speed. He was of the opinion that the vehicle would not be able to stop before reaching the gates and he therefore ran clear. Next moment there was a scraping noise as the lorry squeezed between the stationary car and the parapet before crashing through the gate on the Jedburgh side, completely destroying it. In his evidence the accused said that he was unable to pull up because of a defective foot brake. The servo pipe had burst and he was unaware of this until after the accident. He had been in top gear coming down the hill towards the station and his speed was about 20 mph. He was about to change down through the gears when he spied, about 30 yards away, the stationary car. He did not agree that the servo could have been damaged in the collision with the gates. Sheriff Baillie was not satisfied as to when the foot brake was damaged but said that, in any case, the accused had a hand brake and should have stopped. He found the accused to be guilty of dangerous driving, fined him £4, or, in default, 14 days in prison, and ordered that his licence be endorsed. The report of the trial appeared in *The Scotsman* on 23rd March, 1938.

A very familiar story appeared in the *Southern Reporter* of 17th November, 1938. The item referred to the flooding which was caused by heavy rain the previous weekend, the 13th and 14th November. Once again the water level in the Teviot had risen considerably and on Monday 14th it was necessary to close the line to all rail traffic. About 120 yards of the permanent way near Nisbet station were under water and some 60 yards of the embankment supporting the sleepers and rails was completely washed away. Passengers between Roxburgh Junction and Jedburgh were once again conveyed by bus. Surfacemen worked all day on Monday to effect repairs so that the rail service could be resumed.

A Jedburgh labourer, William James Hunter, appeared at Jedburgh Sheriff Court on 8th February, 1940 charged with the theft of an electric light lamp from the carriage of a train travelling between Roxburgh and Jedburgh, according to the *Hawick News and Border Chronicle*. Hunter said to the court that he had visited the doctor at Galashiels. He bought a newspaper at Roxburgh on his way back to Jedburgh but he could not see to read it in the compartment. He took out a bulb and tried to scrape its surface clean but unfortunately it broke and he 'chucked it out of the window'. He claimed that he was going to report this to the station master but he was not there. He went home to get some tea. He found that the lights in his own house on Headrig were fused and he didn't get the chance to go back to the station to report matters. The Procurator-Fiscal said that he was afraid that the story given to the court by the accused did not coincide with the several statements made to the police. The guard had seen Hunter in the compartment with another man as the train approached Nisbet. The compartment was fitted with a blue bulb. (This was as a result of the wartime restrictions to reduce light levels in the train.) When he was charged with the offence he had first of all said that there was no light in the compartment; later he said that he had removed a bulb to scrape it. Even later he had said that he took out the bulb to get darkness in order to have a sleep. To the court he had stated that he wanted more light! He had no right to interfere with the lighting system on the train and he was committing an offence to do so. The Sheriff-Substitute Mr Anderson said he considered this to be a serious charge. He found the accused guilty and a fine of £2 10s. 0d. was imposed with the alternative of 14 days in prison.

An interesting discussion was initiated by a letter in the *Hawick News and Border Chronicle* of 22nd November, 1940. Writing under the pen name of 'The Rambler', a correspondent referred to statements that had been made regarding Hawick, rather than Jedburgh, being the county town. One of the points for consideration that was offered was that Jedburgh, owing to what the writer called 'the railway arrangements' was just about as awkward a corner to reach as anywhere in the county of Roxburghshire, whereas Hawick was situated on 'the main line' referring, of course, to the Waverley route. He ended by saying that 'Jedburgh must look to its laurels!'

The LNER announced in December 1940 that John Dickson, the station master at Jedburgh had been appointed to the position of station master at Haddington. The *Berwickshire News*, which reported the announcement, also contained the information, in February 1941, that John Johnston, a relief clerk at Hawick, had been promoted to fill the vacant post (*see below*).

We return now to the Jedburgh Sheriff Court for a court case following an alarming incident on a train travelling to Jedburgh station. The incident and the subsequent court case were described in the *Sunday Post* of 30th March, 1941. The incident involved a Jedburgh grocer by the name of William Michie. He appeared in the court charged with having in his possession a Colt revolver without the necessary permit. The Procurator-Fiscal said that the accused was travelling on the train between Edinburgh and Jedburgh and was clearly under the influence of drink. He told some soldiers in his compartment that he had a Colt revolver and some ammunition in his possession. In view of his drunken state the soldiers became somewhat alarmed and when the train arrived at Roxburgh they informed the railway staff of the situation. On arrival of the train at Jedburgh Michie was met and taken directly to the police station. He was searched and the Colt revolver was duly found, but with no ammunition. The accused was represented in the court by solicitor T.Y. Smeall who admitted that Michie had been imbibing but that the drink had loosened his client's tongue. Throughout the entire journey the revolver had been securely inside his suitcase. Sheriff McGregor found the case proven and imposed a fine of £2.

Some happy news was reported in the *Southern Reporter* of 3rd July of the same year when the recently-appointed station master at Jedburgh, John Johnston, was married at the Barony church in Edinburgh by the Revd J.E. McIntyre. His bride was Miss M. Evelyn Arnott, the only daughter of the late Henry Arnott and Mrs Arnott. Despite the wartime clothing restrictions the bride wore a two-piece ensemble of Tudor Rose French crêpe and lace, whilst a cousin of the bride, who acted as bridesmaid, was attired in a dress of turquoise blue and a hat of black straw.

News of the promotion of another Jedburgh railwayman appeared in the *Berwickshire News and General Advertiser* of 9th September, 1941. Albert Wallace, resident in Stratheden Place, Jedburgh, had been one of the station's booking clerks for 11 years. His railway career with the LNER had started at Newcastleton, then Stobs, before he was transferred to Kirkbride on the Silloth branch to the west of Carlisle. From Kirkbride he moved to Jedburgh. His latest promotion was to St Boswell's station on the Waverley route. The paper stated

that whilst at Jedburgh Wallace had played a leading part in the activities of Toc
H, the international Christian movement.

A ceremony to mark the retirement of former Jedburgh station master
William Shaw took place at Stirling in November 1941. Shaw had joined the
NBR in 1895 and worked successively at Galashiels, North Berwick, Manuel,
Caldercruix, Rawyards and Airdrie South before moving to Berwick. After
working at Berwick (as reported earlier) he moved to Jedburgh where he was in
charge of the station for some 13 years from 1915 onwards. A deputation of
railwaymen in LNER service, plus various traders from the town of Stirling,
called upon him to do him honour as he reached the compulsory retirement
age. The Chairman for the occasion was David Bremner. He called upon
William Ramage, cashier of the goods department at Stirling, to make the
presentation. Ramage said that he had great pleasure in handing over to Mr
Shaw a wallet full of notes, the wallet being suitably inscribed. Mrs Shaw was
presented with a handbag. After the presentations Mrs Shaw entertained the
company to tea and a most pleasant time was spent 'in singing and sentiment',
the proceedings being terminated, appropriately, with the singing of *Auld Lang
Syne*. The account of the proceedings appeared in the *Stirling Observer* of 18th
November, 1941.

Yet another former Jedburgh railwayman was referred to in a Borders'
newspaper when T. Lawrence took up the position of station master at Hawick
in 1942. Lawrence was a native of Northumberland and commenced his railway
career as a junior clerk at Plashetts station on the Border Counties line. His
career took him to various other Border stations at Jedburgh and Bellingham
before he moved to Hawick as relief station master. Here he was recognized as
a capable, trustworthy and obliging official and he was appointed as a district
inspector in 1926. Just three years later he was promoted to the post of station
master at St Boswells. After a further 13 years, according to the *Hawick News and
Border Chronicle* of 22nd May, he obtained the post at Hawick.

Because of the restrictions imposed on the press there are few references to
'sensitive' Border activities connected with the prosecution of the war.
However, the *Southern Reporter* of 23rd July, 1942 did make a brief reference to
the inclusion in the local police account estimates of the sum of £500 in the
budget in case it was necessary for the local police to further protect Jedburgh
station. Precisely what the police would be required to do in this connection
was not mentioned.

The *Hawick News* regularly included a column referring to items that had
appeared in the newspaper of 50 years previously. On 23rd July, 1943 this
newspaper column contained a reference to 'The new railway' which had been
proposed late in the 19th century. Provost Craig Brown of Selkirk was reported
as having written a letter to the *Newcastle Daily Journal* as follows:

> Admitting that Hawick is on a straight line between Newcastle and Glasgow, it is not
> admitted that a straight line would be the quickest. It would have to rise and fall and
> tunnel over ridges of bleak, high hills. On the other hand, the railway would find an
> easy course down to Jedburgh. There is an exaggerated idea abroad as to the importance
> of Hawick, whose tweed trade may be said to be incapable of further development,
> while Selkirk has room for twenty mills.

Jedburgh station was earning quite a reputation for its staff being promoted to more senior positions in the LNER system. The *Hawick News and Border Chronicle* reported in August 1943 that Robert Baillie, of the clerical staff at Jedburgh, had been appointed station master at Lundin Links on the Fifeshire Coast near Leven. Lundin Links was then a well-known golfing centre. Mr Baillie was a Jedburgh man and his father had been an engine driver on the local branch line for many years. He had worked at Jedburgh for some 28 years, having been initially appointed to Jedburgh when it was still a NBR station.

There was another change of post in June 1944 when Thomas ('Tommy') Dagg, the station master at Kirkbank, was appointed station master at Edrom station. The announcement appeared in the June 1944 *Southern Reporter*. The following month (on 27th July) the same newspaper indicated that John Johnston had been appointed, from his Jedburgh station master post, to the station master position at Gorgie station on the suburban line, south of Edinburgh; this station was much closer to his wife's family home.

In June 1946 the Sunday School picnic day was said to be able to resume after having not taken place during the duration of the war. However the LNER stated that it was not in a position to convey the party by train (despite being asked to reconsider its decision) and the children had to be transported in the coaches of the Scottish Motor Traction Co. (SMT). Ten buses were to be involved according to the *Berwick Advertiser*. The trip was planned for Monday 2nd July

The 1947 edition of the *Railway Magazine* contained an item relating to the donation to the York Museum collection of a number of items which included 'an old level crossing gate signal' off the former NBR Jedburgh branch. This signal was an old 'vane' signal from Ford level crossing. This level crossing had red diamonds affixed to its gates and North British red-lensed signal lamps on the top rails of its five-barred gates. These unusual (for 1947) items may also have been taken to York.

At the end of World War II all of the railways of Britain were in somewhat of a desperate state. Lack of investment, lack of maintenance during the war, and increasing competition from road transport were all quoted as evidence for taking the railways into state control, particularly by left wing politicians and supporters for whom nationalization was a political ideal. Yet in the early 1920s the railway companies recovered on their own, albeit quite slowly, from the similar effects of World War I without nationalization taking place. In the mid-1940s these railway companies, despite their parlous condition, were still opposed to their takeover by the state. Nevertheless nationalization went ahead and on the first day of 1948 the lines in the Borders found themselves part of the newly created Scottish Region of British Railways irrespective of the companies to which they had previously belonged. At many of the depots and sheds the midnight arrival of the infant British Railways was greeted by the sounding of locomotive whistles. It is unlikely that this happened at Jedburgh where the last train had arrived some hours previously with the train staff, no doubt, having already returned to their homes for a well-earned sleep.

Chapter Thirteen

Branch diary: Nationalization to closure

The extreme weather events that led to the closure of the Jedburgh branch to all traffic in August 1948 are described fully in Chapter Seventeen, together with the work that allowed the line to be re-opened but only for freight, goods and parcels.

The widespread damage caused to the railway system, particularly in the Borders and the north-east of England represented a huge challenge to the newly-formed British Railways with its regionalized structure. That the remedial work was accomplished so quickly and efficiently is a tribute to the management and staff involved, together with the patience of the travelling public.

With the wartime reporting restrictions largely removed the media could return to reporting all aspects of railway operations. The rebuilding after the August 1948 storms was widely reported. *The Scotsman* of 20th August, 1948 reported that a combination of rail and road services had made it possible to book passengers to all railway stations in the area affected by the floods. Based at Dunbar, Berwick and St Boswells bus services linked the railheads with those stations cut off from a direct rail service by the washing away of railway tracks and the destruction of bridges. The services were scheduled to run as nearly as possible to the times at which the stations were served by train prior to the flooding. However, small livestock, horse-drawn road carriages and similar traffic could only be accommodated by arrangement with the station masters of the affected stations. The movement of most livestock, coal and minerals was not yet possible for some stations and Border towns which had become isolated from the main rail network, such as Jedburgh and Eyemouth, had to obtain their household coal, for example, by road rather than rail.

Despite the instigation of a temporary taxi service to replace passenger trains on the Jedburgh branch, its subsequent cessation and the introduction of a replacement bus service, there were continued discussions about passenger train services to Jedburgh. The members of the Jedburgh Town Council meeting held in early January 1949 spent much time discussing the matter and the need for future action. The meeting was reported in the *Berwickshire News and General Advertiser* of Tuesday 18th January. Dean of Guild Elliott moved a motion that arrangements be made to have a meeting with the Railway Executive (Scottish Region) with a view to pressing for reinstatement of the former facilities. In support of this resolution he said that the cutting out altogether of the passenger train service to and from Jedburgh was a heavy blow to the prestige of the county town and an inconvenience to many people in the burgh and district. The chief reason for the discontinuation of the service seemed to be operating costs coupled with loss of revenue , and in order to meet that difficulty the question of introducing a 'diesel-operated railroad car' might be considered. Councillor Clarkson in seconding the motion said that a diesel-operated coach would serve the purpose and was a strong point to put before the Railway Executive. Bailie Campbell, in suggesting that the council should enlist the

This view was taken from the window of Roxburgh Junction signal box. The station buildings are all still intact but the NBR signals on the main St Boswell to Kelso line have already been fitted with replacement upper quadrant arms. The Jedburgh branch signals are still of the lower quadrant type. Compare this with the photo below taken a few years later. *Bill Lynn Collection*

This is a general view of Roxburgh Junction station taken from the St Boswells line around the date of closure. Note the signal box and water tower to the right of the Jedburgh branch tracks, also the North British signal posts, complete with finials, but with replacement British Railways-type signal arms. *Bruce McCartney Collection*

An 0-6-0 shunts the Jedburgh goods in the sidings at Roxburgh Junction. The goods includes both vans and open wagons as well as the six-wheel van which was used to carry parcels and road van traffic to and from Jedburgh. Note the tended flower beds on the platform; these are absent from the pictures on the previous page. *Bruce McCartney Collection*

In this photograph both the starting signal and the advanced starter are 'pulled off' for the Kelso-Roxburgh Junction-St Boswells train hauled by one of the two Standard class '2' 2-6-0s transferred to the line when these trains were reduced to little more than a single coach, though this train seems to have a van or horse box attached behind the locomotive.
David Walsh/Bruce McCartney Collection

Both of the photographs appearing on this page show Jedburgh branch stations after the cessation of timetabled passenger trains, when they were largely unmanned Kirkbank station platform is festooned with weeds, though wild flowers are growing on the embankment opposite.   *Geoff Corner*

Jedfoot station is looking rather unkempt with its buildings crying out for a lick of paint and the weeds, with their new-found freedom, encroaching all over the platform in the foreground. At least the crossing gates appear to be in good repair and well-painted. The post and wire fence on the right appears to be a recent replacement for earlier wooden fencing.   *Geoff Corner*

backing of the county council said that the latter had an important interest in the matter, having regard to the fact that the people who had been in the habit of using the intermediate stations on the branch line were now just as badly off as, if not worse than, those in the town. The motion was unanimously adopted and Provost Moncur, Dean of Guild Elliot and Councillor T. Wilson were appointed to represent the council.

The Roxburghshire County Council at its February meeting decided to support the Jedburgh Town Council's complaint about the rail closure, according to *The Scotsman* of 16th February. If the reinstatement of the railway service was not successful then a strong request was made for a better coordination of bus and rail services between Jedburgh and Kelso. The decision to close the branch railway to passengers, according to Councillor Campbell, was a retrograde step made without any public warning. A large rural area had been completely cut off from public services of this nature.

Of course the termination of the passenger train service reduced the need for station masters at each of the branch stations and grade 1 porters assumed responsibility for the stations at Kirkbank, Nisbet and Jedfoot. The station master's position was, however, retained at Jedburgh. At Nisbet, for example grade 1 porter Mr Tulley was placed in charge of the station succeeding two popular station masters, Messrs Adam Fox and Tom Grieve. His duties combined attending to the signals and crossing gates, the station lighting, also the receiving and dispatching of goods. He was responsible to the Jedburgh station master, Mr Bennett. The local railwaymen expressed some despair at the closures and the loss of jobs.

The Jedfoot water supply was the subject of a *Jedburgh Gazette* article on 3rd June, 1949. At a Roxburgh County Council meeting late in May 1949 the Railway Executive had given an undertaking that improvements would be carried out at the station house, Jedfoot. The water supply to the property was deemed unsatisfactory and the supply had been withdrawn. Water was currently being sent to the house in containers from Jedburgh station. On the report of the medical officer, the council's sub-committee directed that the Railway Executive be pressed to provide a satisfactory water supply and that unless steps were taken in the near future a statutory notice would be served calling on them to provide a supply. The medical officer would provide assistance in this matter.

A strange headline appeared in the edition of the *Berwickshire News and General Advertiser* of 3rd January, 1950: 'Weighbridges wanted'. Branches of the National Farmers Union in the Borders had been appealing to BR for the reinstatement of weighbridges which had been removed from the stations of Nisbet, Kirkbank and Jedfoot. However their application was turned down on the grounds that there was insufficient traffic to justify restoring them. Was it therefore a coincidence that just over two months from this report the *Jedburgh Gazette* reported that a British Road Services vehicle had been stopped near to Jedburgh railway station with an overload of lime? William Russell of Stockbridge, Linlithgow, was fined £10 in the Sheriff Court for permitting this to take place. The driver, David Simpson of Falkirk, was admonished by the Procurator Fiscal for having a load almost 1¼ tons over the appropriate limit. In view of the fact that there had been a previous similar case brought against Russell his fine was doubled.

In both *The Scotsman* (10th February, 1950) and the *Berwickshire News and General Advertiser* (14th February, 1950) there were articles describing the increasing concern that the South Scotland Chamber of Commerce was having over the progressive closures of the branch lines in the south of Scotland. Whilst the Roxburgh to Jedburgh and St Boswells to Duns lines were already closed they feared that the Symington to Peebles line was likely to follow. A rumour was abroad that the Berwick-Kelso-St Boswells line was under consideration for closure. The towns of Jedburgh, Duns and Peebles had a combined population of over 11,000 so the number of people affected was considerable. The effect on local industries was also highlighted.

In May 1950 the *Dundee Evening Telegraph*, the *Dundee Courier*, also the *Fife Free Press and Kirkcaldy Guardian* announced that J. Bennett, the station master at Jedburgh, had been appointed to the post of station master at Ladybank in Fife, also to supervise Kingskettle. Mr Bennett had been station master at Jedburgh during the 1948 floods and the subsequent termination of the passenger train service to the station.

In the *Jedburgh Gazette*, dated 24th February, 1950, there was a report of a statement made by William Scott (Lord Montagu-Douglas-Scott, of the Unionist Party) at a Parliamentary candidates meeting at Jedburgh Public Hall. He was asked about the suspension of the Jedburgh train service. His reply was to say:

If anybody was able to persuade me that the vast majority of the people of Jedburgh find it more convenient to use the bus service then I say the people of Jedburgh are entitled to the bus service, but any inconvenience resulting from the removal of railway passenger services must be more than made up by increased road facilities. I believe that the vast majority of the people of Jedburgh would prefer a really efficient road transport service rather than a railway service. There would be a pretty fair outcry in Jedburgh if anyone suggested stopping the bus service.

(In the following election William Scott's share of the vote went down and he lost his seat to Archie MacDonald of the Liberal Party, a seat he held for barely 12 months before becoming unseated in the 1951 General Election.)

The *Gazette* of 19th January, 1951 announced the passing of another former railway employee at Jedburgh station, namely Archibald Shiels. Mr Shiels had a varied career starting off as an apprentice compositor at McQueen's in Galashiels. He then moved to the office of the *Kelso Mail* and then at the office of the *Jedburgh Gazette*. In 1915 he moved to work at the goods office at Jedburgh station. As he became older he found this work very taxing and he left to go to Boyd's Mill where he stayed until his retirement in 1940.

A railwayman on hire from BR to the North British Rayon works was found guilty at Jedburgh Sheriff Court in March 1951 of the theft of nine sacks of metal, including lead, phosphor bronze and copper from the rayon makers. He was the driver of a mechanical-horse vehicle which had been on hire from the railway for some time. The stolen material could not be found locally but it was recovered at Carlisle. The report appeared in the *Jedburgh Gazette*.

Also in March 1951 the same newspaper contained an article on bus-rail co-ordination, especially as regards passengers for Jedburgh from Newtown St Boswells station. The 7.03 pm bus from Newtown station had been put back two minutes to await a train connection from Edinburgh with the added instruction that it should wait until 7.10 pm if the train was slightly late. Up to the bad spell of weather earlier that year this arrangement had failed on only two occasions, though since the bad weather there had been four occasions when the connection had not been made, with explanations including snow storms and tyre punctures as the reasons. On one occasion the passengers arriving on the late-running train, believed that the bus connection had already left. Consequently they hired a taxi, although, in fact, the bus subsequently arrived at Newtown after the taxi had departed!.

Back in LNER days there were newspaper notices announcing local 'Hunting appointments' together with the meeting points. The various stations on the Jedburgh line were often such venues and this continued into BR days, the Duke of Buccleuch's hunt meeting at Jedfoot station on 10.30 am on Saturday 22nd December, 1951 being listed in the *Gazette*.

In its New Year 1952 edition the *Gazette* conducted a review of the year just ended. Amongst the items referred to was the 'red letter day of the year' – the day when there is a real train with an engine and guard on the Jedburgh line – the picnic day. As usual there had been a trainful of children with adults, and scores more had travelled by road. 'Jethart's streets were indeed empty and echoing as its inhabitants shopped, bathed, paddles or absorbed Forte's ices at Spittal'.

In June 1953 there appeared an announcement in the *Berwickshire News* that John Johnston had been made the new station master at Galashiels. He had begun his career as a clerk for the NBR in 1911. He served in the office at Hawick station from 1913 onwards until transferring to Jedburgh in 1941. After three years there he went to Gorgie station, Edinburgh, then Carstairs, before accepting the Galashiels post.

The 21st August, 1953 edition of the *Jedburgh Gazette* reported that BR were proposing to withdraw the 'porter-unit' from Jedfoot station. The station would retain its ability to deal with 'passenger train and freight train traffic in full truck loads.' The station master at Jedburgh station would be responsible for providing any staff for Jedfoot if the occasion arose. Freight traffic of less than a full wagon load would be dealt with at Jedburgh with collection and delivery, if required, being undertaken by the Railway Executive vehicle based at Jedburgh. The Provost said that his main observation was that there was no passenger service. In practice Jedfoot was reduced to the status of an unstaffed public siding from 30th August, 1954, with Jedburgh responsible for supervision of less-than-full truck loads

An unusual road traffic accident took place close to the garage of Messrs Butler & Oliver at Jedburgh station. A gun-tractor with a 7-ton 4.5 pounder gun attached collided with a car driven by a John Beveridge. Two people in the car, including Mr Beveridge, were injured. In Jedburgh Court Sheriff Murray found the gun-tractor driver, gunner Robert James Gowan, of the Royal Artillery, guilty of driving without due care and attention and imposed a fine of £10. The incident was reported in the *Gazette* of 11st December, 1953.

Local transport provision continued to fall under the spotlight. In December 1954 the transport committee of Jedburgh Town Council, as reported in the

Gazette, had been dealing with complaints from bus and rail travellers who were complaining about the paucity of lighting on trains between Edinburgh and Galashiels and on the failure of Scottish Motor Traction (SMT) buses to wait for train connections at St Boswell's station. BR promised to remedy matters and to take steps to avoid inconvenience in the future. The SMT traffic manager wrote: 'On the 5.20 pm journey from Edinburgh to Jedburgh or Newcastle the conductor will, on arrival at Newtown station, get in touch with the station master [*sic*] and ensure that the train from Edinburgh has arrived and that Jedburgh passengers have been given the opportunity of joining the bus before the journey is continued to Jedburgh.' Arrangements were made for the bus to wait if the train was running slightly late.

The *Berwickshire News and General Advertiser* of 14th December, 1954 reported yet another former Jedburgh railwayman who was continuing a successful railway career elsewhere. A Jedburgh native, Tom Brown, had started his career in the booking office at Jedburgh. He then served successively at Hawick, Duns and Galashiels, before relief work took him to almost every station in the Borders. He became station master at Grantshouse and then at Belses and Hasseldean before his latest promotion to the station master post at Langholm.

Another promotion was reported almost two years later when the Scottish Region of British Railways announced that G. Paterson had been promoted from the post of station master at St Boswells to station master at Fort William. The *Gazette* (21st September) described Mr Paterson's career as having started in the Lime Road goods station at Falkirk before appointments at Abernethy, Easterhouse, Reston and Jedburgh.

A fine of £15 was imposed upon a Jedburgh railway clerk in the Sheriff Court in December 1955 when George Todd pleaded guilty to having charge of a motor-assisted invalid carriage and attempting to drive it, whilst under the influence of drink to such an extent as being incapable of proper control. The *Gazette* said that the court clerk reported that Todd lived in Ancrum but needed his vehicle to travel to work in Jedburgh. The same month, the other side of the 'motoring coin' was shown as reported again in the *Gazette*. In a pleasant ceremony at Jedburgh station, BR lorry drivers, John Haig (for some reason known in local sporting circles as 'H. Jones') and James W. Lowrie were presented with oak leaf bars for accident-free driving for periods of 11 and 14 years respectively. Provost Elliot handed over the decorations and said it was a great pleasure to perform the ceremony, the awards being important in that they contributed to road safety at a time when large numbers of lives were being lost through road accidents. Richard A. Lumsden who had been station master at Jedburgh for about three months (having transferred from a post at Riccarton Junction) said he was very pleased when the notification of the awards came through.

Also in December 1955 a gift was presented to Ronald Cameron, a railway employee at Jedburgh, prior to his sailing from Southampton to America on board the *Queen Elizabeth*. The presentation was made by John Brown, senior member of the goods office staff, who extended the best of good wishes to Mr Cameron for his future on the other side of the Atlantic.

The same edition of the *Gazette* informed readers of the 'not-well-known' fact that ordinary railway tickets for passengers joining trains at Hawick,

St Boswells and Kelso could be purchased at Jedburgh station. Occasionally bus and train times left passengers with very little time to buy tickets before the departure of the train and time could be saved by purchasing the tickets in advance. A further reminder was issued via the same newspaper in May 1956. The *Jedburgh Gazette* was well-known for publishing letters or articles which looked back at local history. The edition of Friday 30th March, 1956 contained two such items. Under the heading of 'Another might-have-been' the first item, in referring to BR's desire to close the line, known as 'The Borders Railway', between Hawick and Newcastle via Hexham, reminded readers of another route which was surveyed and costed for a line between Glasgow to Newcastle via Jedburgh. What had killed the plan was the likely cost of the tunnelling beneath Carter Bar. The newspaper report speculated that if constructed it might have made all the difference to Jedburgh's size and prosperity. The second article related to the siting of Jedburgh's railway station, which was built to 'dodge' the local rates in being placed outside the town. When built it was at a distance from the centre and eventually raised quite an outcry, with attempts, on at least two occasions, to have it extended into the town, with one plan for a new station at what became Stratheden Place and the other for a station between Queen Mary's building and the Jed.

If there had still been an honest-to-goodness railway service here, with passenger trains and all the doo-dahs, we would doubtless have been celebrating Jedburgh's railway centenary this year. We once read in the 1856 *Teviotdale Record* about all the jollifications that attended the opening, with the town council and the band taken on a free trip all the way to Roxburgh and back and free drinks for everybody. What they didn't seem to supply (and what may have been badly needed) was free transport from Jethart's station back home!

In mid-May 1956 under the headline 'Jedburgh-Hawick Railway' the *Jedburgh Gazette* reported on being handed a map by a local resident, A. Muir Sturrock. The map bore the title 'Proposed Jedburgh and Hawick Junction Railway, 1866' and was drawn up by R.A.J.A. Cayne, CE. In its 25th May edition the newspaper said that it had 'never heard' of this scheme to link these towns by rail but that it must have been seriously considered. The line was to start at Jedburgh station (opened some 10 years previously) to cross the road where the prefabricated buildings stood (in 1956) staying on that side of the road and passing Bonjedward a little towards Monklaw. It was to swing left, following the fields, at Cleikiminn, passing some distance behind Knowesouth and Newton until it crossed the Dunion road. Keeping on the same side of the main road it would pass below Denholm where Denholm Dene used to be. Still running parallel with the main road it appeared, from the map that the line would terminate in open ground close to the entry to Hawick. The paper commented that this would imply two stations in Hawick, not that this was uncommon in some towns at that time. 'The question is asked as to whether this line would have made any difference to Jedburgh.' The answer was 'Anyone's guess', but that it would have made less of an impact than if the Glasgow to Newcastle line had passed through Jedburgh, not that either of these schemes got beyond the paper stage!

Jedburgh station viewed from the north in 1963. There are some wagons in the sidings but there is not the 'bustle' associated with earlier years. The roadside hoarding advertises a popular beer of the time (McEwans Export Ale). The 'pre-fabs' on the right were soon to disappear when the entire site was re-modelled after closure of the railway.   *David Stirling*

Jedburgh station viewed from the run-round loop and shed road. The only rolling stock visible is the six-wheel van parked in the platform. There were occasions in the early 1960s when this was the only load-carrying vehicle in the goods train. The North British Railway starting signal at the platform end lasted until the branch closure.   *Armstrong Railway Photographic Trust*

John Brown, the goods office chief clerk, was called upon to make another presentation at Jedburgh station on the occasion of the retirement, on 21st April, of J. Anderson, who had been a railway employee for 37 years, most of which had been spent at Jedburgh. The report appeared in the *Gazette* of 4th May, 1956. The station master, Mr Lumsden, congratulated Mr Anderson and offered him good wishes for a long and happy retirement when he would have time to develop his hobby of breeding budgerigars!

Two months later, on 29th June, the *Gazette* contained the headline 'Jedburgh boys stole railway fog signals'. Three youths, George Thomas Scott (aged 15), Johan Larsen (14) and William Syme Swan (15) were charged with a charge of theft by housebreaking. Although they were under-age the newspaper was allowed to publish their names. They were accused of breaking into the wash-house of the unoccupied dwelling house known as 'The Gatehouse' by the railway at Nisbet. Having gained access to the premises they stole a red coloured flag and one detonator from a box of detonators kept there. The break-in and theft was discovered by a railway employee, Mr Tully, who had been patrolling the line and who visited the Gatehouse to open the crossing gates to let the goods train through. In the boys' defence it was said that they had thrown stones at the detonator to explode it and that there had been no risk to others. Nevertheless the newspaper's sub-heading read 'Contain enough explosive to cause serious injury'. The two elder boys were found to be guilty. The boys' parents or step-parents were fined £2. The youngest, Larsen, was deemed to have been led astray and was let off with a severe warning.

Bad weather in August 1956 once again caused flooding in the Jedburgh area including the vicinity of the station. Such was the amount of rainfall that the Jed burst its banks and the level of water in the old slaughterhouse was measured as two inches higher than it was during the floods of 1948 which had led to the closure of the line.

Also reported in the *Gazette* in August 1956 was a court case in which the owners of a lorry allowed it to be driven whilst carrying an overweight load. The lorry had been laden with granite and police suspected it was overloaded. It was taken to the weighbridge at Jedburgh station where it was measured as showing well over the 14 tons weight allowed on the front wheels and 9 tons allowed on the rear wheels, the values being exceeded by well over a ton in each case. Sheriff-Substitute Martin issued the driver, Duncan Stewart of Carlisle, with a firm reprimand.

On 3rd November, 1956 it was John Brown's turn to receive a presentation, on the occasion of his marriage, when he was the recipient of a gift from his colleagues on the station staff. Station master Richard Lumsden presided over the ceremony, but the gift was actually handed over by Mr Haig (*see above*) who extended his good wishes on behalf of the donors.

The last edition of the *Jedburgh Gazette* for 1956 described the circumstances of a crime that had been committed at Jedburgh station on Saturday 22nd December. It was found that someone had gained access to the workshop at the maintenance premises at the station and stolen coupons as well as petrol from a lorry. The thieves had entered the workshop by breaking a window and had taken the coupons. Using tools found there they had removed the petrol tank

The station site at Jedburgh looks very down-at-heel in this photograph taken from the buffer stops end. The replacement locomotive shed roof is visible beyond the roof-mounted water tank. Weeds are beginning to encroach onto the trackbed though with closure imminent their treatment could not be justified.   *Bruce McCartney Collection*

In this early 1950s photograph the overall station roof has been replaced and the new brickwork, roof and smoke vents can be seen on the shed. The tracks now terminate at the buffer stop in front of the shed which has now been switched to road vehicle housing and maintenance. A 'J37' class 0-6-0 waits departure from the platform with the branch goods.   *Geoff Corner*

from a lorry and emptied it. The empty tank was found at about 4.00 pm. Two men, regarded as suspects, had been seen in the vicinity of the workshop around the time of the thefts.

The *Aberdeen Free Press* of 20th December, 1963 contained an advertisement for a 'Public protest meeting' against the raft of railway closures that were planned for Scotland. The Scottish Vigilantes Action Committee required representatives from all over Scotland to attend the meeting planned to take place on 23rd December at the City Hall, Perth. It is not known whether anyone attended from the Jedburgh district. In any case the writing was already on the wall for the Roxburghshire branch which was to close, very quietly, to the remaining goods traffic on 10th August, 1964. The line between St Boswells and Berwick-on-Tweed via Kelso had already closed to through passenger trains and this cross-country link would shortly be closed to all traffic as a result of the 'Beeching cuts'.

After the final closure of the line, items appearing in the local press largely disappeared, though the *Aberdeen Press and Journal* contained several advertisements in 1971 for the availability, at Jedburgh, of wooden items including railway box vans, telegraph poles and crossing timbers. These were to be sold by a concern named as 'Hub of the Wheel' with a Jedburgh telephone number, though the location of their base has not been traced.

(In his excellent three-part feature, 'The Jedburgh Branch', which appeared in *Back Track* magazine in the first decade of this century, author Alastair F. Nisbet included several tales and reminiscences, particularly from BR days, arising from interviews with former branch employees; as these have already appeared in print, it is not appropriate to repeat them here.)

Taken when the track on the engine shed road had been completely lifted. The station platform has been shortened and a way has been laid across the platform track and run-round loop to allow road vehicles to access the shed. The starting signal is now some way beyond the platform end and the shed water crane has been removed.   *Bruce McCartney*

Chapter Fourteen

Locomotives used on the line

The Directors of the Jedburgh Railway had formed an agreement with the North British Railway to provide locomotives and to operate all trains on the line from its opening. Lieutenant-Colonel Yolland's inspection report commented on the fact that the turntable at Jedburgh had not been constructed and that therefore he would only sanction the opening of the line if tank engines were used. The immediate reply from the Chairman and Secretary of the Jedburgh Railway was that a tank locomotive was already in the course of construction for use on the line.

The only locomotives that fit the bill, in that they were being constructed at the right time, are a pair of 2-2-2 well-tank locomotives. The locomotives were numbered 31 and 32. These have an important position in NBR history in that, up to the year 1856, the railway had a policy of 'buying-in' its locomotives mainly from R. & W. Hawthorn of Newcastle, whereas this pair of locomotives were 'home-built' at the NBR's own works at St Margaret's, Edinburgh. One of the locomotives was destined for use on the Jedburgh branch, the other for the Selkirk Railway which also opened in 1856. They were almost identical in having 5 ft 0 in. driving wheels and leading and trailing wheels of 3 ft 6 in., with cylinders measuring 12 in. x 18 in., later increased to 13 in. x 18 in. They had weatherboards, not full cabs for the crew. The main difference between them was that No. 31 had spacings of 6 ft 10 in. and 6 ft 0 in. between the wheels whilst the figures for No. 32 were 6 ft 0 in. and 6 ft 0 in. These locomotives were transferred to the NBR 'Duplicate' list in 1874 suggesting that they had been replaced by other locomotives on the Jedburgh and Selkirk branches. They ended their careers on the Wigtownshire Railway.

It has often been stated that 0-4-2 tender locomotives were the planned motive power for the goods trains on the Jedburgh line. Of course these were not acceptable to Inspector Yolland until the turntable came in to use at the Jedburgh terminus. Depending on exactly when the turntable was completed, it is possible that the first 0-4-2 tender engine allocated to the branch was one of the batches of locomotives with that wheel arrangement, built in 1855, which had originally been ordered for the Lancashire & Yorkshire Railway (L&Y) from Fairbairn & Son of Manchester. When William Hurst left the L&Y to become locomotive superintendent of the NBR he transferred the order to alleviate the severe locomotive shortage which the NBR was experiencing. They were certainly sent from the L&Y to St Margaret's. They had 5 ft 0 in. driving wheels with trailing wheels of 3 ft 6 in., their cylinder size being 17 in. x 24 in. Two of the four locomotives were renumbered in the duplicate series in 1880 and all were withdrawn in 1882. It is a matter of speculation as to whether these locomotives worked on the line; it may be that the tank engine was in charge until the following class of locomotives became available.

No. 18 was the locomotive that was involved in one of the accidents at Heiton. This was a goods engine, also with the 0-4-2 wheel arrangement but whether it worked over the line to Jedburgh is not recorded. According to the Stephenson Locomotive Society's handbook it was withdrawn in 1872.

Members of a subsequent class of 0-4-2s are recorded as working on the line. These were in the NBR number series 317-334. The first 12 of these were built by Beyer, Peacock, in Manchester, between 1859 and 1862; the remaining six were built at Cowlairs Works in 1864. (Note that the Jedburgh turntable appears on the first edition of the 25 in. Ordnance Survey maps surveyed in 1859; this allowed tender locomotives such as these 0-4-2s to be used.) Nos. 324, 327 and 328 are locomotives from the Beyer, Peacock batch which were seen on the line whilst 329 from the later batch is recorded as working a St Boswells to Kelso service through Roxburgh. Whilst still carrying its original NBR number of 99, No. 327 was observed on the Jedburgh branch on a passenger train. It was a Hawick engine at the time. These locomotives had coupled wheels of 5 ft 1 in. in diameter with trailing wheels of 3 ft 6 in. and they were powered by angled cylinders measuring 16 in. x 22 in. There were detail differences between members of the class involving their boiler domes (or lack of them!), their weatherboards or cabs and their cab windows. All, however, had lavish brasswork and open splashers. They were successful locomotives, surviving to be rebuilt in 1895 and being renumbered between 1903 and 1906. No. 327 (by then on the duplicate list as No. 1068) was withdrawn in 1911. Nos. 324 (by now 1065) and 329 (now 1029) were withdrawn and scrapped in 1912; 328 (now 1069) survived for just one more year. Some of the class were given names, often of places at which the locomotive worked. No. 325, for example, was named *Peebles*, though the other three mentioned did not receive names.

At least two of the 0-4-2 tender engines built by Beyer, Peacock for the North British Railway between 1859 and 1862 have been recorded on the Jedburgh branch. No. 324 was photographed in front of Jedburgh signal box in 1893 whilst No. 328 (then shedded at St Margaret's) was observed on 9th July, 1913 hauling an extra passenger train for the Jedburgh Games. The SLS handbook reports that No. 329, one of the class built at Cowlairs in 1864, worked on the St Boswells to Kelso service and may thus also have made an appearance on the Jedburgh line. All of the engines were rebuilt from their original form by Holmes. They had Stephenson valve gear and their lever reverse was on the left-hand side.

Records exist of another relatively long-lived class of engines working on the Jedburgh branch. This was a class of 4-4-0Ts designed and built when Dugald Drummond was the locomotive superintendent of the NBR. They were constructed at Cowlairs Works in several batches between 1880 and 1884 as class 'R'. They have been described as being 'extremely neat'. They possessed coupled wheels of 5 ft 0 in. and solid bogie wheels of 2 ft 6 in. They were 30 ft long overall and their total wheelbase was 17 ft 6 in. In their long lives of 40-50 years they underwent few modifications. Their coal bunkers were enlarged by the addition of a fender and between 1908 and 1911 they were fitted with Holmes-type boilers. In their early days they were all fitted with nameplates, and, as with earlier locomotives, these were often associated with the areas in which they worked. No. 99 (allocated to Hawick shed) is recorded by NBR historian Bill Lynn as working a passenger train on the branch in North British days. It was renumbered 1458 in 1922. It originally bore the name *Roxburgh* but all of the class had lost their names in about 1883-4. In addition to this locomotive there is a picture of No. 299 (formerly named *Hamilton*) attaching a horsebox onto a train at Kelso. Another photograph of the same locomotive shows it at Jedburgh heading a passenger train. This was taken in NBR days, but after its renumbering as 1411 in 1921. Originally it had worked on the Corstophine branch. One other locomotive of the same class, No. 79 (later 1469) is known to have worked on the Kelso branch and may have visited Jedburgh. The LNER renumbered these locomotives again, in 1924 and 1926, into class 'D51'. No. 1458 became 10038, then 10458, 1411 became 10029, then 10451, whilst 1469 became 10048, then 10469. Carrying its post-1925 number locomotive No. 10456 (first of all 74, then 01456, later 10036) was recorded at Jedburgh with a passenger train on 30th May, 1928. This locomotive originally carried the name *Coatbridge*, then *Whiteinch*, before reverting to its first name for a further brief period. The first of these engines to be withdrawn was No. 10469 in January 1927. The days of No. 10411 ended in October 1930 and those of No. 10456 in September 1931. Finally, locomotive No. 10458 was withdrawn in May 1933, making it one of the last of the class to survive. Railway observer, artist and writer C. Hamilton Ellis observed this locomotive serving out its very last days at Kittybrewster, near Aberdeen in 1932. He painted a picture of it, entering Maxton station, against a background of the Eildon Hills in 1926. Two photographs appeared in the *Railway Magazine* of August 1928, one showing a locomotive of this class in the Jedburgh platform at Kelso, the other showing the engine at the head of a train ready to depart from Jedburgh.

Photographs dating from 1906, taken in the large storms of that year, show an 0-6-0 of NBR class 'E' on snowplough duty on the Jedburgh branch. Unfortunately its number cannot be identified. This was a long-lived class. Built between 1867 and 1875 the class survived to become LNER class 'J31'. Successive rebuilds of these useful engines were undertaken by Holmes and Reid.

A photograph exists of a member of what became LNER class 'J34' taken at Jedburgh pre-1924. The locomotive is carrying its NBR livery as No. 557. Built at Cowlairs in April 1883 as a 'Standard Goods', it was rebuilt by Holmes in 1907 and fitted with Westinghouse brakes. It was allocated No. 9557 by the LNER but this number was never carried, the locomotive being withdrawn in October 1924.

On the 6th August, 1926 an 0-4-4T was working on the Jedburgh branch hauling a passenger train. It was a Hawick-allocated locomotive and belonged to the class which became LNER class 'G9'. It was built by the NBR at Cowlairs in 1910, some sources state October 1909, as No. 354 and the '9' prefix was applied by the LNER in January 1926. It was later allocated No. 9557 by the LNER but this number was never carried as the locomotive was withdrawn before the number could be applied These Reid-designed locomotives, belonging to his class 'M', were similar to earlier Holmes engines but were built larger for passenger train working. Their duties included suburban trains around Glasgow and Edinburgh as well as branch line work. They were fitted with steam heating and Westinghouse brakes. No. 9354 arrived at Hawick shed

NBR 'D'/LNER 'J34' class 0-6-0 No. 557, in North British Railway livery, is pausing in the shunting a brakevan at Jedburgh. This type was the standard goods locomotive for the NBR. No. 557 was built in 1883 at Cowlairs Works in Glasgow and withdrawn for scrap in October 1924, not having received its new LNER allocated number of 9557.

Bill Lynn Collection

in January 1933, having been transferred from St Margaret's in Edinburgh. It was photographed at Jedburgh shed around 1935 when it was out-stationed from Hawick. It did not survive for much longer for it was one of the first of the class to be withdrawn from stock at Hawick on 21st September, 1936. There were only 12 locomotives in this class, Reid's later locomotives for local passenger trains being 4-4-2 tanks.

Bill Lynn has supplied a photograph from his collection of a member of LNER class 'C15', No. 9134, when it had worked a passenger service to Jedburgh. Nicknamed 'Yorkies' this class of 4-4-2Ts was designed by Reid and built at the Yorkshire Engine Co. (hence their nickname). Locomotive No. 9134 had started out in life in July 1912 as No. 134, gaining its new number, 9134, in May 1925. The LNER renumbered it again in January 1946 when it became 7459. Under the British Railways renumbering scheme it became No. 67459 in September 1950 before being withdrawn in October 1955. In the early 1950s it was allocated to Hawick, 64G, depot. Three years after nationalization a member of the same class, No. 67457, was photographed approaching Roxburgh with a train from the Kelso direction and about to cross Roxburgh viaduct. This was also a Hawick-allocated locomotive. These Hawick-based 'C15s' were regulars on the Jedburgh branch. Seven different engines of this class of locomotives were based at Hawick at times between the late 1920s and 1955. They had the power classification of '2P' in British Railways' days.

Another class of 0-6-0 tender locomotives to be seen on the Jedburgh line was the LNER class 'J36', designed by Holmes for the NBR in 1888. No. 9788, for example, was a Hawick engine seen on 11th July, 1939 working the branch goods. Another seen on the line was No. 9748. Originally numbered 788 and 748 respectively they both survived into BR days, becoming 65340 (withdrawn in

The 4-4-2Ts of LNER 'C15' class were nicknamed 'Yorkies' as they were built by the Yorkshire Engine Co. in Sheffield. No. 9134 was photographed, in between turns, at Jedburgh. Originally NBR No. 134 it ended its days in 1955 as BR No. 67459. It was one of about a half dozen allocated to Hawick, and its sub-shed at St Boswells, and was regularly employed on passenger turns to Kelso and St Boswells.   *Bill Lynn Collection*

No. 67472, formerly NBR 265 and LNER No. 9265, then 7472, was photographed at Tweedmouth station in the first half of the 1950s with a through train for Kelso, Roxburgh Junction and St Boswells. This was another of the Hawick-based engines regularly employed on the Jedburgh branch. Note its Westinghouse pump at the side of the smokebox.

Armstrong Railway Photographic Trust/D.R.Dunn collection

1952 from Hawick shed) and 65305 (withdrawn in 1962). These locomotives had 5 ft 0 in. wheels and were placed in the power classification of '2F' by BR. One is preserved.

It was in 1944 that a member of NBR class 'K', later LNER class 'D32', worked a cattle train throughout between Blaydon, near Newcastle, and Jedburgh. The locomotive concerned was No. 9888. Designed by Reid it had entered service in December 1906 as a mixed traffic 4-4-0. It was renumbered 2449 by the LNER in 1946 and then a '6' was added after nationalization. It was withdrawn in November 1948 as 62449.

Sometime in 1946, on an unrecorded date, No. 3065, a Henry Ivatt-designed 4-4-0, of LNER class 'D1', was observed at Roxburgh Junction and Jedburgh, working a passenger train. Dating from 1911 and designed for the Great Northern Railway, this was certainly an unusual engine to find in this location, but all of the class had been transferred to the Borders after becoming redundant on the former Great Northern lines in the early 1920s. They were converted to Westinghouse brakes and adjusted to the NBR loading gauge. This class of engines gained the nickname 'Ponies' but were not popular with NBR crews, being rough-riding and with draughty cabs. All were to be withdrawn by 1950, the last to go being No. 62209 of Stirling shed. This particular locomotive, No. 3065, was allocated to Hawick shed in 1946. These locomotives had huge driving wheels of 6 ft 8 in., having been designed for fast passenger train work.

Another 4-4-0 was observed and photographed at Jedburgh in 1948. The locomotive concerned was No. 2358, of class 'D20', about to depart with a passenger train for Roxburgh. The locomotive was allocated to Tweedmouth and was no doubt rostered for the working which involved a Jedburgh engine, normally a 'C15', spending a night at Tweedmouth shed whilst a Tweedmouth engine, in this case a 'D20' spent the night at Jedburgh. The Jedburgh engine worked the 2.30 pm Kelso to Berwick via Tweedmouth. At the intermediate station of Twizell the Jedburgh crew exchanged footplates onto a Tweedmouth engine working a train towards Kelso, with the Tweedmouth crew taking over their 'steed'. At the end of the day the Jedburgh engine would spend the night at Tweedmouth shed before working the 6.30 am from Berwick and, also the 9.30 am and 2.35 pm train with a Tweedmouth crew. At Twizell, on the last of these trains, the crews would exchange once more, the Jedburgh crew returning home whilst the Tweedmouth crew headed eastwards to Tweedmouth and Berwick. The Jedburgh men never worked east of Twizell on this roster. The 2.35 pm train from Berwick was an interesting one in that it was advertised to the public as a train from Berwick to Kelso. However, in the working timetable it was shown as a through train from Berwick to Jedburgh. It ran in the last days of the LNER and also into British Railways' days until the great storm and floods in 1948 put an end to scheduled passenger trains on the branch.

In the 1950s a variety of locomotive types was recorded on the branch goods train. On 29th May, 1950, for example, 'J39' No. 64948 of Carlisle (Canal) shed, 12C, was seen as was No. 64880 on 17th October, 1953. The reason for the appearance of the Carlisle locomotives was that the morning pick-up goods, serving all station sidings on the branch, became a Carlisle working. An evening

On 13th July, 1946 Ivatt-designed 'D1' class No. 3065 is employed on the through working from Berwick and Tweedmouth to Jedburgh. Here it is pulling out of the main platform at Roxburgh Junction before running round its train of 'North Eastern' carriages and working tender first to Jedburgh. These locos were not liked by NBR crews and were nicknamed 'Ponies'.

Bill Lynn Collection

'J35' class 0-6-0 No. 64478 was photographed awaiting departure with the goods for St Boswells after completing its shunting in Jedburgh yard. This was a Carlisle Canal-allocated engine and would have worked the Carlisle to St Boswells goods before being employed on the Kelso and Jedburgh line as a 'fill-in' turn. It has done some hard work in view of the state of the lower part of the smokebox door! *Armstrong Railway Photographic Trust/M. Halbert Collection*

goods train was worked from St Boswells to Carlisle, arriving there at 10 o'clock in the evening. The locomotive returned to St Boswells soon after midnight arriving at St Boswells at 3.45 in the early morning. It was then used on the 'fill-in' turn to Kelso and Jedburgh before returning to St Boswells to work the evening goods to Carlisle. The fill-in turn consisted of a departure from St Boswells around 10.30 am to Roxburgh Junction then on to Jedburgh (about an hour earlier on Saturdays). Leaving at about 1.35 pm it would return to Roxburgh, reverse and set off for Kelso, shunting as required at sidings en route. Leaving Kelso at about 2.20 pm it would return direct to St Boswells. Locomotives observed on this working included 'J35' 0-6-0s including No. 64463 (of Hawick depot, 64G), 64478 and 64499 (both 12C, Carlisle Canal, engines) also Nos. 64948 and 64880 (*see above*) which were members of the Gresley-designed 'J39' class. The 'J35s' were designed by Reid for the NBR and introduced in 1908. The more powerful 'J39s' were nearly 20 years 'younger' having been introduced in 1926. After the closure of Canal shed on 17th June, 1963 the responsibility for providing the locomotive for this duty was transferred to other Carlisle sheds and on the 29th May, 1964 spectators would have been rather surprised to see '6P5F' 'Jubilee' class 4-6-0 No. 45696 *Arethusa* working the turn. Fortunately railway historian and photographer John Spencer Gilks was on hand to record the event for posterity, taking pictures as the train worked on the branch and also shunting in the sidings at Jedburgh (*see page 103*).

Yet another 4-6-0 class was observed on the goods when 'B1' class No. 61029 *Chamois* of St Margaret's depot was in charge on 26th May, 1962. Bill Berridge recalls 'B1' No. 61007 *Klipspringer* working the goods on an unspecified date; the appearance of a 'B1' on the line he rated as 'very occasional'. This locomotive belonged to Hawick at the time. The 'B1' class was a relatively modern Thompson design for the LNER, introduced for mixed traffic duties in 1942.

Bill Berridge also recalls the presence of several 'Scott' class 4-4-0s in the area because of their memorable names. Some that he brought to mind were *Ellangowan* (62425), *Wandering Willie* (62440), *The Talisman* (62428), *Quentin Durward* (62432) and *Jingling Geordie* (62430). He was in a good position to study the locomotives on the goods as he often played at the station house at Jedburgh with George Lumsden, the son of the station master, who was one of his classmates at school.

Although 'D34' class 4-4-0s were occasionally to be seen on some of the special passenger trains on the line in its latter years, it was quite rare to see one appearing on the Jedburgh branch goods. However on 1st August, 1959, No. 62484 *Glen Lyon* was so employed. These locomotives were designed by Reid for the NBR and entered service starting in 1913. BR rated them as '3P' locomotives.

Other locomotives observed on the Jedburgh goods in the late 1950s and early 1960s included the Reid-designed 0-6-0 'J37' class introduced for the NBR in 1914. Individual engines recorded were No. 64606 in June 1960 and No. 64577 on 30th July, 1962. Both engines were allocated to 64A, St Margaret's depot in Edinburgh. Another Gresley-designed 0-6-0 visitor at this time was 'J38' class No. 65912, also of St Margaret's, on an unrecorded date. Both the 'J37s' and 'J38s' were in power class '4F' whereas the 'J35s' were '3F'.

Hawick-allocated 'J37' class 0-6-0 No. 64539, with 'pick-up goods' headlamps, awaits its afternoon departure for Roxburgh Junction and St Boswells with a mixture of open wagons and vans. It required it would shunt Jedfoot sidings on its way to St Boswells.   *Transport Treasury*

In the years just before closure of the Jedburgh branch and the remaining services on the St Boswells to Kelso and Tweedmouth line most of the pre-Grouping and LNER locomotives were replaced by ex-BR Standard types including the class '4' and class '2' 2-6-0s. No. 78048, photographed at St Boswells on 4th September, 1963, was quite a regular engine on passenger trains through St Boswells and was also seen on the Jedburgh line.

Armstrong Railway Photographic Trust/J.M. Boyes

Towards the end of the life of the branch both Tweedmouth and Hawick sheds received an allocation of the H.G. Ivatt-designed 2-6-0s. These modern-looking machines, power class '4MT', were introduced for the LMS system in 1947 though many appeared after nationalization. No. 43138 was one of the Hawick-based engines which appeared on the Jedburgh goods on 18th June, 1964. The BR Standard version of this class also appeared on the branch, No. 76050 photographed leaving Roxburgh for Jedburgh is an example (*see page 104*). Other modern types of locomotive to appear included the BR's Standard design of '2MT' 2-6-0. Those in the No. 78045 to 78054 series were all allocated to Scottish sheds including St Margaret's and Hawick, and No. 78049 allocated to the latter depot, appeared on the goods on 3rd August, 1964. (Sister engine No. 78048 was regularly seen at Roxburgh Junction on Berwick and Kelso to St Boswells' services shortly before the line closed to passenger trains.)

Although photographs have been taken of a class 350 hp diesel shunter at Roxburgh Junction with the daily goods from Kelso to St Boswells after the closure of the Jedburgh line (*see page 102*), it is very unlikely that such machines ever worked on the branch.

Returning to passenger workings, there were several 'specials' in the late 1950s and early 1960s. The retention of the passenger platforms at the branch stations and Jedburgh terminus meant that passengers could still safely alight and climb back into carriages. The full details of these workings have been described in the previous chapter so it is sufficient here to summarize that on 4th April, 1958 'D34' class No. 62471 *Glen Falloch* worked a special train. Then on 9th July, 1961, 'J37' class No. 64624 and 'D34' class No. 62469 *Glen Douglas* (running in NBR livery and as No. 256) were in charge of a 'special'. Finally on 14th April, 1963 'B1' class No. 61324 headed an Easter-time tour.

Shunting at Kelso

As an aside it is worth briefly mentioning that until early 1922 all of the shunting of goods wagons at Kelso was performed by horses as the sidings were short and sharply curved. In 1921 the NBR purchased a 'Simplex' 40 hp chain-driven locomotive from the Motor Rail Co. It was a two-speed chain driven machine. This locomotive could shunt a maximum of five wagons at one time. The LNER gave it the classification of 'Z6', then 'Y11' in 1943. Although it is reputed to have saved much money, in that one member of staff could be dispensed with, and it was cheaper to run than conventional shunters, it did not prove to be a great success. It was transferred to Ware in Hertfordshire in August 1928. It received the LNER No. 8431. It was re-engined in January 1954, reputedly with the engine from a World War II tank. It survived for over 30 years until it was eventually withdrawn from Ware in 1956.

On leaving Kelso the Simplex was replaced by a Sentinel steam shunter of class 'Y1/2', built in 1927. This arrived at Kelso numbered 9529 but in 1946 the LNER renumbered it as 8138 and British Railways added 60000 to this number in July 1952, making it No. 68138. It was officially allocated to Hawick shed to where it travelled for attention such as minor repairs or boiler washouts.

The water tank was located on the platform at Roxburgh Junction station and the water crane at the platform end. Train crews preferred to take water here, rather than at Jedburgh, because the Jedburgh water was polluted by the effluent from the rayon factory which entered the Jedwater. Locomotives steamed much better on Roxburgh water. Note the small integral fire devil attached to the water crane: essential in Border winters!
(Both) Armstrong Railway Photographic Trust/
J.M. Boyes

General repairs required return visits to Edinburgh. It would thus have been seen traversing the tracks at Roxburgh Junction but there is no written record or photographic evidence of it visiting the Jedburgh branch. After 27 years' service at Kelso it was transferred to Ayr but withdrawn just two years afterwards.

Jedburgh locomotive shed

Jedburgh possessed a small locomotive shed from the earliest days of the line. It was located between the station building and the Jedwater. It was a single-road shed with stone walls and a slate roof. It could house two small locomotives. The shed road was connected via a single point to the run-round road. In very early days the run-round line led towards the small turntable which was located inside the boundary fence above the waters of the Jed. There was no additional stabling road leading from the turntable.

It was in the early 1940s that Jedburgh station lost its overall roof. A surviving LNER document, dated 1939, lists the proposed changes. The result was that the engine shed became a stand-alone building. The former dividing or separating wall between the locomotive shed and train sheds became the outer wall of the engine shed only, no longer having an overall station roof to support. At this time the shed retained the gabled roof which had been constructed in LNER days presumably to replace the original. However, the shed was in generally poor condition and in the 1940s a decision was made to carry out

'G9' class 0-4-4T No. 9354, the branch passenger engine, rests inside the engine shed at Jedburgh. These Reid-designed locomotives belonged to a small class of just 12 engines, built in 1909. They were all withdrawn between 1936 and 1940. Note the original pointed roof on the shed with its smoke vent, and, on the right, the station's overall roof, partly supported by the shed wall.   *Bill Lynn Collection*

improvements. Firstly, several brick and cement mortar courses were laid to replace the upper courses of stone on the shed walls; the brickwork was extended around the end of the shed also. Secondly, the roof was replaced by a new corrugated one of lighter construction, possessing a much lower pitch. This roof was slightly shorter than the previous one. A central smoke trough completed the change. However, the shed was finally closed in February 1949 so the improved shed saw little locomotive use! The track which had formerly run into the shed was cut back and a buffer stop was placed a few yards north of the shed doors. It gained a new role when it became the garage for the road vehicles which distributed, locally, the parcels and goods traffic arriving on the surviving goods trains. A 'new' water column was erected on the run-round loop for supplying the locomotives before they returned with goods to Roxburgh and St Boswells. St Boswells' shed was formally closed in November 1959 and after that time the workings in the Jedburgh branch came under the auspices of Hawick shed, though watering was still possible at Jedburgh.

The water tank was located on the roof at the rear, town end, of the locoshed. It was filled with water obtained from the River Jed. The water was pumped up using locomotive steam to power a Tangye engine. Unfortunately the river was much polluted at this point with effluent from the rayon factory and crews would experience steaming problems with their locomotives. Water was thus usually taken at Kelso or Roxburgh Junction.

This view of Jedburgh engine shed shows its final role as a garage and depot for the road vehicles which delivered from the station. The new roof and barely-used smoke vents are evident. A van and a trailer stand where the track of the shed road was located. This picture can be contrasted with the photograph on the previous page.

Armstrong Railway Photographic Trust

Chapter Fifteen

Accidents and incidents: Jedburgh and Jedfoot

Our tale of the accidents and incidents at Jedburgh after the line's opening begins with a gruesome and unfortunate event. During the construction of the Jedburgh Railway children, no doubt attracted by the novelty of the situation, much frequented the line, taking particular pleasure from playing about on empty trucks which had been left by the workmen. It was on the afternoon of Wednesday 16th July, 1856 that three or more children, according to the *Caledonian Mercury* of 19th July, were amusing themselves about 20 yards away from Jedburgh station. They were told to leave on more than one occasion by an adult but, after this man had left the scene, they returned to continue their game. Soon afterwards there was a cry from one of the children in the trucks. Some stone masons had been working close by. They approached the trucks and found one of the children suffering from hideous injuries. He was lying close to the line with his hand very badly crushed and blood flowing copiously from his nose, mouth and right ear. He was lifted up and supported but died very shortly afterwards. Medical aid had arrived quickly but to no avail as the boy was already dead. He was later identified as Thomas Purves, the son of a labourer, also Thomas, who lived in Jedburgh. The father was away at the time but returned to the news that his son was a mangled corpse. It was deduced that young Thomas had been crossing the rails between two trucks which had been set in motion either by himself or his companions. Whilst creeping out from between the trucks his head had been caught between the protruding buffers causing the serious injuries which ended his life.

The newspaper went on to say that it was fortunate that other accidents of this nature had not taken place as there had been other incidents of boys playing with wagons. Apparently it was only a few days previously that another boy had been knocked over in the same manner though on this occasion the boy had fallen between the rails and thus escaped being crushed by the collision of two wagons.

It is inevitable that any accidents and incidents taking place at a newly-opened railway are considered newsworthy, and the Jedburgh branch was no exception in this respect. The *Jedforest and Teviotdale Record*, being a new arrival in the publishing world, was particularly interested in such events. On 26th August, 1856 this newspaper reported an incident close to Jedfoot station. A certain John Wood, employed by a merchant, W. Brown of Jedburgh, was driving his cart past the station when several cart-loads of coal, likely from the station yard, passed closely by. Wood stopped and held his horse's head but his cart was contacted by the second of the coal carts. The wheels became entangled and the coal cart turned over on its side discharging the coal onto the road. The driver of the coal cart, who had not been paying close enough attention, realised his mistake and had to gather up all of the coal whilst John Wood 'stood laughing into his sleeve at his neighbour's reward for his unconcern, which to say the least, certainly deserved him right.' Fortunately no-one was hurt in this incident.

The same newspaper reported that on Friday 4th September, 1856 a 'smash' occurred at Bonjedward Mill as a result of an error by the crossing gate keeper. An excursion train had passed the crossing on its return to Jedburgh from Edinburgh. The gate keeper, in error, thought that, what the newspaper described as 'locomotive business', was over for the day. However, he was wrong as a short time after he had closed the gates, supposedly for the last time, the engine returned with the empty carriages and smashed the gate into pieces. The lococrew must have been totally unaware of what had happened for they steamed on as if nothing had taken place. The newspaper surmised that it was probable that the gatekeeper had either neglected or mistaken his instructions as it was likely that the officials along the line would have been made aware of the arrangements for bringing back the empty carriages. The paper went on to comment that it was fortunate that the gates had not been closed before the laden excursion train went past 'else there is no saying what might have happened to a number of our most respected townsmen'.

In December 1856, on the same day as flooding caused damage to the track near Nisbet, a quantity of loose timber stacked in the station yard at Jedburgh, was recovered after it had been found floating around in the water. Fortunately the train service had been suspended.

The New Year of 1857 had barely started when the *Record* reported that on Saturday 10th January the train expected at Jedburgh at 10.10 am did not reach the station until nearly 1.00 pm. The cause of the delay, apparently, was what was described as the failure of the 'spindles' of the new locomotive recently set to work on the branch. Another locomotive had to be brought in so that the train could reach its destination.

An accident took place in Jedburgh station on 24th August, 1859. The *Teviotdale Record* stated that at about two o'clock in the afternoon of this date the passenger guard on the Jedburgh line, whilst performing his normal duties, stumbled over the iron lever which was used in shunting the carriages. He fell in front of the train and a wheel passed over his foot, severely bruising it and crushing one of his toes. He was fortunate not to suffer greater injuries!

Such accidents and incidents were not untypical of those that occurred on relatively newly-opened lines, especially branch lines, at this time. It appears, in view of a decline in the frequency of their reportage, some lessons were learned, and that both railway employees and passengers became more aware of health and safety matters. However, some incidents, especially those with more serious consequences, continued to be described in both the local and regional newspapers.

The *Kelso Chronicle* of 4th August, 1865 reported on an incident which, though frightening, did not result in any death or injuries to the passengers intending to travel on a train from Jedburgh to Roxburgh or beyond. The date of the incident was Friday 28th July and was attributed, according to the newspaper's reporter to the engines on the Jedburgh line being 'old and rickety affairs, discreditable to the railway company, and also dangerous'. The 30 or so passengers travelling on the 7.30 am train had just taken their seats and the train was just about to depart. They were startled by a noise like the firing of a cannon causing them to jump up from their seats. A loud hissing noise then emanated from the engine and the station became filled with steam. The passengers left the carriages and fled along the platform. The cause of the alarm was the bursting of a pipe 'connecting the water and steam tanks'. The damage was so great that another locomotive had to be called for, using the railway telegraph. Even so it was some time before some of the passengers could be persuaded to re-enter the station and re-join the train. Eventually an hour behind schedule the train departed but Kelso passengers had to wait a further considerable time at Roxburgh, presumably having missed their connection onwards.

A severe snow storm on New Year's Day at the start of 1867 caused disruption to the train service on the Jedburgh line. In the evening the wind rose considerably and much drifting took place. The train which was due to arrive at Jedburgh on the Sunday morning at 10.15 am did not arrive until after one o'clock, some three hours late. The 5.25 pm departure back to Roxburgh did not leave at all. However a rapid thaw soon allowed services to return to normal though a careful watch had to be kept on the River Jed which was in full flood, carrying large pieces of timber and tree branches.

The *Newcastle Journal* of 13th September, 1869 recorded a 'melancholy death' at Jedburgh station. John Ormiston, a blacksmith, aged 75, disappeared from his home in Newcastle-upon-Tyne. On 9th September a police officer stationed at Camptown on the Scottish side of the border met with a person matching Ormiston's description. On satisfying himself that he had the right man he set out for Jedburgh. About two miles from Jedburgh they were overtaken by the man's son who agreed to look after his father and return him home by train. The police officer returned to Camptown whilst Ormiston was taken on to Jedburgh station. Whilst waiting at the railway station some bread and cheese were sent for but no sooner than the old man had started eating then he began to choke. In a few minutes he was lifeless on the ground. His body was conveyed to the police office in Jedburgh. The deceased was said to have been in a weak state of mind for some time and it was thought that his death was as a result of exhaustion.

There was a narrow escape for a train approaching Jedburgh station on 8th February, 1871. The engine driver of the train due at Jedburgh at 9.30 pm noticed something lying on the rails. He applied the brakes at once and tried to stop his train before he reached the obstacle but could not do so. Fortunately the locomotive was not derailed and carried on past the spot. The track was inspected immediately afterwards and it was found that two rail chairs, weighing about 14 lb. each had been placed on the rails. Fortunately for the train they had been laid in such a way that the locomotive had pushed them off without any damage being done. Had they been placed differently then the result could have been very serious. The police proceeded to investigate the matter, believing that young boys were probably responsible but the *Kelso Chronicle* said that by a week later they had not been able to identify and apprehend the guilty parties.

The *Scotsman* newspaper of Wednesday 29th May, 1872 and the *Southern Reporter* of 30th May, both reported on an unusual incident which happened on a through return excursion train from Jedburgh to Edinburgh. John Haig, a labourer from Jedburgh, was a passenger on the train on the returning journey. Before the train had reached St Boswells station, the engine driver observed Haig perform a highly perilous act. He climbed out of the carriage on which he was travelling onto the step and then tried to pass from this carriage to an adjacent one. Not content with this he attempted to climb on to the carriage roof. The driver stopped the train at St Boswells where Haig was removed, with the intention of ejecting him from the station. However by some means Haig escaped from the custody of the station master and chased the now-departed Jedburgh train along the track. He succeeded in jumping in via the window of a carriage just a short distance from the platform. Haig was brought before the local Sheriff at Jedburgh and charged with contravening the by-laws of the NBR by jumping into a train whilst it was in motion. The Sheriff imposed a fine of 32s. including costs. If he failed to make the payment he was to experience a fortnight's imprisonment. Around the same time another Jedburgh labourer, a certain Thomas Anderson, was charged under similar by-laws. As a passenger train approached the platform at Jedburgh station, Anderson was seen to jump from a carriage. The Sheriff fined him 22s., including court expenses, with the alternative of eight days' imprisonment if this sum was not paid.

Three years later on there was another accident at Jedburgh, this time involving a railway employee, a certain William Young. He was one of the porters who worked at Jedburgh station. Some wagons were being shunted in the sidings and Young was caught between the buffers of two of them. He was so severely crushed that he died 12 hours after the accident took place. According to both *The Scotsman* and *Dundee Courier* newspapers, he was just 46 years of age.

Jedburgh station in the mid-1870s was suffering from a series of thefts. The *Southern Reporter* of 24th June, 1875 reported an incident beneath the headline: 'Jedburgh, another alleged theft by railway guards'. On Sunday 20th June two men were apprehended near Edinburgh on a charge of having stolen a gallon of ale (or half a gallon in the report in *The Scotsman*) from a cask at Jedburgh railway station. They had both, until recent times, been in the employment of the NBR as goods guards. Named as David Russell and Thomas Scott they were brought to the court in Jedburgh, convicted and sent to prison.

Another Jedburgh railway-porter with the surname of Young was involved in an incident at the station later the same year which was described in the *Southern Reporter* and *The Scotsman* newspapers. George Young was accused, together with a local carter named James Hunter, of assaulting John Miller, another carter, at Jedburgh station on the 13th September, 1875. Hunter and Young unbuttoned some of Miller's clothes and rubbed sheep dip onto his person causing severe injury and pain! When brought to court on 11th October both pleaded not guilty but after the presentation of evidence Sheriff Russell found them both guilty and sentenced them to 30 days' imprisonment.

An accident involving livestock took place in the sidings at Jedburgh station on 3rd August, 1882. According to *The Scotsman* and the *Southern Reporter* four waggons [*sic*] of lambs were being drawn out from the cattle-loading bank. One of the waggons was for Kelso and it was shunted onto the front of the 2.10 pm passenger train, clearly running as a 'mixed' train on that day. This wagon came into contact with the van at the front of the train, the end panel of which was broken by the buffer-end of the cattle-wagon which was full of the lambs. This waggon overturned but fortunately all of the lambs escaped unhurt. *The Scotsman* reported that with the exception of the smashing of the van all of the damage done was 'trifling'. The departure of the branch train was held up by just 15 minutes!

On 10th December, 1885 the *Southern Reporter* recorded the death of a man on the railway below Jedburgh station on the 3rd December. Apparently the man was walking along the railway line when a train approached and knocked him over. His body was much mangled but was conveyed to the local police station. He was described as a stranger, apparently of between 30 and 40 years of age. In one of his pockets there was a time and pay book, with several addresses near to Newcastle. His pockets also contained two railway tickets: a half return railway ticket from Edinburgh to Lochgelly (dated 21st November), and another, from Edinburgh to New Hailes (dated 23rd November). On the day after the accident the body was identified as that of William Anderson, a pit-sinker, of New Craighall, near Niddry [sic]. He left a widow and three children.

The *Teviotdale Record* for 5th November, 1887 contained an item referring to the engine of the early morning train becoming derailed at 'the distance points' (presumably those located some way from the signal box or station platform) at Jedburgh whilst performing shunting. The train, referred to as being from Edinburgh, but presumably with only a through carriage from the capital, had arrived on time. However, the efforts to return it to the rails resulted in the passengers for the 9.47 am train being delayed for some considerable time, it being necessary to obtain another engine from Roxburgh. Fortunately the derailment caused no permanent damage to the locomotive or to the permanent way.

The same newspaper, on Thursday 27th April, 1893, reported on a 'somewhat serious accident' which took place at about 10.30 am on 24th April in the sidings at Jedburgh railway station. A woodman by the name of William Craig was engaged in loading a truck with some trees of considerable size, using a crane. One of the trees slipped and fell onto Craig's right leg. His leg was broken just above the ankle; his foot was dislocated and bruised severely. He was attended to by a local doctor, Dr Blair, but was afterwards able to be taken to Hawick 'in a conveyance'.

It was in 1920 that an incident, fortunately not resulting in injury, took place at Jedburgh. At that time the regular branch goods engine was a somewhat aging 0-6-0 tender engine of the NBR's class 'D' and on the day in question it was shunting the station sidings. Apparently the train crew (driver, fireman and guard) did not have their attentions devoted to railway matters; they were discussing cricket on the locomotive's footplate along with the Jedburgh station master. During the shunting manoeuvres the locomotive managed to over-run some points and became derailed. It is said that the station master was not in uniform at the time but after the incident happened he changed into his uniform so as to produce a report of what had taken place. Apparently there is no record of whether the crew received an official reprimand. Mr Shaw had been appointed station master at Jedburgh during 1920.

The level crossing at Bonjedward was the location of the two following accidents; both involved trains running through the crossing gates. There is a strange coincidence, that in both cases the crossing keeper responsible for the opening of the gates was the wife of one of the train crew. Firstly a train in the hands of Jimmy Grieve, the driver, and his fireman Bob McDonald, demolished the gates after Jimmy's wife had failed to open them. In the second case it was the wife of driver Davy Lamb who failed to open the gates because she had overslept. The rules stated that the gates should be opened 10 minutes before the time that the train was expected to pass. Bonjedward crossing was the site of other collisions with the level crossing gates. Although a fixed distant signal at Jedburgh warned lococrews to keep a look out at the crossing they apparently seemed to ignore the warning.

On at least three occasions the crossing gates at Bonjedward were demolished by trains, one being soon after the line opened and the other two being in BR days. The crossing keeper's cottage survives today. *Alexander Turnbull*

One further potentially serious accident took place at Jedburgh station. It was reported in the *Southern Reporter* of 26th August, 1926. On the morning of Friday 20th August a team of men were engaged in dismantling the old bridge at Jedburgh railway station. A certain William Adams, resident in Hawick, was working on a wooden structure when he lost his balance and fell a distance of six feet onto the ground. His fall dislodged a number of huge stones which fell on top of him. Medical aid was called for and he was examined by a doctor. Fortunately he did not suffer very serious injury though there were some minor injuries to his back.

An article in the *Hawick News and Chronicle* newspaper reported on a fire that had taken place in the shed of the locomotive department at Jedburgh station on 22nd December, 1938. This could have been a serious incident especially if the fire had spread to the station building or if the branch locomotive had been damaged. The Hawick fire brigade (directed by a Mr Ridley) responded to a phone call from Jedburgh. On their arrival they discovered that the fire had been put out by some local men using extinguishers. However, in view of the initially alarming nature of the fire and the proximity of other station buildings, it had been considered necessary to summon a fire appliance. When they had satisfied themselves that there was no chance of the fire starting again, the fire crew returned, with their appliance, to Hawick. About six yards of the roof of the shed was burned through.

Members of the Hawick Fire Brigade are photographed in front of their appliance in 1936. Some of those shown, plus the appliance, would have attended the locomotive shed fire in December 1938. *Museum of Fire, Scottish Fire and Rescue Service*

Chapter Sixteen

Accidents and incidents between Jedfoot and Roxburgh and on towards Kelso

It was the newspaper with the grandiose title of the *North & South Shields Gazette and Northumberland and Durham Advertiser* that provides the first report of an incident on the section of the branch from Jedfoot to Roxburgh. In its edition of 14th August, 1856 the newspaper headlined a 'Malicious Attempt to Overturn a Train upon the Jedburgh Railway'. The event took place on the morning of Saturday 2nd August, 1856, when a person unknown described as a 'heartless villain', gained access to the point levers and changed the points at Jedfoot station. Furthermore a quantity of stones was placed upon the rails with the obvious intention of derailing the engine of the train. Fortunately the work of the villain was discovered and the stones were removed from the line before the arrival of the early train, otherwise the consequences for the newly-opened railway could have been very serious indeed. The Directors of the Jedburgh company immediately offered a reward of 10 guineas to anyone who could identify the person or persons involved. Reports appeared in the *Kelso Chronicle* of 8th August and the *Belfast News-Letter* of 12th August. The *Chronicle* further commented:

> What the motive could possibly be which prompted any one to perpetrate so horrid a crime, as mercilessly to imperil the lives of an unknown number of human beings is difficult to conceive of. There are, we trust and believe, few such persons. Rare as they are, however, they seem numerous enough to place the lives of railway travellers in eminent danger …. We trust that the culprit will be caught. Depend upon it, whoever he may be, he is a coward of the first water [*sic*] and richly deserves being held up to universal contempt amongst civilised men.

Another accident reportedly took place towards the end of September 1856 which resulted in inconvenience, but fortunately no harm, to the persons travelling from Jedburgh to the Rood-Day Fair at Kelso. A train became derailed near to Old Ormiston as a result of a section of rail becoming out-of-place. So as to get the passengers to the Fair the newspaper reported that a locomotive, the *Blucher*, reportedly of 'former days', was put into 'travelling trim' to convey the passengers to Kelso.

Three months later, in December 1856 there was a period of inclement weather and heavy rain resulting in the local rivers becoming very swollen. It was dark when the 6.40 am train from Jedburgh to Roxburgh made its journey, nothing untoward or dangerous being noticed because of the darkness. It arrived at its destination safely. However, on its return towards Jedburgh, about half an hour later, it could proceed no further than Nisbet. The embankment leading to the bridge over the Teviot had been carried off by the flood. It was necessary, for the rest of the day and for a period thereafter, for all passengers to be conveyed by road coach between Nisbet and Jedburgh. Team of railway workers was set to work when the water level subsided and the rails were returned to their former course within a few days.

A far more serious happening took place on 21st September of the following year when one of the surfacemen, employed by the Jedburgh Railway, met with an accident when working close to his home village of Nisbet. He was employed in tarring the southern portion of the railway bridge over the Teviot near to Nisbet. The rails that morning were very wet and slippery as a result of an overnight frost. He missed his footing and fell to the ground between the sleepers. This portion of the bridge was not filled in with earth or ballast between the rails. His cries for help were heard by some workers at the nearby Nisbet Mill. They carried him home immediately and medical aid was obtained. One of his legs was found to be broken and he had also sustained injuries to his head and chest. Fortunately he made a recovery from his accident. All three of these incidents were reported in the *Kelso Chronicle* and the *Teviotdale Record.*

The *Teviotdale Record* reported that two accidents occurred on successive days on the Jedburgh branch, specifically on 7th and 8th December, 1858. In the first a train from Kelso to Jedburgh came off the rails near to Nisbet station. Fortunately no one was hurt, another engine was procured, and the passengers continued their journey. The second took place just as the 5.10 pm train was leaving Nisbet station. An unspecified accident happened to the engine. As a result of this the passengers were held up for one hour.

The length of the line between Roxburgh Junction and Old Ormiston station was the site of a serious derailment on Thursday 29th March, 1860. The accident was attributed to the wet weather and the 'shaky state' of the track according to the *Kelso Chronicle.* About 120 yards after leaving Roxburgh the 3.30 pm train left the rails and ran along the cutting. The engine nearly overturned and the end of a first class carriage, fortunately not carrying any passengers, was entirely smashed in. A neighbouring second class carriage (containing, according to the newspaper, a representative of Clarke & Co. of Paisley, a certain Mr George Armstrong, and Mrs Oliver of the Cross Keys Hotel in Kelso) was also damaged. The passengers were uninjured. About 30 yards of track was torn up in the incident. The traffic on the line was suspended as a consequence until the line could be repaired, about 100 men being called in to repair the line. They worked through the night and normal services were able to resume on the Friday morning. Whilst the work was going on the Harrow and Spread Eagle hotel omnibuses transferred passengers between the branch and the main line. The newspaper editor put forward the theory that the accident had been caused by sleepers sinking into the soft ground. The use of ash ballast, rather than stone, during the construction of the line cannot have helped drainage.

Some five years later it was the severe weather that posed a threat to the branch services according to the *Southern Reporter* of 1st June, 1865. The water level in the local rivers had risen dramatically and at the Teviot bridge the water was almost up to the level of the rails. The broad haughs and meadows nearby were deep under water and the water reached some way into the garden of the Nisbet station master. A nearby field of potatoes was completely covered with water. Fortunately the water levels abated quickly and the threat to the bridge went away.

It is not known whether any goods wagons or passengers emanating from the Jedburgh line were involved in the first of the two accidents that took place at Heiton sidings between Roxburgh Junction and Kelso on 18th November, 1865.

In the first of these accidents, described in the *Manchester Courier and Lancashire General Advertiser* of 25th November as 'serious and alarming', a passenger train from Roxburgh was in collision with the rear of a goods train, the passenger locomotive striking the guard's van and driving it into the remainder of the goods train. The goods train had been dispatched from Roxburgh at 5.58 pm after the 5.10 pm from Jedburgh, which left Roxburgh at 5.37, would have arrived safely at Kelso. The passenger train from St Boswells was running 19 minutes late and so did not leave Roxburgh until 6.13 pm. The accident report, signed by Captain F.H. Rich after his inquiry, stated that the passenger train consisted of a tank locomotive, a horse box, a second class carriage with a break [*sic*] compartment, one first class, one third class carriage and a break-van [*sic*] with a guard in it. It had reached between 15 and 20 mph when the crew sighted the Heiton distant signal in the 'clear' position. The driver then spied the goods train but did not know immediately that the goods train was on the same line of rails and it was not until he was about 70-80 yards away that he applied the brakes. There was no time to whistle for the guard's brake or reverse the engine. The passenger train locomotive was completely wrecked and the wagons in the collision were, according to the newspaper report, reduced to firewood. At least 15 passengers, plus the three members of the train crew, received injuries such as being rendered unconscious, becoming concussed, and receiving cuts and bruises, some serious. The guard's van and three wagons of the goods were broken and a fourth was derailed. The goods train driver had not acted in accordance with the instructions he had been given at Roxburgh, having left six wagons on the main line whilst he shunted a further two into Heiton sidings.

This 2019 view shows the remains of the loading platform of the goods depot at Heiton Siding, just 60 yards or so from the site of the two accidents in 1865. A public footpath now passes the site.   *Author*

Any Jedburgh residents, having spent that day in Kelso, or indeed any other passengers from Kelso or points east, would have needed to make alternative arrangements for their journeys to or from Kelso that evening. The track blockage would have prevented the last branch train of the day, the 6.50 pm from Kelso, scheduled to depart from Roxburgh for Jedburgh at 7.00, from running close to its proper timings.

The second Heiton accident, also investigated by Captain Rich, took place on the 29th November, just 11 days after the first one. On the day in question a special goods train was started from Kelso at 7.10 pm for Edinburgh via St Boswells. This train was a heavy one with 14 loaded, and five empties, with just one brake van and the crew had lost a minute or two on their schedule of 19 minutes from Kelso to Heiton. The train stopped at Heiton, the guard's van (carrying red tail lights) was uncoupled, and the driver received instructions to pull up his train and put the empties into the siding. The passenger train had left Kelso on time at 7.25 pm. The locomotive was No. 18, an 0-4-2 tender engine, originally built by R. & W. Hawthorn in 1846. It was hauling a train consisting of a guard's van, one third, one first and one second class carriage, with a brake compartment for the guard. The crew of the passenger train believed that the goods train was not going to stop at Heiton where the collision actually occurred. The passenger train driver appeared not to have noticed that the Heiton distant signal was in the 'on' position. On realising that a collision was imminent he reversed the engine but appears not to have whistled for the guard's brake. The engine collided with the brake van of the goods at between 12 and 15 mph. The frames of the engine were bent in the accident; both the buffer beam and eccentric straps were broken. All of the carriages were derailed. The van next to the engine had one spring and its brake screw broken. The guard's van of the goods train was smashed but nevertheless was driven forward into the wagons of the goods train, four of which were broken to pieces. Captain Rich considered that the accident was caused by gross neglect on the part of the passenger train driver who had failed to keep a proper watch. On this occasion passengers on the last train from Kelso to Jedburgh via Roxburgh would not have been inconvenienced as their train would have arrived at Jedburgh by the time of the accident. Both accidents were reported by Rich on the 9th December to the Lords of the Committee of Privy Council for Trade who, after examining them, transmitted copies to the North British Railway.

There was a follow-up letter regarding the two accidents at Heiton in *The Scotsman* in December of 1865. A correspondent to the newspaper, using the *nom-de-plume* of 'A Traveller' stated that he believed that the accidents were not caused by the culpable carelessness by the railway's servants, but by the general mismanagement by the company. He considered that the stations were understaffed and that the engines, carriages and plant were disgracefully bad. He proposed that Heiton sidings should be closed once a cart bridge had been constructed over the Teviot and facilities transferred to Roxburgh. He concluded that savings resulting from the Heiton sidings closure would be more than adequate for the bridge construction and would result in an 'obvious improvement'.

The Teviot bridge near Nisbet features in a report of a fatality which appeared in the *Glasgow Evening Citizen* of 1st February, the *Edinburgh Evening Courant* of 3rd February, the *Southern Reporter* of the 4th February and the *Illustrated Berwick Journal* of 5th February, 1869. A man, subsequently identified as John Haig, a hawker of Berwick, had been walking along the line near to Nisbet station. As he crossed the bridge over the Teviot a goods and luggage train was approaching. This train had left Roxburgh Junction at 1.40 pm. The bridge at that time was the original, rather narrow, timber-built structure. The driver of the engine had observed Haig upon the bridge and used every endeavour to use his brakes to check the speed of the train to allow time for the man to escape from the bridge. However, despite Haig having heard the warning whistle and broken into a run his efforts were unsuccessful. Realising that he would not be able to cross in time he made for the side of the bridge but was knocked down by the buffer beam of the engine. The wheels of the locomotive passed over his neck, fracturing his skull and smashing his small neck bones. An arm was also fractured. Of course he died instantaneously. After the train stopped Haig's body was conveyed in the guard's van to Jedburgh station, whence it was taken to the police office where it was examined by Dr Hume. Here it was identified by the keeper of the Model Lodging House where Haig had spent the previous evening. The deceased was said to be of about 35 years of age and he left a widow and family. This very sad accident took place on the afternoon of Saturday 30th January.

An accident took place at Roxburgh Junction on Tuesday 27th September that year on the NBR line towards Kelso. Whilst not occurring on the Jedburgh branch itself it had an impact upon the branch passenger train service. As reported in the *Glasgow Evening Post* of the following day, a goods train was passing along the line when several 'waggons' left the rails, broke the parapet of a small bridge and ran onto the road below. In the accident the waggons were smashed and part of the goods they contained was destroyed. Fortunately no persons were injured or killed in the accident. It has been recorded that the remains of these waggons were hauled back onto the track by connecting them with a steel hawser and using an engine to haul them up the bank by the bridge.

The *Edinburgh Evening News* of Tuesday 29th July, 1873 reported an unfortunate accident which occurred at the Teviot bridge on the previous Saturday. A certain John Watson, a resident of Jedburgh and a shoemaker by trade, was returning home from the Kelso Games on the last train of the day. At Roxburgh Junction he and several others got out of the carriages as they had been told of some delay. He mistook the train departing for Kelso for the Jedburgh train and jumped into an empty van. After the train had started Watson became aware of his mistake and he leaped from the van near the Teviot bridge. His head made violent contact with a strong wire attached to a telegraph pole which probably killed him instantly. His body rolled down the embankment towards the river where it was discovered a little before 11 o'clock the following morning. He left a widow, Jane, and two young children, John and Robert.

A sad incidence of suicide, reported in both the *Southern Reporter* and the *Dundee Evening Telegraph*, took place on the Jedburgh line on Tuesday 9th July, 1878. One of the surfacemen (platelayers) had been walking along the track about a quarter of a mile from Kirkbank station, on the following morning. He discovered the body of a dead man lying at the side of the track. The body as later identified as that of Alexander Durie, lately a commercial traveller in Newcastle, and formerly of Galashiels. The deceased had, apparently called at Kirkbank station on the evening of Tuesday 9th July. He had written a letter to a friend in Jedburgh intimating that before it was delivered he would be no more. After this it was believed that he had gone along the line and placed himself in front of the last train to Jedburgh, by which means he met his death. His skull was found to be fractured but the train had not passed over his body.

A 1st January, 1880 court case resulted in the dismissal on a technicality of two masons and a labourer, all resident in Jedburgh, who were accused, under the Poaching Prevention Act of 1852, of being in possession of a sack of game and sending it by train from Kirkbank station to Jedburgh station, addressed to a certain Henry Miller. Thomas Waugh, Thomas Gallacher and William Lamb pleaded not guilty but were not convicted after 'a difficulty arose during the evidence'. The *Southern Reporter* covered the court case.

The same year three men, William Landores, Alexander Stewart and Charles Smith, all of Kelso, were convicted of a serious and unprovoked assault committed on a railway guard, James Grant, on a train somewhere on the Jedburgh line. As summarized in the *Reporter* of 16th December, 1880, Landores was found guilty and, in view of his previous convictions, received a prison sentence of six weeks. The other two were also convicted and received one month's imprisonment, all with hard labour.

The *Southern Reporter* of 5th July, 1883 contained details of an accident at Roxburgh station which had consequences for the Jedburgh line. The previous Thursday, 28th June, had been Jedburgh Fast Day [*sic*] and the train in question was heavily laden with people who had set out to spend the day as a holiday. It was the first branch train of the day from Jedburgh to Kelso and as it crossed a set of points at Roxburgh station two of the carriages left the rails and were overturned against the water columns. The roofs and sides of the carriages were smashed and the footboards torn off. A panel in the door of the guard's van was knocked in whilst the water columns were damaged. The platform surface was torn up for a short distance. The passengers were much alarmed by the mishap but fortunately no one was injured, although it was some time before several of the passengers fully recovered from the nervous shock which they sustained. No reason was identified for the occurrence of the accident.

An accident involving livestock was reported in the *Glasgow Evening Post* of 11th October, 1883. On the evening of the 10th the last train of the day (from Jedburgh with passengers for Edinburgh) had reached the neighbourhood of Nisbet station. It ran over a bullock which had strayed onto the line. The collision resulted in several of the carriages being thrown off the rails but fortunately none of the passengers was hurt. The train was consequently much delayed and the passengers missed their connection at Roxburgh onto the Kelso to St Boswells train. As a result they also missed the Carlisle to Edinburgh express which they would have caught at St Boswells.

An NBR foreman painter was accidentally killed at Nisbet station on 26th May, 1886. The *Edinburgh Evening News* of the 28th May gave no details of how the accident took place. However the *Southern Reporter* of the following day contained much more detail of his death. The painter was Robert Atkinson Downes (or Downs in the 1881 census) who lived at 33 High Street, Balleyfield, Portobello, in Edinburgh. He was 38 years old and had been in the NBR's service for over 16 years working at the Baileyfield Works. He had left Edinburgh earlier that morning to inspect some painting on the Nisbet bridge. Shortly after noon he had arrived at Nisbet station where he left the train and proceeded to walk along the line in the direction of the bridge. He hadn't walked more than 30 yards when he was overtaken by the train which he had just left. Somehow the locomotive ran over his body and severed it in two. The engine driver immediately shut off steam and stopped the train. Downes left a widow, Margaret, and a son, James, in Portobello. He was buried at his local cemetery on the following Sunday, 1st June. The unfortunate incident was also reported in the *Portobello Advertiser* of Friday 28th May.

Just over 10 years later, in 1896, the same newspaper reported a 'very unpleasant experience' for passengers on the 1.25 pm train from Jedburgh on Friday 9th October. This train had departed some 15 minutes late from Jedburgh and was double-headed. About 100 yards from Nisbet station an empty horse box was seen to be lying across the single line of rails. Further progress was thus blocked. The incident had apparently occurred during shunting operations at Nisbet. The *Edinburgh Evening News* report went on to say that at that time there was no telegraphic communication at the station and thus 'the engine between which and the goods train the overturned horsebox lay, proceeded on to Jedburgh'. This statement certainly lacks clarity as to precisely what happened as the report goes on to say that it was found to be impossible to clear the line. However, the Kelso and Edinburgh train was brought up from Roxburgh and the passengers from Jedburgh, who had scrambled along the banks at the side of the line, were picked up by this train, running 45 minutes late. (In the absence of the telegraph how was this train summoned?) The Jedburgh train had been carrying Lady Ramsay of Banff and some distinguished citizens of Jedburgh on their way to Lord Roseberry's race meeting.

On 25th April, 1902 an incident took place at Nisbet and a description appeared in the *Edinburgh Evening News* dated the following day and the *Southern Reporter* of 1st May. A boy, with the surname of Marchbanks, was travelling with his mother and some other children in a railway carriage between Jedburgh and Roxburgh. The boy had been playing with the door handle. The door swung open and he fell from the train. He received bruises to the head and some other injuries, fortunately none of them serious.

During the major rail strike of 1919 there was a minor incident at Roxburgh. As mentioned earlier one elderly driver, named Rutherford, did not agree with going on strike and he agreed to work one passenger train between Jedburgh, Kelso and St Boswells. The fireman, Pat Nolan also agreed to work, and a guard John Cullen, with a large family, could not afford to give up his pay by going on strike. The station master at Roxburgh, Thomas Dagg, aged 47, operated the points and signals from the Roxburgh Junction signal box. Unfortunately Dagg was very much an amateur when it came to operating the box. Also there was a fault in the signalling system and the locomotive was derailed at some catch points. This resulted in the locomotive sliding down the bank into the station master's own garden. His wife Annie's reaction is not recorded!

On a September morning in 1924 the crossing gates at Nisbet were damaged by a train of empty livestock wagons running as the 4.15 am special from Hawick to Jedburgh in the charge of driver Rutherford. Instructions (originating in the February 1879 *NBR General Appendix*) stated that crossing gates should be kept shut until 10 minutes before the passage of the next train with a red light on the gates to warn locomotive crew if they were still closed against the train. Also the level crossing at Nisbet was protected by a home, or stop, signal with a distant signal giving an advance warning. On the morning in question there was dense fog in the area as the station master at Nisbet came on duty. Driver Rutherford on the locomotive said that as he approached Nisbet the distant signal was in the 'off' position. This should have indicated that the following 'home' signal was cleared for the train to proceed over the crossing. However, on approaching the latter he observed that the home signal was at danger. He applied the brakes to try and stop the train. He was unsuccessful and both the locomotive and the first wagon had passed the crossing by the time the train came to a stand. Now it is a fact that hot days cause signal wires to expand and can cause signals some way from the signal box to show a false reading. On the previous day to this accident the Nisbet station master had adjusted the wires to allow for the high temperature. Unfortunately he had forgotten to reverse the adjustment for the severe frost that had occurred on the following night. As a result the distant signal was falsely showing clear. The station master received a mild reprimand and was reminded of the need to be vigilant when adjusting the wires as he should have been aware that the wires could contract overnight and should have adjusted them accordingly.

A hurricane rainstorm from the west caused the Jedburgh branch train service to be suspended briefly on Tuesday 30th December, 1924. The storm caused the level of water in the River Jed to rise rapidly and a little to the north of Jedfoot station, opposite the junction of the Jed and the Teviot, the line was undermined at several points over a stretch of some 50 yards. At one point, according to the report in *The Scotsman*, the bank was washed away to such an extent that the metals and the sleepers were suspended three feet above a strong rush of water. A rapid fall in the water level allowed the railway gang to repair the track the following morning allowing trains to run over the repaired track that same afternoon, the morning service having been cancelled.

A similar heavy rainstorm, reported in *The Scotsman* on 6th November 1926, caused damage to the railway line in precisely the same location as the previous incident some two years earlier. On the 5th November, just to the north of Jedfoot station a considerable length of the railway line was submerged beneath the waters of the Teviot which was in full flood. It was necessary, once again, to suspend the train service. Throughout the day the mails and passengers were conveyed between Nisbet and Jedburgh by motor buses. Railway traffic outward from Jedburgh was also taken by road to Nisbet which acted as the temporary terminus of the trains from Roxburgh Junction. As a result of a tree being uprooted by the gale, causing damage to 60 wires, telegraphic and telephonic communications broke down and for a time Jedburgh was isolated from the outside world. Some damage was also caused to a bridge near Jedburgh railway station.

It was in the 1930s that the first aid knowledge and training of the Nisbet station master was more than useful. A lady, Jessie Gibb, worked at West Nisbet Farm, for which establishment cattle cake arrived by rail. A cake-breaker, known locally as a 'cake-bricker' was used to crush the oily cattle cake before it was fed to livestock at the farm. Jessie managed to get her sleeve and arm trapped in the device and suffered extensive injuries to her arm. As the farm was at a distance from the nearest doctor (whose surgery was in Jedburgh) the station master was called for and, by the use of a tourniquet, he was able to stop the bleeding and save the unfortunate lady's arm.

As a result of further flooding caused by heavy rain on the weekend of the 12th and 13th November, 1938 the Roxburgh to Jedburgh branch line was closed to all traffic. About 120 yards of the permanent way was under water at Nisbet station and 60 yards of the embankment supporting the rails were completely washed away. Passengers between Jedburgh and Nisbet were conveyed by motor bus, with Nisbet once again becoming the temporary terminus for trains from Roxburgh. Surfacemen worked all day on Monday 14th to repair the track so that rail traffic could be resumed. Reports of this flooding appeared in both *The Scotsman* and the *Southern Reporter*. (This incident is alluded to in the next chapter on the closure of the line.)

There was interference with the Jedburgh branch goods service and its onward connections when a derailment occurred at Roxburgh Junction in early October 1948, the branch passenger train service having already finished by this date. At that time the Tweedmouth-Kelso-Roxburgh Junction-St Boswells line was being used by diverted Newcastle to Edinburgh trains following the damage caused to the East Coast main line in the floods of August of that year. A goods train was derailed at Roxburgh Junction on Friday 1st October, but speedy work by the engineers allowed the Kelso to St Boswell's line to be reopened at 2.00 am on the Saturday morning. Fortunately no casualties resulted from the derailment. A report on the derailment appeared in the *Berwickshire News and General Advertiser* on Tuesday 5th October.

Finally a heavy shunting incident at Kirkbank in early 1951 caused the buffer stop at the end of Kirkbank siding to be pushed backwards. The short length of track to which the buffer stop was attached was also pushed backwards resulting in a gap appearing between the rest of the siding track and this short length. Things would not have been so difficult to remedy if it were not for the fact that a vacuum-braked van was left standing on this short length. This occurred just before Tom Little, relief station master at Roxburgh, came to inspect the station for the first time. Although the contents of the van, namely fertilizer for farm use, had been emptied out, the incident had not been reported. Tom used his initiative and asked one of the Roxburgh team of platelayers to fetch two sleepers with grooves cut into the ends which could be laid in place across the gap between the wagon and the siding rails. A locomotive was obtained and drawn up to the end of the rails. It was then attached to the wagon coupling and very gently the wagon was hauled across the sleepers until all four of its wheels were back on the track. With the wagon now removed it was much easier to move the errant buffer stop towards the siding rails and re-attach them with new fishplates.

Chapter Seventeen

Meteorological matters
and the closure of the line

The consequences of inclement weather badly affected the train services on the Jedburgh branch on numerous occasions. In both 1875 and 1906, for example, it was very heavy snowfalls which stopped all traffic. In each case clearance of the snow allowed services to resume. Heavy rainstorms were another matter.

The 37 mile-long River Teviot has its source at Comb Hill on the border of Dumfries and Galloway. It flows generally eastwards until it discharges into the River Tweed. On the way its flow of water is increased by the discharges from various tributaries. Slitrig Water and Rule Water drain the slopes of the Cheviot Hills south of Hawick and Bonchester Bridge whilst the Alewater, joining the Teviot near Ancrum, drains the area to the north of Hawick. At Jedfoot the Teviot is joined by the Jed (itself over 20 miles long with several tributaries) that carries water down, through Jedburgh, from the slopes of Carter Fell in the Cheviots. Following heavy rainstorms the water level in the Teviot can rise very rapidly, so that the river bursts its banks and spreads water over its adjacent floodplain. It is unfortunate that the lowest point on the Jedburgh branch railway is at the bridge where it crosses the River Teviot.

As early as January 1861 there was a newspaper reference to a rapid thaw breaking up the ice on the local rivers with the high water levels depositing floes over large areas on the adjoining haughs. Fortunately the flow of water and ice down the Jed did not affect the station and line at Jedburgh, and the wooden bridge carrying the railway over the Teviot at Nisbet emerged unscathed, though bridges further down the river were broken. Perhaps it was further events such as this which stimulated the NBR into replacing the timber-built Teviot bridge with something more substantial. The *Southern Reporter* of 15th April, 1875 reported the railway's intention to erect an iron bridge over the river.

On 5th June, 1894 there were newspaper references to flooding in Teviotdale close to the railway. The large 'haughs' near Crailing were covered in water to a depth of several feet with the tops of the hedgerows being barely visible At the Teviot railway bridge an observer reported that the water was near to the top of the structure. On this occasion the damage to the track was not recorded. A device known as the 'Tweedometer' registered a rise of 5 ft in one morning just below the confluence of the Teviot and Tweed!

On Saturday 27th December, 1894 Jedfoot station wired to Edinburgh to say that there was flooding between the up home and distant signals. The permanent way was undermined and the track had become unsafe. The last train to pass safely had been the 11.40 am passenger service from Roxburgh Junction. Repairs were carried out by 4.30 pm the same day and the line was reopened on the Monday morning. However on the 30th December, a hurricane force wind bore down the Teviot Valley from the west. Jedburgh had already received a heavy rainstorm on the previous Saturday and the local rivers were already very swollen. A little to the north of Jedfoot station, opposite the junction of the Jed and Teviot, the railway line was undermined at several points over a length of about 50 yards. At one point the ballast was completely washed away so that the metals and sleepers were suspended 3 ft above a torrent of water. The cattle train from Gorgie to Jedburgh was cancelled as was the first train from Jedburgh, the 7.12 am 'mixed'. Passengers and parcels were carried to Roxburgh by a bus. Later a bus linked Nisbet with Jedburgh and a shuttle service of trains connected Nisbet with Roxburgh. The bus service was run by Moore's of Jedburgh.

Fortunately the level of water fell rapidly and the railway repair gang were able to get to work and make good the damage. Their speedy efforts allowed the train service to be resumed in the afternoon of the following day, the 1.46 pm Jedburgh to Roxburgh being the first train to travel cautiously over the repaired track. The service was short-lived as the track was once again washed out for some 30 yards on 1st January and once again a bus service had to be instituted.

In November 1926 the same section of line was affected once more. The Teviot was in high flood and in the Crailing and Nisbet areas hundreds of acres of grassland were under water. Near the junction of the Jed and the Teviot, not far from Jedfoot station, a considerable section of the railway was completely submerged. The train service had to be suspended and throughout the day both passengers and mails were transported between Nisbet and Jedburgh by Moore's motor buses. Outgoing traffic from Jedburgh also had to be taken to Nisbet station which was just above the water level. The Tweedometer registered over 12 ft of flood water.

The water level at Nisbet reached an even higher level on 12th-13th November, 1938 when about 120 yards of the permanent way at Nisbet were under water. Sixty yards of the 'banking' supporting the rails were washed away as a result of the flooding. Surfacemen worked all day to restore the track once the water level subsided. The train service was, as usual, replaced by buses between Roxburgh and Jedburgh. In all of these cases the full railway service was soon restored after the floods had subsided. However, the storms and resulting floods of 1948 were to have major consequences for the future of the railway to Jedburgh.

According to the *Monthly Weather Report of the Meteorological Office* for August 1948 the first week of that month brought very heavy rain to most of the British Isles. However, a few days later a depression located over the Bristol Channel moved north-eastwards across England towards the North Sea. Heavy thundery rains occurred in the Midlands and North-East England on 11th August spreading into the Borders on the 12th. For example 6.21 inches of rain fell in just 24 hours at Kelso onto already saturated ground. Similar figures were recorded throughout the Borders region with some locations in Berwickshire receiving a third of their annual rainfall in the first two weeks of August. The heavy rainfall caused widespread destructive flooding and the destruction of crops. Damage was caused to infrastructure, especially roads, bridges and railways. At Kelso the Tweed was reported as rising to a level over 6½ inches higher than the previous highest flood of 1831.

The damage was catastrophic. In the east of the region the torrent on the Eyewater and its tributaries swept away a pillar on the railway viaduct at Eyemouth. On the East Coast main line between Berwick and Dunbar there were breaches in many places with 11 bridges and culverts being washed away. South of Berwick the trackbed was flooded between Goswick and Scremerston whilst ballast was washed from under the track at Chathill. Rails and sleepers were often left suspended in mid-air. As reported in *The Scotsman* and on BBC radio news bulletins, rail traffic on the Eskbank and Penicuik branches ceased, also between St Boswells and Reston. There were landslides on the Waverley Route to the west, one at Gorebridge and one at Tynehead. All services were suspended on the Kelso to Tweedmouth line, also the branch lines to Selkirk and Peebles. On the Jedburgh branch the swollen waters of the Teviot burst their banks and the embankments on the approach to the railway bridge over the River Teviot were washed away.

We are fortunate that the Jedburgh station master at the time, John Bennett, published his memories of the events at that time. He records his personal relief that on Thursday 12th August, 1948 the last train of the day from Roxburgh arrived safely at Jedburgh with the locomotive adjourning to its shed. Throughout the afternoon his signalman had relayed periodic reports on the information he was receiving about successive bridges on the East Coast coming down and trains being held up.

At 1.30 am the next morning Mr Bennett made an inspection tour of the Jedburgh station and goods yard, being concerned about the levels of water in the River Jed which flowed close to the station site. He recorded that the rain had ceased and the river was just contained within its banks, but that the nearby main road was flooded. Police were in attendance and road traffic was stopped.

Later, at 6.00 am Bennett was back on duty and spoke with the driver of the first morning train. The driver made the suggestion that it would be a good idea if the locomotive were to be uncoupled from its carriages and run up the line for a preliminary inspection to investigate any possible damage. Some 300 yards beyond Jedfoot station the locomotive had to stop because the ballast had been washed away (into the field behind Mounthooly Farm) for a distance of between 50 and 60 ft leaving the rails, with their attached sleepers, being suspended 6-8 ft in mid-air above 'a big yawning gap'. He records that dozens of soaking wet rabbits were marooned on small islands throughout the surrounding fields. 'There was no escape; they either perished there or were picked up by poachers'.

Both passenger and goods services were immediately suspended though the railway cartage crews and their vehicles maintained a service of sorts with Hawick and St Boswells on the Waverley route. At the start of the suspension of the passenger service a bus service was instituted between Jedburgh and Roxburgh Junction. Onward connections were not as good as normal due to the stopping train service on the St Boswells, Kelso and Tweedmouth line being severely curtailed because of the necessity of diverting the main line Edinburgh-Newcastle-London expresses onto this route. Being mostly a single line the number of train paths was very limited. At St Boswells these trains ran onto the Waverley Route whilst at Tweedmouth they resumed their normal route southwards. There were inevitable delays and extensions to the schedules of these trains.

One other incident associated with the flooding was the derailment of several goods wagons in the sidings of Jedburgh yard. Local efforts to get them back on the rails with ramps proved to be unsuccessful. A breakdown crane was requested from Tweedmouth but there was no path for it between the diverted expresses on the Tweedmouth to Roxburgh line. A young assistant engineer arrived at Jedburgh by road and he approved the method of trying to haul the wagons back onto the track. This was tried and was successful. However, it was achieved at the expense of the breaking of several of the rail chairs, something that the local permanent way crew had been trying to avoid. At the time rail chairs were in short supply.

On 20th August the *Railway Gazette* referred to the closure of the Jedburgh branch because of the floods, whilst on the same day *The Scotsman* reported on a statement from British Railways (Scottish Region) that it was now possible to book passengers to all stations in the flood area through a combination of rail and road services. The bus services would be based at Dunbar, Berwick and St Boswells and would run as closely as possible to the scheduled times of the trains that they were replacing. It was pointed out that horses, other livestock, carriages and similar traffic could only be conveyed by road after consultation with the station master at the sending point. Livestock, coal and mineral traffic by goods train could not be accepted yet. The article mysteriously ended with the statement: 'Train services between Roxburgh and Jedburgh were resumed yesterday'! On 27th August the *Railway Gazette* also reported that the branch service had been resumed on 19th August. In fact the service was still maintained by a bus.

However, after a short time, and as a result of the paucity of passengers, the bus service was reduced to a taxi. This, like the bus, called at the intermediate stations on the branch and was to continue until the date when normal passenger services on the line could be resumed. Meanwhile some discussions took place at a high level and the question of the resumption was debated. A date at the start of February 1949, probably 2nd February, was the date scheduled for the restart of passenger services. Bennett therefore cancelled the taxi service from this date. However on the evening before, Mr Bennett received a telephone call from a member of BR's Scottish Mobile Squad in Edinburgh, a Mr Ian Forrester, to say that the decision had been made not to resume the passenger train service. The taxi service was therefore to continue for the time being. Unlike on the Eyemouth branch to the east where a large viaduct was repaired allowing passenger trains to resume (and continue for more than 10 years), there was to be no reprieve for the Jedburgh branch passenger trains. The cessation of public passenger trains had thus taken place on the 12th August, 1948.

The Jedburgh Town Council met in early January 1949 to discuss the 'discontinuance' of the passenger train service on the branch. Dean of Guild Elliot recommended that talks be entered into with the Railway Executive (Scottish Region) with a view to pressing for a reinstatement of all of the former facilities. Bailie Campbell in suggesting that the council should enlist the

This was a regular scene on the Jedburgh branch between Nisbet and Jedburgh. Here the River Teviot has burst its banks in the vicinity of the Black Bridge, overflowing onto the surrounding meadows. *Jedburgh Historical Society Collection*

These are the remains of the Boss Brig, the weir which allowed water to drain from the haughs (flat meadowland) on the south side of the river in an attempt to minimise the erosion of the trackbed. The track was removed some time previously. *Photos from the 50s/James C. Todd*

backing of the county council said that the latter had an important interest having regard to the fact that the people who had been in the habit of using the intermediate stations on the branch line were now just as badly off as, if not worse than, those in the town. The motion to arrange a meeting with the Railway Executive was adopted unanimously. Provost Moncur and Dean of Guild Elliot, plus Councillor T. Wilson, were appointed to represent the council.

The Roxburgh County Council met on 14th February. They decided that they would protest against the Railway Executive's decision to close the branch line to passenger traffic. The convener's committee placed before the full committee a recommendation that they support the Jedburgh Town Council in their complaint about the service withdrawal. In the event of the reinstatement not being successful they made a strong request for a better coordination of bus and train services to serve Jedburgh and the villages between Kelso and Jedburgh which were formerly served by the railways. Bailie C. Campbell and Councillor W.L. Johnston proposed that the county council should make separate representations to the Railway Executive. The resolution was passed.

However, all representations and discussions were unsuccessful and the decision to end the public passenger service on the line was confirmed leaving the goods trains as the principal traffic on the line. But a few more passenger trains traversed the line, namely the Jedburgh Sunday School charters and the enthusiast rail tours.

As an aside, even the through line from St Boswells to Tweedmouth via Kelso was under considerable threat of closure and only its goods traffic continued to produce reasonable revenue. In 1955 the number of through passenger trains on this line was reduced from four in each direction down to two and even this service eventually ceased on 15th June, 1964, the line closing completely on 1st April, 1968. In the 1950s the line, already singled in places, was occasionally used for diverted trains when, for example, there was engineering works or blockages on the East Coast main line. Also the siding accommodation at Roxburgh Junction was reduced as goods services declined.

One consequence of the end of the passenger service was the ending of the employment of level crossing keepers at Ormiston, Nisbet Gatehouse and Bonjedward. With the relatively small number of passenger trains, and just the daily goods on the branch, occupying these positions cannot have been an arduous job.

The Jedburgh branch was declared open again to rail traffic on the 18th August, 1948, though this was solely for the daily goods train which, at that time, made a single return journey on the branch. Undoubtedly the goods service was maintained because of the considerable traffic linked with the North British Rayon factory at Jedburgh. Much of this was coal though there was some sundries traffic carried in vans rather than open wagons. When North British Rayon entered receivership in July 1956 the writing was on the wall for the goods train service, though it struggled on until 1964. The last goods train ran on Friday 7th August of that year, having run on just three days a week for some time, usually Mondays, Wednesdays and Fridays. The goods trains were steam-hauled to the end.

The branch has been closed and the demolition and recovery teams have done their work. This is the site of Jedfoot station and yard looking towards Jedburgh. The station building has been demolished though part of the loading gauge survives. Fencing has replaced the gates at the former level crossing.   *Photos from the 50s/James. C. Todd*

A second photograph of the site of Jedfoot station looking along the trackbed towards the Boss Brig and the Teviot Bridge. The further portion of the trackbed now forms a very pleasant footpath accessed from the main road via gate and the station yard.   *Jedburgh Historical Society*

The two pictures on this page show stages in the demolition of the Black Brig over the Jedwater. The first picture shows the demolition contractor's crane, fitted with caterpillar tracks, lifting the transverse girders of the bridge decking. The second picture shows what was left once the demolition engineers had left the site. Just one pier remains standing with rubble littering the site.   *Alexander Turnbull (upper)/Jedburgh Historical Society (lower)*

Local rail enthusiast, historian and author, Bruce McCartney, recalls seeing the Jedburgh goods on several occasions at Jedfoot and its locomotive shunting Jedburgh station yard. On one visit to Jedburgh he spied the notice advertising the withdrawal of the goods trains and the closure of Jedburgh goods depot from Monday 10th August. He therefore determined to make a visit to photograph the train on the 'last day' which he calculated would be Saturday 8th August. He planned to start at Kirkbank and then shadow the train to Jedburgh on his motor-bike. No train appeared at Kirkbank so he biked into Jedburgh where he was told that the last train had, in fact, run on the day before. He hadn't been aware of the three days per week, Monday, Wednesday and Friday, 'runs-when-required' nature of the goods as the end approached. He thus missed the chance of a final day photograph!

The *Railway Observer* of October 1964 provided the following epitaph:

JEDBURGH BRANCH. The Roxburgh Junction to Jedburgh Branch, latterly used by the daily freight train, was completely closed with effect from 10th August.

Some sad pictures taken after the closure of the line, show some of the stations and various engineering features on the branch in differing states of demolition.

The site of Jedburgh station after all has been demolished and levelled apart from the remains of the locomotive shed and the small mound where the yard crane was located. Shortly the site will become a hive of activity as the works associated with the A68 road re-alignment and the development of the trading estate commence.   *RCTS Image Archive*

Chapter Eighteen

The line today

For two reasons it is hardly necessary for a *full* description of remains of the Jedburgh branch line to be described in detail here.

Firstly, visitors to the tourist information offices in Jedburgh or Kelso, or even to the former telephone boxes in Eckford or Nisbet, which have been converted to contain racks of tourist information literature, can obtain helpful leaflets. These describe the public walkways which have been created over most of the former Jedburgh railway line. These excellent leaflets, such as the one entitled *The Borders Abbeys Way* contain maps, photographs and detailed instructions as to how to gain most benefit from a walk along the old railway.

Secondly, modern technology allows views of much of the line to be discovered from the comfort of an armchair. For example using Google Earth or Google Maps (the usual disclaimer applies) and the 'little yellow man' allows substantial parts of the line to be inspected and followed. For example the route of the line between the A68 road and Jed-Forest rugby ground and the entire length of the line between Nisbet and Kirkbank can be followed this way and views over the route of the former line can be obtained elsewhere. In addition aerial views of the Jed and Teviot valleys, also available on the internet, can identify the position of the former stations, road crossings, former bridge sites and other features associated with the line.

However, an outline guide may be useful to indicate where inspection of the line's remains can be made.

At the Jedburgh end of the line the station site has been completely obliterated as a result of the re-alignment of the A68 road and the development of commercial and industrial units. The filling station is a useful marker as to where the former station building lay. To the north of this area and on the east side of the A68 the alignment of the railway can be followed between the trees and adjacent to the town's Jed-Forest Rugby Club ground at Riverside Park. The alignment then disappears into impenetrable undergrowth beyond a small bridge over the Jed.

At this point it is worth mentioning that some of the trackbed, especially at the former station sites, is now private property and permission *must* be requested to approach or walk along such land even for such 'harmless' pursuits as taking photographs.

From the A68 road between Jedburgh and Bonjedward it is possible to look over the roadside hedge and follow the alignment close to the River Jed in the valley beneath. The tarmac road leaving the A68 on its east side leads down to the site of the former crossing keeper's cottage protecting the line at Bonjedward Mill Farm. This cottage still survives and the route of the trackbed northwards can be seen from this point.

The trackbed between here and the A698 at Jedfoot is on private land but can be seen, in part, from the Jedfoot to Jedburgh minor road via Walkersknowe. Between Jedfoot and the approach to the site of the former Teviot railway bridge the

Drivers entering Jedburgh from the north on the A68 from Edinburgh, and visitors to the adjacent retail outlets, would not suspect that this filling station was built on the site of the former station. The demolition of the station site after closure allowed the road to be re-aligned, widened and landscaped.   *Author*

Only a few relics of the Jedburgh branch survived to be entered into museums. This collection of platform barrows was more lucky for, on closure of the station, they were obtained by local residents and preserved, as attractive garden features, in their house on Kenmore Bank, Jedburgh.   *Author*

Jed-Forest rugby ground was located between the railway line and the River Jed. The straight length of the line opposite the ground has now been converted into part of the 'Jedburgh Paths' network. The small signpost on the right identifies this length as part of both the 'Jedforest Trail' and the 'Dere Street Dash', a reference to the name of the old Roman road.   *Author*

This is Bonjedward crossing keeper's cottage situated adjacent to the line close to the Jedwater. The road crossing the alignment of the former railway line now leads to farm buildings and part of the line here is used for field access. Several accidents, described in the text, occurred here and the crossing gates were renewed on several occasions.   *Author*

Towards the end of the life of the railway the narrow bridge over the river was replaced and the road re-aligned. A small lay-by is located at the site of the entrance to Jedfoot station yard and the 'new' gates allow pedestrians and dog-walkers to gain access to the footpath which passes the station site. *Author*

In the former Jedfoot station yard the footpath follows the old railway trackbed past the site of the confluence of the Jedwater and the Teviot rivers and passes adjacent to the former goods platform. All buildings have long disappeared but a small section on the platform edge is exposed, particularly after the vegetation has died down in autumn. *Author*

trackbed is now a public footpath. Access is gained via a gate and part of the former rear platform edge is immediately visible on the left of the former yard at Jedfoot. The trackbed provides easy walking and glimpses are seen of the former ballast and railway fencing. In recent years soil was washed away revealing some of the piles of the Boss Brig. So as to allow pedestrians to reach Nisbet, the public path then makes a detour leaving the trackbed in an easterly direction to reach the B6400, Crailing to Nisbet road. However, it is possible, by following the Teviot's southern river bank, to walk to the site of the former railway bridge where the pier bases still survive. This area can be very boggy after periods of flooding. After joining the B6400 it is necessary to turn left and follow the road over the somewhat delicate-looking road bridge towards Nisbet. The former Nisbet station house is on the left-hand side and is now in private ownership. Beyond the house, the lane to the left, the former trackbed, can be followed for a short distance. On its left are the remains of the edge of the former platform and, until recently, the yard beyond on the left contained a grounded passenger carriage body. Storms have caused the sides and ends to fall down and the remains now consist of little more than a pile of timber almost lost amongst the weeds. This is, of course, on private property.

Retracing one's steps to the road, and the site of the former level crossing, it is possible to carry straight onwards and walk along the entire length of the former line as far as Kirkbank station. This is the section of track which can be viewed and followed on Google Maps. From this section of the trackbed there are excellent views eastwards towards the Teviot and Ormiston House is visible to the right. Agricultural vehicles, and others for the cottages use this track and care should be taken.

The gently curved trackbed straightens as it approaches the site of Kirkbank, formerly Ormiston, station. Here the path makes a deviation to the right via the former station yard to avoid the private property associated with the former station house and garden. As at other stations some remains of the platform edging exist and in the front garden is a relocated sign which formerly indicated the route to the station from an adjacent main road. The path descends towards the minor road leading down to the A698 via Kalemouth bridge near to where the Kalewater joins the Teviot. At this minor road it is necessary for pedestrians to turn left and approach the remains of the former railway bridge. Here the footpath onto the Kirkbank to Roxburgh section can be accessed on the right. Once again this section, now partly shaded by trees, provides views towards the river and over some delightful countryside and parts are in cutting where spring flowers thrive!

Approaching the site of the former Roxburgh Junction branch platform the path deviates and descends to the right allowing access to the village road between the remains of the two former overbridges, the piers of which still survive. (The gardens of a private house now occupy the last few yards of the trackbed and access is not possible.) A short walk to the right brings the visitor to the village bus shelter inside which is a very interesting display of photographs and information regarding the viaduct which formerly conveyed the Roxburgh to Kelso line over the Teviot.

From here it is possible, if one wishes, to retrace one's steps and then gain access on the left, to the footpath, signposted 'Kelso', which continues across the

A short deviation from the footpath along the old trackbed allows inspection of the remaining pier which supported the bridge carrying the railway over the River Teviot between Jedfoot and Nisbet stations. This area has always been subject to flooding after heavy rainfall, necessitating repeated repairs to the approach embankments. Clearances were not generous on the bridge and at least one fatal accident occurred here. *Author*

Nisbet station house was formerly occupied by the station agent and, for a time, also doubled as the local Post Office. Now it is a private residence near the location where the road from Crailing crosses over the weight-limited bridge as it enters Nisbet village. The site of the former level crossing is clearly visible, the former trackbed crossing the road at right angles. *Author*

A short walk from the Nisbet station house along the former trackbed in the direction of the River Teviot allows inspection of the edge, and part of the surface of the former Nisbet station platform. What survives is part of the rebuilt platform with concrete coping stones and upright panels. Most of the platform forms part of the fenced-in garden of the occupants of the station house. *Author*

Until the early years of the 21st century the remains of an old North British Railway coach were in use as a garden store in the former Nisbet station yard. The storms of the winters of 2017 and 2018 caused considerable damage and the carriage is now in a derelict and collapsed state. *Author*

Left: The Kalemouth bridge is a suspension bridge, almost 200 years old, linking Kirkbank station with Kalemouth on the Kelso to Jedburgh road (now the A698). Intending passengers from the villages of Morebattle and Eckford would have crossed this bridge en route to Kirkbank station, following the direction shown on the surviving 'finger-post'. Today it carries a severe weight restriction and is Category A listed.   *Author*

Below left: In the garden of the former station agent's house at Kirkbank, formerly Ormiston, station is this finger post indicating the way to the station. It is not a railway sign as such but was formerly half a mile away at the side of the road near the Kalemouth bridge over the River Teviot. It is nicely painted to aid its preservation.   *Author*

Top: This photograph was taken from the permissive footpath from Nisbet to Kirkbank at the side of the Kirkbank station site. It shows the remains of what may have been a replacement for the original weigh-house at the exit from Kirkbank station yard. One other former yard building survives nearby, also in a semi-derelict state.   *Author*

Right: Walkers along the footpath between Nisbet and Roxburgh have to divert from the trackbed as the bridge over the Kalemouth road was demolished some time after the railway closed. On regaining the footpath on the Roxburgh side of the bridge this is the view that greets them: a pretty sylvan glade! *Author*

Kirkbank yard and sidings were located to the east of the line, behind the station platform and buildings. This photograph was taken from the footpath which bypasses the station and visible in the foreground is the ramp leading up to the goods platform surface. This is now private property with vegetation hiding much of the original station.   *Author*

viaduct in the direction of Heiton. The viaduct provides excellent views over the river, particularly towards Nisbet to the south. At the north end of the viaduct is the site of Heiton sidings where the two major accidents took place in the 19th century. At the sidings' site the remains of the goods unloading platform still exist. At this point the footpath leads onwards towards Kelso, or alternatively it is possible to use the path to descend from the sidings site towards the Heiton Mill road where the stone piers of the viaduct can be inspected or photographed from the adjacent small car park.

Fortunately some individuals saw fit to purchase, and look after, relics related to the line. The former signpost indicating the route to Kirkbank station has already been mentioned as has a surviving single-line staff. Also in this category of preserved items must be included some former Jedburgh station platform hand trolleys which are decorative features in a private garden in the town. Finally the Museum of Transport in Glasgow contains the preserved NBR 'K' class No. 256 *Glen Douglas*, which worked a rail tour over the line shortly before closure.

The Jedburgh branch may have closed many years ago but its remains can still give much pleasure to those who come to visit this delightful part of the Borders.

In the foreground are the abutments of the bridge which formerly carried the Jedburgh track into the branch platform at Roxburgh Junction station. A few yards beyond are the abutments of the bridge which carried the double-track line from Kelso into the station. The public footpaths paths leading along the trackbeds towards the Kirkbank and the River Tweed viaduct commence on the right-hand side between the two sets of abutments.   *Author*

Many trains from Jedburgh continued beyond Roxburgh towards Kelso crossing the magnificent viaduct over the River Teviot. This photograph was taken from the riverside field between the two former rail lines. The site of Heiton sidings is hidden in the trees beyond the viaduct on the right-hand side.   *Author*

Bibliography

The Directory of Railway Stations (R.V.J. Butt), Patrick Stephens, 1995
Border Railways Remembered (Bill Peacock) Cheviot Publications, 1984
'Railway Days at Jedburgh', article by John Bennett in the above, 1984
Memories of Lost Border Railways (Bruce McCartney), published by the author, 2016
Roxburgh Village (Brian Wain), printed by Kelso Graphics, 1983
Old Jedburgh (Judy Olsen), Stenlake Publishing, 2003
Scottish Railways (O.S. Nock), Thomas Nelson & Sons, 1950
A Regional History of the Railways of Great Britain, Vol. 6, Scotland: The Lowlands and the
   Borders (John Thomas), David & Charles, 1971
The First Railway Across the Borders (George Dow), issued by the LNER in 1946 to
   commemorate the opening of the North British Railway
Random Reflections of a Roving Railwayman (J.M. Bennett), published by the author, 1975
British Locomotive Catalogue, 1825-1923 Vol. 6 (Bertram Baxter, David Baxter and Peter
   Mitchell) Kestrel Railway Books, 2012
The North British Railway - A History (David Ross), Stenlake Publishing, 2014
The Northumberland Central Railway (N.D. Mackichan), published by the author, 1998
The North British Railway (Hamilton Ellis), Ian Allan, 1955
The North British Railway Vols 1 & 2 (John Thomas), David & Charles, 1969/1975
Berwick to St Boswells via Kelso (Roger Darsley and Dennis Lovett), Middleton Press, 2015
Border Country Branch Line Album (Neil Caplan), Ian Allan, 1981
The Great Borders Flood of 1948 (Lawson Wood), Tempus
Locomotives of the North British Railway 1846-1882 (Stephenson Locomotive Society),
   published by the SLS 1970
The Silk Mill at Jedburgh (Derek Rae), Jedforest Historical Society, 2016
Auld Roxburgh (Brian Wain), published by author, 2002
LNER Carriages (Michael Harris), David St John Thomas, 1994
Sectional Maps of the British Railways (Railway Clearing House Maps), Ian Allan, 1948
Slater's Directory Scotland, 1893
Meteorological Office monthly weather reports especially 1948
British Railways Locomotives Combined Volume and Locoshed book published by Ian Allan
   from 1944 onwards (various editions)
North British Railway Study Group Journal (various editions including articles by Mike Smith)
'Focus on the Jedburgh Branch' by David Stirling in Scottish Railway Preservation Group:
   Blastpipe No. 50 (Winter 1980/1)
'Sir Walter Scott and Two Early Railway Schemes' (Michael Robbins) in Railway Magazine,
   February 1951
Spittal Point Development Brief (Berwick-upon-Tweed Burgh Council), 2004
'Jedburgh' (A.E. Wallace) London & North Eastern Railway Magazine, 1938
Various editions of Back Track, Steam Days, Railway Observer, Scots Magazine, Railway
   Magazine, London Gazette and the Edinburgh Gazette
Various issues of The Jed Eye Community News Magazine
Various railway passenger timetables and working timetables (NRM, NBRSG and in
   private ownership)

Websites referred to, and providing useful information, included those of Ancestry UK,
Institute of Civil Engineers Virtual Library, RailScot, Railways Archive (Accident
Archive), Wikipedia, Grace's Guide, Geograph, Jedburgh Border Games, Jedforest
Instrumental Band, LNER Encyclopaedia, Sixbellsjunction, the Stephenson Locomotive
Society, the Railway Correspondence & Travel Society, Smugmug, Crailing, Jedburgh
Town Online, Eckford and Nisbet Community News and the Ordnance Survey (Scotland)
plus those of many of the organizations acknowledged below.
Many newspapers have been consulted either on-line via their own websites, via the
British Newspaper Archive or in hard copy when not available online. They are identified
and acknowledged individually in the text.

Acknowledgements

I would like to acknowledge, with much gratitude, the assistance provided by the following organizations and individuals who have been very patient and generous in responding to my questions and requests for assistance:

North British Railway Study Group; Scotland's People; Dollar Academy Archives; Stirling Council Archives; Scottish Railway Preservation Society Archives; Stirling Library; Stirling Archives; Jedburgh Library; Armstrong Railway Photographic Trust; British Newspaper Library; Parliamentary Archive, Westminster; Northumberland Archives, Woodhorn; The Hub, Hawick; Search Engine, National Railway Museum; Museum of Science and Industry, Manchester; Museum of Fire, Scottish Fire and Rescue Service; Scottish Borders Council; Crailing, Eckford and Nisbet Community Council; Jedburgh Jail and Museum; Mary, Queen of Scots, House, Jedburgh; Photos of the 50s; the Clapperton Collection, the rugby clubs of Galashiels, Hawick and Jedforest; the Rugby Football Union; World Rugby Museum, Twickenham; the National Archive, Kew; the National Archives of Scotland; The National Records of Scotland; Jedburgh Local History Society; Borders Family History Society; *Border Telegraph*; the Jed Eye; Transport Treasury; the Lothian Estate; the Monteviot Estate; the Buccleuch Estate; Scottish Border Council; Stenlake Publishing; Transport Treasury; Institution of Civil Engineers; St John's church, Jedburgh.

Alastair Nisbet; Bill Black; Chris Veitch; James Black; Bruce McCartney; Jimmy Cook; Ken Fotheringham; John Burgon; Geoff Corner; Stuart Bouglas; Donald & Nancy Mathieson; David Dunn; Mrs Anne Brydon, Steve Armitage; Jim Sedgwick; Graham Watt; Chris Milner; Barrie Forrest; Graham Dolan; Jim Hall, Alexander Turnbull, Dave Farries; Mrs Margaret Casserley; Douglas Nicol; Thomas Welsh, David Stirling, Bill Berridge, Deborah Mason, Zilla Oddy; Francis Dalrymple-Hamilton (Signalling Record Society).

Especial thanks are due to Bill Lynn of Gateshead, who has willingly provided me with much information from his extensive records and collections: locomotive lists, train timings, working timetable information and photographs.

Most of all I would like to offer grateful thanks to my wife Diana for walking many miles in search of on-the-ground evidence and for accompanying me to various archives and museums, both searching for evidence and in taking notes.

The internet, generally has been an invaluable research tool and has allowed me to identify and access records which otherwise may have remained undiscovered. Those who have offered photographs will see their name appearing below those that have been used. Even if offered photographs or other items have not been used as illustrations they may have provided some useful information which has been incorporated into the text. Every effort has been made to identify the copyright owners of the illustrations. However, some were obtained as unmarked photographic prints, engravings or old picture postcards which were purchased at postcard fairs or 'on line'. These are described as being from the 'Author's Collection'. My sincere apologies if your material has been used without permission. I am sure that some readers may identify errors in, or omissions from, the text or photographic captions. I accept full responsibility for these. I would be delighted to hear from these readers so as to make the story of The Jedburgh Railway complete and accurate!

Index

THE OAKWOOD PRESS, 54-58 MILL SQUARE,
CATRINE, KA5 6RD 01290 551122

PRICE £22.95

www.stenlake.co.uk